ALLEGORIES OF CONTAMINATIO

PIER PAOLO PASOLINI'S *TRILOG*

The *Trilogia della vita* (*Trilogy of Life*) is a series of three films that Pier Paolo Pasolini completed before his horrifying assassination in 1975, and it remains among the most controversial of his cinematic works. In *Allegories of Contamination* Patrick Rumble provides an incisive critical and theoretical study of these films and the Marxist filmmaker's complex, original concept of the cinematic medium.

With the three films that make up the *Trilogy of Life* – *The Decameron*, *Canterbury Tales*, and *The Arabian Nights* – Pasolini attempts to recapture the aura surrounding popular, predominantly oral forms of storytelling through a pre-modern vision of innocent, unalienated bodies and pleasures. In these works Pasolini appears to abandon the explicitly political engagement that marked his earlier works – films that led him to be identified with other radical filmmakers such as Bellocchio, Bertolucci, and Godard. However, Pasolini insisted that these were his 'most ideological films,' and his political engagement translates into a mannerist, anti-classical style or what he called a 'cinema of poetry.' Rumble offers a comparative study based on the concept of 'aesthetic contamination,' which is fundamental to the understanding of Pasolini's poetics. Aesthetic contamination concerns the mediation between different cultures and different historical moments. Through stylistic experimentation, the *Trilogy of Life* presents a genealogy of visual codes, an interrogation of the subjectivity of narrative cinema. In these films Pasolini celebrates life, and perhaps therein lies their simple heresy.

(Toronto Italian Studies)

PATRICK RUMBLE is Assistant Professor in the Department of French and Italian, University of Wisconsin–Madison. He is co-editor, with Bart Testa, of *Pasolini: Contemporary Perspectives*.

PATRICK RUMBLE

Allegories of Contamination: Pier Paolo Pasolini's *Trilogy of Life*

UNIVERSITY OF TORONTO PRESS
Toronto Buffalo London

© University of Toronto Press Incorporated 1996
Toronto Buffalo London
Printed in Canada

ISBN 0-8020-0428-8 (cloth)
ISBN 0-8020-7219-4 (paper)

(∞)

Printed on acid-free paper

Toronto Italian Studies

Canadian Cataloguing in Publication Data

Rumble, Patrick Allen, 1963–
    Allegories of contamination

    (Toronto Italian studies)
    Includes bibliographical references and index.
    ISBN 0-8020-0428-8 (bound)   ISBN 0-8020-7219-4 (pbk.)

    1. Pasolini, Pier Paolo, 1922–1975 – Criticism and
    interpretation.   2. Decameron (Motion picture).
    3. Racconti di Canterbury (Motion picture).   4. Fiore
    delle mille e una notte (Motion picture).   I. Title.
    II. Series.

    PN1998.3.P37R85 1995   791.43'0233'092   C95-931198-X

University of Toronto Press acknowledges the financial
assistance to its publishing program of the Canada
Council and the Ontario Arts Council.

To my family

'tra il corpo e la storia
c'è questa musicalità che stona'
Pier Paolo Pasolini

Contents

Acknowledgments

This project would not have been possible without the financial support of the Mellon Foundation during the research and writing of early drafts of the book. I would like to thank Laura Betti, director of the extremely valuable Fondo Pier Paolo Pasolini in Rome, as well as her assistant Giuseppe Iafrate. Like all those interested in Pasolini, I owe a debt of gratitude to Nico Naldini, for his work on Pasolini as well as for his encouraging words and anecdotes during his visit to Toronto in 1990. I would like to acknowledge the excellent research facilities and staff at the Robarts Library of the University of Toronto, and at the Memorial Library of the University of Wisconsin–Madison.

For their instruction, help and/or constructive criticism at the University of Toronto I would also like to thank Amilcare Iannucci, Domenico Pietropaolo, Maddalena Kuitunen, Bart Testa, Roman Luperini, and Wlad Godzich. I especially thank Massimo Ciavolella, for reasons too numerous to list. I would like to express my gratitude to Ron Schoeffel, John St James, and Anne Forte at University of Toronto Press for all their help in preparing the volume for publication, and for their patience. Thanks, as well, to my colleagues and students at the University of Wisconsin–Madison. Special thanks go to Piero Aragno, Stefania Buccini, Gino Casagrande, Tom Cravens, Silvano Garofalo, Doug Kelly, Christopher Kleinhenz, Elaine Marks, Yvonne Ozzello, Peter Schofer, and Robert Rodini. To Grazia Menechella, le parole non bastano.

Pier Paolo Pasolini

Rosso Fiorentino's *Descent from the Cross* as model in Pasolini's *La ricotta* (Fondo Pier Paolo Pasolini)

Jacopo da Pontormo's *Deposition* as model in Pasolini's *La ricotta* (Fondo Pier Paolo Pasolini)

The Adoration of Ser Ciappelletto in *The Decameron*

Pieter Bruegel the Elder, *Battle between Carnival and Lent* (Kunsthistorisches Museum, Vienna; Art Resource, New York)

Scene from *The Decameron*

Pasolini as Giotto's
disciple in *The Decameron*

Pieter Bruegel the Elder, *Flemish Proverbs* (Kaiser Friedrich
Museum; Art Resource, New York)

The Painter's Inspiration in *The Decameron* (Fondo Pier Paolo Pasolini)

The Painter's Vision in *The Decameron*

Giotto, *Last Judgment* (Scrovegni Chapel, Padua; Art Resource, New York)

Giotto, *Ognissanti Madonna* (Uffizi, Florence; Art Resource, New York)

Pasolini as Chaucer in *The Canterbury Tales*

Public execution in *The Canterbury Tales*

Hieronymus Bosch, *Hell*. Detail from right panel of *The Millennium* (Museo del Prado, Madrid)

Hieronymus Bosch, *Hell*. Detail from *The Table of Wisdom* (Museo del Prado, Madrid)

Bosch's infernal imagery in Pasolini's *The Canterbury Tales*

Hieronymus Bosch, detail from *The Temptation of Saint Anthony* (Museu Nacional de Arte Antiga, Lisbon)

Seventeenth-century Rajput miniature (Phyllis and Eberhard Kronhausen, *The Complete Book of Erotic Art* [New York: Bell Publishing 1978])

The Arabian Nights

ALLEGORIES OF CONTAMINATION

1

Pasolini *regista civile*

'I live hour by hour, frame by frame.'[1]

From the Novel to the Screen

By the time Pier Paolo Pasolini made the *Trilogia della vita* (1971–4), the last three films that he would ever see completed and released to the public in his lifetime, he had already established his reputation in Italy as poet, first of all, and only secondarily as novelist, filmmaker, playwright, theorist, and journalist. But as many of the letters he received from friends and followers show (and Nico Naldini's recent publication of Pasolini's collected correspondence makes it possible to see this),[2] the call to renounce the cinema and return to his position as the *poeta civile* (national poet) of postwar Italy was insistent. For intellectuals such as Franco Fortini (with whom Pasolini had worked during the late fifties as part of the editorial committee for the journal *Officina*), Pasolini's cinematic activities indicated irresponsibility or even immaturity.[3] But certainly Fortini wasn't the only writer who considered the cinema a suspect medium, given its historical ambivalence as a technologically based form riding an ideological pendulum between the twin peaks of business interests and artistic expression. Even Moravia, during his emotional speech in Rome before a mass of people mourning Pasolini's death in early November of 1975, called for a memory of Pasolini as poet – *poeta civile* – and he was right.

However, Pasolini himself felt little hesitation, around the late fifties and early sixties, when he found himself on the road to cinema. Indeed, as he often remarked, he felt a pull towards the medium even before he published his first book of poems in the Friulian dialect in 1942.

Besides his 'infantile' attraction to paracinematic signs, especially the sensational and colourful posters advertising the coming attractions at the movie-theatres, his first movie-going experiences in Bologna as a member of a *cineguf* (a Fascist film club, much like many other clubs set up throughout Italy) contributed to a growing desire to study at the Centro Sperimentale di Cinematografia, the state film school instituted in Rome by Mussolini in 1936. This desire was compounded following the war by his first encounters with the new style of Neorealists such as Roberto Rossellini, Vittorio De Sica, Cesare Zavattini, and Luchino Visconti. He was especially struck by Rossellini's *Rome, Open City* (1945). His Neorealist debt would be partially paid during the filming of *Accattone*, his first film (1961), when he wrote a poem relating the impact that this film had upon him[4] and also hinted at some of the reasons for his decision to abandon the novel and pick up the camera:

entro nell'arena, all'ultimo spettacolo,
senza vita, con grige persone,
parenti, amici, sparsi sulle panche,
persi nell'ombra in cerchi distinti
e biancastri, nel fresco ricettacolo ...
Subito, alle prime inquadrature,
mi travolge e rapisce ... l'intermittence
du coeur. Mi trovo nelle scure
vie della memoria, nelle stanze
misteriose dove l'uomo fisicamente è altro,
e il passato lo bagna col suo pianto ...
Eppure, dal lungo uso fatto esperto,
non perdo i fili: ecco ... la Casilina,
su cui tristemente si aprono
le porte della città di Rossellini ...
ecco l'epico paesaggio neorealista,
coi fili del telegrafo, i selciati, i pini,
i muretti scrostati, la mistica
folla perduta nel daffare quotidiano,
le tetre forme della dominazione nazista ...
Quasi emblema, ormai, l'urlo della Magnani,
sotto le ciocche disordinatamente assolute,
risuona nelle disperate panoramiche,
e nelle sue occhiate vive e mute
si addensa il senso della tragedia.

E' lì che si dissolve e si mutila
il presente, e assorda il canto degli aedi.

I enter the cinema, at the last showing,
without life, with drab people
with relatives, friends, spread out over the benches
lost in the shadow of whitish and distinct circles
in the cool theatre ...
Immediately, at the first frames
I am overwhelmed and carried away by ...
l'intermittance du coeur. I find myself
in the mysterious rooms where man
physically is another
and the past washes him with its tears ...
And yet, having become an expert through long use
I don't lose the threads: Look at the Casilina
where the gates of the city of Rossellini
are sadly opening:
Here is the epic neorealist landscape
with its telegraph wires, its sidewalks, its pines
and crumbling walls, the mystic crowd
lost in daily affairs,
the grim shapes of Nazi domination.
Almost an emblem by now, Magnani's cry,
beneath her locks disordinately absolute,
it resounds in the desperate panning shots
and in her glances, alive and mute,
the sense of tragedy is growing.
And it is there the present dissolves
and changes, and deafens the song of the bards.[5]

It is precisely the realization, expressed in the final lines of this poem, that a new culture or, better, a new form of storytelling (and thus of knowledge) was arising to 'dissolve' and 'change' the present and 'deafen the song of the bards' that leads Pasolini to engage in the medium and apparatus of the cinema.[6] Furthermore, he accepts the perhaps inherently compromising character of the new medium, given its technological basis, and the density of the commercial interests that mediate between any filmmaker and his or her spectators. And while acknowledging an ever-ambivalent complicity, he also implicitly rebukes Fortini and others who would criticize his change in technique for ever conceiving of any form of intellectual or literary expression as not being complicit, to some degree, with the forces of profit and alienation: what Pasolini will call the forces of 'neocapitalism' and 'false tolerance,' as we shall see.

Pasolini's choice, in the early 1960s, to switch focus from the novel to film was a function of his overriding desire to engage in the reality of the present, to make an impact upon an audience quickly abandoning the book for the more immediate gratification of the movie-theatre (and later, television). This Gramscian urge to renew the intellectual's mandate during a period of great cultural and political transition explains his adoption of the role of *regista civile*.

'The cinema of poetry' and a Post-National *Trilogy*

[Il cinema] rappresenta dunque la realtà attraverso la realtà. In concreto, attraverso gli oggetti della realtà che una macchina da presa, momento per momento, riproduce ... Ecco, a questo punto si può individuare il rapporto della mia nozione grammaticale del cinema con quella che è, o almeno io credo essere, la mia filosofia, o il mio modo di vivere: che non mi sembra altro, poi, che un allucinato, infantile e pragmatico amore per la realtà. Religioso in quanto si fonda in qualche modo, per analogia, con una sorta di immenso feticismo sessuale. Il mondo non sembra essere, per me, che un insieme di padri e madri, verso cui ho un trasporto totale, fatto di rispetto venerante, e di bisogno di violentare tale rispetto venerante attraverso dissacrazioni anche violente e scandalose.

[Cinema] thus represents reality through reality. In concrete terms, through the objects of reality that a camera reproduces, moment by moment ... And so at this point one can identify the relationship between my grammatical concept of cinema with what is, or at least I believe to be, my philosophy or my way of life – which does not strike me in the final analysis as being other that a hallucinated, infantile, and pragmatic love for reality. It is religious in that in some way it is fused, by analogy, with a sort of immense sexual fetishism. The world does not seem to me to be other than a totality of fathers and mothers, toward whom I feel an absolute rush of feeling, composed of respectful veneration and the need to violate said respectful veneration through even violent and scandalous desecrations.[7]

As we noted, in Italy Pasolini is known principally for his poetry. For many, his other artistic and journalistic activities are all mere distractions from his poetic calling. For Pasolini, however, the distinctions between these various 'techniques' do not hold: they are, for him, precisely techniques adopted along the path of his search for 'reality.' Driven by this 'love for reality,' Pasolini will come to identify cinema as the technique able to communicate reality most completely, without – he polemically insists – any intermediary system of symbols or signs; signs whose materiality, and arbitrary relations to the world of objects, interrupts our full understanding of our environment and of the positions we take up within it.

The optimistic (or even positivistic) naiveté of such a view – for which he was roundly attacked by other theorists of the cinema (such as Umberto Eco and Stephen Heath, as we shall discuss in a later chapter) – is reproduced and reaffirmed in the title Pasolini gives to the collection of essays on film and language that he published in 1972 (collecting together essays written between 1964 and 1971). In *Empirismo eretico* (*Heretical Empiricism*), Pasolini offers his formulations concerning cinema as 'the written language of reality,' and it is here also that he accounts for his own 'poetic' approach to filmmaking. The 'heresy' indicated in the title is not only derived from the scandalous nature of his work (regularly attacked as obscene, and morally suspect), but also, and more important, from the way he views film as the reproduction of 'concrete' reality; film that becomes the articulation of reality, which is itself nothing but 'cinema in nature': an 'infinite sequence shot' as Pasolini would say, in an extreme version of a Bazinian 'realist' position.

Furthermore, as he often repeated, his turn to cinema, and the highly experimental style he adopts, should be viewed as functions of a desire to abandon his own language and national identity. As his cousin and biographer Nico Naldini remarks:

Nel confronto con la poesia scritta che è sempre definita da una serie di limiti storici nazionali, il cinema rappresenta un linguaggio transnazionale e la sua scelta in questo momento ha anche il significato di un'abiura della lingua italiana, e assieme, un po' alla volta, della sua letteratura e di 'tutto ciò che fa italiano.'

Compared with written poetry, which is always defined by a series of national-historical limits, cinema represents a transnational language, and his choice during this time also has the sense of an abjuration of the Italian language along with, little by little, its literature and of 'all that is Italian.'[8]

For Pasolini, then, cinematic language offered a possibility of moving beyond national cultural identities (in a way that novels and poems cannot), and perhaps inherently resisted or even subverted any nationalistic discourse. This audiovisual language offered itself as a new model of mass communication, a form that, unlike the novel, was not to be identified either in plot structure or in language with the form of the bourgeois nation-state. Indeed, the crisis of the novel in Europe is symptomatic of a crisis of national forms of political, economic, and cultural organization. In Italy, where the novel as a genre is so closely identified with the history of the nation, the type of linguistic contamination (or *plurilinguismo*) experimented with in the 'post-novels' of Carlo Emilio Gadda, Giorgio Manganelli, and Pasolini himself indicates a moment of extreme social and cultural instability.

Pasolini gains his homological understanding of the novel, that is, his understanding of how the linguistic or stylistic structure of the novel offered insights into analogical structures of conviviality as well as epistemological paradigms, from his studies of Lucien Goldmann's *Sociology of the Novel*. The problem here is one of theorizing the relationship between literary/artistic texts and historical/economic contexts (which has usually been approached in terms of mimesis, of mediation – especially by Marxist or otherwise engaged forms of criticism – or of a mutual irresponsibility of text and context – as theorized especially by structuralists and especially post-structuralists).[9] While Pasolini criticizes Goldmann for being too content-oriented, and not sensitive enough to questions of style, he does adopt Goldmann's general structural approach.[10] Pasolini's studies of Goldmann in the early 1960s, along with his knowledge of the work of the Russian Formalists, underpin his approach to the 'proto-novels' he will adapt in the *Trilogia della vita*: the *Decameron, Canterbury Tales*, and the *Arabian Nights*. That is, the first two texts exist as prototypes of the European novel,[11] and both cultivate the language they adopt as a potentially unified and unifying national koiné. The entirely alien, and quite mysterious, author-less origins of the *Arabian Nights* and the complexity of its narrative structure offer Pasolini alternative models of narration, drawn from a non-European tradition.

Furthermore, we find in the *Trilogia* a continuation of Pasolini's desire to reinterpret past texts or myths in terms of the present, as found earlier in the films *Il Vangelo secondo Matteo, Medea*, and *Edipo Re*. These texts also were thought capable of generating new insights when projected upon the modern world of industrialization and consumerism. And, as our discussion of the *Decameron*, in particular, will demonstrate, Pasolini's desire to adapt these texts was rather ambivalent: on the one hand, he detects something in the 'open' structures of these texts (and the way their episodic nature calls attention to issues of narrative organization or 'framing') that offers a possible linkage between the contexts surrounding their production and the context of the *Trilogia*; and, on the other hand, his adaptations, especially of Boccaccio and Chaucer, may be seen as acts of aggression towards texts that had such important foundational roles to play in modern Western culture. In other words, there may be something within these proto-novels that is shared with the 'post-novel' of the culture of late capitalism.

Moreover, for Pasolini, the fact that these texts derive from moments or geographical zones predating or untouched by the historical and cultural processes involved in the later phases of formation of the nation-state makes them inherently resistant to any nationalist claims upon them – notwithstanding centuries of especially academic energies expended to ensure just such a canonical identification. For Pasolini, it would be necessary to join this structural resistance found in the original texts to the 'transnational' and 'transclassist' language of film in order to displace nationalistic cultural paradigms, and to engage in a search for a *società futura possibile*: a society glimpsed in the self-generating but also self-destructive structures of his films *da farsi* (a term that translates poorly as 'in process'), as we shall discuss in chapter 2.

The language of the cinema, according to Pasolini,[12] is particularly appropriate for this endeavour insofar as the filmic signifier, the *imsegno* (image-sign: all that is contained within the frame), as visual sign, has overcome any notion of national linguistic identity. This faith in the 'universality' of *imsegni* helps to explain Pasolini's tendency, seen especially in films such as *Teorema* (1968) and *Medea*, to produce what Gian Piero Brunetta calls Pasolini's 'silent' film style – films with little dialogue that depend upon the brute expressivity of the image and the significance generated through processes of montage.[13] In the *Trilogia della vita*, this style translates into a drama of usurers, artists, lovers, carpenters, millers, poets, hunters, and genies made more accessible and immediate to more spectators by a medium of audiovisual reproduction (and let us leave off the discussion of this ostensibly positivistic belief in reproduction until chapter 2). As Pasolini writes in the 1966 essay 'La fine dall'avanguardia':

Voglio dire che, la ipotetica e potenziale lingua del cinema – se cè – e se non cè, se non è definibile – l'insieme dei 'linguaggi d'arte' dei vari films – è una lingua internazionale e interclassista, per la sua stessa natura (anche se non ancora morfologicamente definita). Ora è vero che in ogni film c'è la lingua parlata dei personaggi, che ne costituisce un momento particolaristico e nazionale; tuttavia tale lingua è in qualche modo diacronica col linguaggio tipico del cinema: per cui un im-segno è formato dalla presenza fisica audiovisiva del personaggio – della sua azione, da *lui stesso* – con l'integrazione della sua lingua (che diventa così soltanto, appunto, un elemento particolare).

I mean that the hypothetical and potential language of the cinema – if it exists, and if it doesn't, if it isn't definable, the whole of the 'languages of art' of the various films – is an international and interclassist language, given its nature (even if it is not yet defined morphologically). Now it is true that every film contains the spoken language of the characters which makes up its specific, national instance; nevertheless, this language is in some way diachronic with the typical language of cinema, through which an im-sign is formed by the physical audiovisual presence of the character – by his action, *by himself* – with the integration of his language (which thus becomes only one particular element).[14]

It is precisely his 'transnational' conception of 'im-signs' that leads to a *potential* break with Goldmann's theory of a structural homology between a text and the socio-economic structure it is embedded within, since, for Goldmann, this structure can only be national in character. Pasolini explains:

Bene: una lingua fondata sulla riproduzione audiovisiva della realtà tout court, non può non possedere delle strutture strettamente omologhe a quelle della società storica riconosciuta, dove il film è prodotto. La riproduzione audiovisiva della realtà è una lingua o un linguaggio identico in Italia o in Francia, nel Ghana o negli Stati Uniti. Le possibili e non ancora definite strutture narrative di questa lingua del cinema, che 'esprime la realtà con la realtà,' non sembrerebbe dunque rispondere alle leggi dell'omologia – essenzialmente nazionali in quanto tipiche di nazioni dominate da borghesie capitalistiche – così accutamente descritte dal Goldmann: se un carattere omologico c'è nelle strutture del cinema in rapporto a quelle della società, tale società si configura, allora, in modo amorfo e generale, *come l'intera umanità civile* – comprendendovi i paesi in 'via di sviluppo.' Le strutture della lingua del cinema si presentano dunque più che come internazionali e interclassiste, come transnazionali e transclassiste: *prefigurano una possibile situazione socio-linguistica di un mondo reso tendenzialmente unitario dalla completa industrializzazione e dal conseguente livellamento implicante la scomparsa delle tradizioni particolaristiche e nazionali.*

Okay: a language founded on the audiovisual reproduction of reality, that is, on reality as such, cannot possess structures which are strictly homologous with those of the historically recognizable society where the film is produced. The audiovisual reproduction of reality is an identical linguistic system or language in Italy or in France, in Ghana or in the United States. The possible and not yet defined narrative structures of this language of cinema which 'expresses reality with reality' would therefore not seem to suit the laws of homology – which are essentially national inasmuch as they are typical of nations dominated by capitalist bourgeoisies – so acutely described by Goldmann. If there is a homological characteristic in the structures of cinema in relation to those of society, this society thus takes form, in an amorphous and general way, *as the whole of civilized humanity* – including the 'developing' countries. The structures of the language of cinema therefore present themselves as transnational and transclassist rather than international and interclassist. *They prefigure a possible sociolinguistic situation of a world made tendentially unitary by complete industrialization and by the consequent leveling which implies the disappearance of particular and national traditions.*[15]

For Pasolini, film presents itself as the language appropriate to a world in which national economies are giving way to multinational trading aggregates, and traditional cultures and ethnicities are being overrun by the expanding, cosmopolitan culture of consumer capitalism. Within his search to be ever more faithful to the often distressing realities in the world around him, Pasolini found film to offer not only the most 'mimetic' medium, but also the medium whose very material – as a means of technological reproduction – contained within itself (in its chemical processes, in its technological dependencies) the very elements of destabilization he bemoans throughout his entire *opera*. That is, film contains within itself the technological 'poison' as well, he would hope, as an ideological 'cure.' As poison and antidote, film becomes for Pasolini what Virgil's 'tongue' was for Dante in the *Divina Commedia*: 'wounded' by the first touch of it, he could be healed only by a second touch. In a society steadily moving from a print-based culture towards one based upon photographic and magnetic information-storage technologies such as film and video, the only way to avoid complete *disimpegno* (disengagement) was to engage in the audiovisual techniques of late modernity – engage, however, in an ironic or, better, 'heretical' manner.

It is Pasolini's understanding of the 'transnational' nature of film, found in the *material* of the signifier itself, along with an ironic choice of medieval texts for adaptation, that helps us to understand how he could claim that the *Trilogia* was his most ideological film project.[16] That is, both the thematic world of the original texts as well as the very nature of *imsegni* open Pasolini's films out onto a history that transcends the

Italian national experience, pushes them beyond this national prehistory, towards a new and necessarily undefined idea of social aggregation. Pasolini insists that this gesture towards a *realtà irrealizzata* (an 'unrealized reality') can be located in a work's 'style' or linguistic structure. As he writes in 'La reazione stilistica,'

> No, la storia
> che sarà non è come quella che è stata.
> Non consente giudizi, non consente ordini,
> è realtà irrealizzata.
> E la lingua, s'è frutto dei secoli contraddittori,
> contraddittoria – s'è frutto dei primordi
> tenebrosi – s'integra, nessuno lo scordi,
> con quello che sarà, e che ancora non è.
> E questo suo essere libero mistero, ricchezza
> infinita, ne spezza,
> ora, ogni raggiunto limite, ogni forma lecita.

> No, the history that will be is not like that which has been. It allows no judgments, it allows no orders, it is un-realized reality. And language, if it is the fruit of contradictory centuries, contradictory – if it is the fruit of obscure origins – it integrates itself, let no one forget, with what will be, and what does not yet exist. And this its being free mystery, infinite richness, now ruptures every reached limit, every proper form.[17]

The *Trilogia* continues this stylistic reaction insofar as the plurilinguistic experimentalism initiated in his writing style, as seen in his 'Roman novels,' *Ragazzi di vita* (1955) and *Una vita violenta* (1959) – very much influenced by the style of pastiche found in Pascoli's poems or in Gadda's novels – is carried over into the *cinema di poesia* (cinema of poetry). As we shall discuss in chapter 2, this *plurilinguismo* is found in certain 'citational' or 'mannerist' aspects of his visual language, to the extent to which Pasolini's frames are often composed with certain painterly models in mind.[18]

Pasolini's intent, whether it be in adapting the *Decameron* or translating paintings by Giotto, Bruegel, or Bosch to the screen, is extremely coherent: to present 'double-voiced' or hybridized signifiers that stage a conflict between the *pre-formato* ('pre-formed') and the energies of innovation or linguistic renewal. Furthermore, Pasolini composes his frames very often with clear models in mind: Rosso Fiorentino and Pontormo as they are reconstructed in *La ricotta* (1963); Giotto, Bruegel, and Vermeer in the *Decameron*; Bruegel and Bosch in *I racconti di Canterbury*; or the Rajput and Persian miniatures in *Il fiore delle mille e una notte*. What Pasolini stages through this sort of *riscrittura* (rewriting or quotation) is a conflict between the transnational language of cinema and those 'particular' cultural models, taken from tradition, that resist, on a metaphorical level, the processes of transnationalization. His films exist as stylistic oxymorons. He presents images and models drawn from specific historical moments of the past, or from particular regional and indeed national traditions and heritages, images that require diverse competencies in interpretation or different ways of seeing (Bakhtin would say different chronotopes). He introduces these other models as alien languages within the dominant language of film, alien languages that threaten to subvert the transparent, international, and inter-class capacities of the filmic communication – subvert it, but not completely disable it.

Pasolini presents superseded visual models and traditions as the repressed memory of cinema, and of the culture it expresses. His re-animation of pre-modern visual sources presents the origins of the cinematic image – pre-technological origins that cinema must repress in order to assert itself as the most objective and unbiased technique of audiovisual reproduction (thus his radical break with neorealist or naturalist theorizations of film language as expressed in the 1940s and 1950s by Zavattini, Aristarco, and others). His style contaminates the transparency of the image with the stains of other styles, styles that call attention to the material of the filmic signifier, thus offering a series of challenges to communication or comprehension. Pasolini's style of pastiche or contamination reveals cinema's 'political unconscious' (Jameson's formulation, which will receive further attention in subsequent chapters): he traces cinema's indebtedness to past models and in so doing reveals, through the allegory of his style, how the global project of post-national neocapitalism spreads throughout the world at the expense of local identities and particular traditions. To use Salman Rushdie's line, Pasolini's style is an allegory of the coca-colonization of the planet.

To put it more briefly, the dialectic of tradition and innovation, the forces of conservation in conflict with the counterforces of transformation, is to be found in the ambivalence of Pasolini's signifiers. This dialectical tension, unresolved given the continual deferral of the moment of synthesis, translates into a style of contamination and excess. As Pasolini explains:

Il segno sotto cui io lavoro è sempre la contaminazione. Infatti se voi leggete una pagina dei miei libri noterete che la contaminazione è il fatto stilistico dominante, perché io, che provengo da un mondo borghese e non soltanto borghese ma, almeno in gioventù, dalle sedi più raffinate di quel mondo, io lettore degli scrittori decadenti più raffinati, ecc. ecc., sono arrivato a questo mio mondo. Conseguentemente il *pastiche*, per forza, doveva nascere.

I always work under the sign of contamination. In fact, if you read just one page from my books you will find that contamination is the dominant stylistic fact because, coming from a bourgeois world, and not only bourgeois but, at least during my youth, from the most refined areas of that world, a reader of the most refined decadent writers, etc., etc., I arrived at this world. Consequently, *pastiche* had to be born, necessarily.[19]

The contradictory nature of Pasolini's *cinema di poesia* forces the spectator into new or altered patterns of reception, beyond the conventional horizon of expectations presumed in the dominant *cinema di prosa* (a hegemonic 'prose' film practice that subordinates style to the necessities of communication). The British filmmaker Peter Greenaway, commenting on his own interest in presenting images of conflicting visual competencies, offers an instructive perspective on this matter: 'I have always been fascinated by the viewer's relationship with paintings, one which is completely different from the "empathy" with which we often react to film, or literature, almost always to the theatre and of course to opera. I want to introduce this viewer-painting relationship, this distance, into my cinematography ... I like to make reference to painting as an example of perfection, a metaphor for looking and vision.'[20] For Pasolini, the contamination of cinematic and painterly codes is a function of a formalist ethic of defamiliarization that provides the ground for his practice.[21] Not only offering 'metaphors of vision,' Pasolini's films present metaphors of 'bound' vision or visual regimes; they recall a history of human image-making, allude to the unconscious of the eye, in order, ultimately, to give looking, vision, and representation – and the socio-economic structures that in large measure determine their forms – a history (and therefore a future).

Pasolini's stylistic optimism, this belief in what he will call a 'revolutionary' potential of the *cinema di poesia*, offers a possibility of renewing the cultural-ideological mandate of the poet-director, the *regista civile*. This resistant potential, ostensibly denied following the completion of the *Trilogia* when Pasolini writes the 'Abiura dalla Trilogia della vita,' offers to return the poet his or her traditional function not only as custodian of the memory of a people, but also as *storyteller*. That is, as we shall see especially in chapter 2, Pasolini attempts to re-create the collective reception of stories (a form of reception analogous to that presumed by the very texts he adapts), and to constitute a community of spectators and bring them, through the narrative experience, to an understanding of the processes involved in the building and maintenance of hegemony – be it the current one or, to recall Giorgio Agamben's utopian concept, a 'coming community.'[22] That is, the *Trilogia* presumes 'una coralità, insomma, d'ascolto e di riconoscimento delle esperienze da cui è nata la deduzione della norma' ('a chorus listening to and recognizing the experiences from which the deduction of the norm is born').[23]

Pasolini's 'Abiura,' as we shall discuss in chapter 3, forms an ironic recantation both of the *Trilogia* and of this belief in the poet's mandate. However, it seems clear that here the rhetorical strategy of *concessio* is adopted to defend his works from the moment of institutionalized censorship – a strategy that Pasolini suggests he would use in defence of his last film, *Salò*, though he did not live long enough to carry it out.[24] Indeed, the 'Abiura,' published posthumously, serves more to sharpen and focus the messages of contestation found in these works, rendering their ideological portion all the more indigestible. That is, the 'Abiura' serves as an ambivalent conclusion to the *Trilogia della vita*, as it will to the present work: a conclusion that indicates, in what is perhaps a utopian gesture, the possibility but also the necessity of such contestation, and points towards a time and place beyond the present, where, Pasolini wrote, 'ogni mattina ricominciava la tragedia dell'essere' ('every morning began the tragedy of being').[25]

Allegories of Contamination in the *Trilogy of Life*

My cinematic taste is not of cinematographic origin, but figurative. What I have in my head, as a vision, as a visual field, are the frescoes of Masaccio, Giotto – who are the painters I love the most, together with certain mannerists (Pontormo, for example). And I am unable to conceive of images, landscapes, compositions of figures, outside this initial painterly passion of mine.

P.P. Pasolini[1]

As the Western world has invested every aspect of its waking life with visual order, with procedures and spaces that are uniform, continuous and connected, it has progressively alienated itself from needful involvement in its subconscious life.

M. McLuhan and H. Parker[2]

One of the paradoxes of Pasolini's cinema, born of the 'visual order' described by McLuhan and Parker, and beholden to a technology largely responsible for the ideological *guarantee* of such an order, is the extent to which it is 'needfully involved' in subconscious life. Indeed, for Pasolini, cinematic language is 'primitive,' 'irrational,' 'oneiric,' belonging to 'untamed thought.'[3] In this chapter we shall focus upon how such an understanding of the origins of cinematic language translates into elements of style in Pasolini's *Trilogia della vita*. Stylistic *contamination* (an ideological form of pastiche) is, for Pasolini, as it was in a similar manner for Gadda, the formal expression of such a 'poetic' understanding of cinema. Pasolinian contamination forms a 'mannerist' response to what

McLuhan and Parker call the 'visual order' of things. His cinema provides a structural attack upon hegemonic codifications of perception (we shall describe this as a problem of perspective). It is an 'anticlassical' or genealogical form of filmmaking that disrupts traditional patterns of reception and perception along with the material basis that provides their foundation.

In a subsequent chapter we will explore how Pasolini's adaptation of Boccaccio's *Decameron* led to a metadiscursive examination of the filmic medium itself: Pasolini's film repeats the examination of a hegemonic literary discourse just as Boccaccio's vernacular prose text had. In this chapter we will develop our discussion of the qualities of contamination, along with related issues of pastiche and parody, in the *Trilogia*. The 'citational' aspects of Pasolini's work, as we mentioned with regard to the novel, will be examined in terms of the presence of Medieval and Renaissance figural traditions, or oriental pictorial models, in his films. Just as the episodes and dialogues of the *Decameron* present us with 'reported speech,' reanimated or cited discourse, so do many of the *images* of the films appear as 'reported vision,' as quotations of preceding perspectives. This approach lends the image a recycled quality, what we shall call a mannered quality. The recycled image leads us to a melancholic gaze insofar as we are often led to adopt a perspective of an 'other': we are periodically forced to share our viewpoint with another consciousness, which actually envelops our own in its precedence. Thus, viewing Pasolini is always something like a *déjà vu* experience. This sensation of repetition leads to a heightened awareness of location and of the perspective one has *adopted*: because, in *déjà vu*, one experiences the uncanny sensation of adopting a forced perspective. The spontaneity of vision, the everyday illusion of the freedom of vision, or of 'unfettered sight,' collapses with the consciousness of repetition.

Pasolini's *Trilogia* often presents its spectator with such a doubled (or doubling) gaze, thus calling the very activity of watching into question. The innocence of viewing, as one is led to feel in nearly any film of the classical narrative style (built according to the 'Hollywood code's' system of continuity editing),[4] is displaced by the sensation of taking on a second-hand viewpoint. The classical style offers the spectator the illusion of being the *subject* of vision, of controlling the seen. Pasolini's spectator is led to a consciousness of being *subjected* to the gaze, of being under the control of the image. Psychoanalytic studies of the mechanisms of identification and of the problem of the gaze in Hollywood cinema have revealed the scopic sadism of traditional terms of spectatorship (and a sadism thematized in films such as Hitchcock's *Psycho*). Pasolini's spectator, rather, is led to struggle with the image that openly requires his or her submission but holds out, at the same moment, the possibility of resistance to the persuasive power of the image (thus the oft-noted masochistic appeal of his films).

The 'realism' of the classical style, as Burch, Bordwell, Thompson, Heath, and others have shown,[5] is the product of a set of conventions established early in the 1900s (synthesized by D.W. Griffith) and long interiorized by spectators (and Bordwell has shown the continuity between theatrical and cinematic codes of representation).[6] These conventions depend upon a moment of identification with the viewpoint offered by the film. The naturalism or realism of the classical style depends upon mechanisms, which we shall describe below, that assure such an identification. But as Heath, especially, has shown, the awareness of the fact that one is led or coerced to adopt a specific perspective, a coercion with obvious ideological consequences, has been lost since the Hollywood code established itself as the standard, hegemonic rhetoric of film production, and thus since it established the terms of spectatorship. (Even the Soviet filmmaker Pudovkin asserted that continuity editing followed 'natural' habits of perception,[7] while never acknowledging what the Russian Formalist Victor Shklovsky called the ethical necessity to break with or 'defamiliarize' such habitual patterns of perception, as we shall discuss further below).

All along the history of cinema there have been filmmakers who have contested any 'hardening' of cinematic language. The experiences of the Italian Futurists,[8] the French Impressionists (Delluc, Dulac, Epstein, and L'Herbier), the Surrealists (early Buñuel, Dalí, Clair, and Man Ray), and North American experimental filmmakers such as Joseph Cornell, Maya Deren, Stan Brakhage, Hollis Frampton, Michael Snow, and others show a long history of 'countercinema,' with one of its principal aims being the rejection of any standardization of filmic language. Unfortunately, their relegation to avant-garde positions in culture (by art-business institutions) has often functioned to neutralize their impact upon cinema.

Pasolini himself mentions the importance of Surrealist experiments (along with neorealism) in his own understanding of a possible cinema of contestation. But he would reject much of the avant-garde forms of contestation insofar as their absolute rejection of established conventions (*qua* conventions), and thus their illegibility, situate them securely within an avant-garde 'ghetto':

Superano la linea di fuoco, e si trovano dall'altra parte, in territorio nemico; quivi, automaticamento, vengono chiusi in una sacca, o per continuare più brillantemente la metafora, ammassati in un lager, che essi poi, come succede, trasformano altrettanto automaticamente in un ghetto. Là dove tutto è diventato trasgressione non c'è più pericolo.

They go beyond the firing line and find themselves on the other side, in enemy territory. Here, automatically, they are closed into a bag, or, to extend the metaphor more vividly, they are crowded together into a concentration camp, which they then, as happens, transform equally automatically into a ghetto. There, where everything has become transgression, there is no more danger.[9]

In this 'ghetto,' the actual struggle over the terms of production and reception of films is never to be found. Avant-garde filmmakers such as Stan Brakhage, Michael Snow, Luigi Veronese, Gianfranco Baruchello, and even Andy Warhol are easily categorized, fetishized, and neutralized, whereas 'revisionist' filmmakers such as Pasolini, and sometimes Godard (both with one foot securely within cinematic tradition and the other certainly somewhere outside it), resist such categorization, and must be reckoned with. They have not abandoned what Pasolini calls the 'linea di fuoco,' or the moment of conflict.

While avant-garde filmmakers often offer 'impossible' or 'incoherent' points of view (since coherence of vision is ideologically suspect) in experimenting with the untapped visual possibilities of the medium (Brakhages's search for innocent looking, for example),[10] Pasolini rejects from the outset any notion of 'unfettered sight.' He would insist upon an awareness of the 'structure' of appearances; he writes that 'reality is a language,' the 'code of codes,' or the Ur-code.[11] Vision is the decoding of the language of reality; and furthermore, since reality is 'nothing but cinema in nature,' spectators, both inside and outside the movie-theatre, interpret the signs of reality in the same manner (given the supposed iconic nature of film-signs or *imsegni*): 'By now I have repeated many times that the Code of Reality and the Code of Cinema ... are the same Code.'[12] And as Marco Vallora writes, this 'anti-naturalism' is a characteristic of Pasolini's 'mannerist' attitude:

La natura, insomma, è già artificio, cultura, spettacolo; non esiste più nulla di elementare, primario; ogni cosa rimanda ad un codice preesistente, l'arte scende nella vita.

Nature, therefore, is already artifice, culture, spectacle; there no longer exists anything elementary, primary; everything defers to a pre-existing code, art descends into life.[13]

Our ability to interpret the signs of reality demands a kind of apprenticeship in looking, a disciplining of the gaze. This is most clearly communicated to us by Pasolini in the Prologue sequence to *Edipo Re* (1967), where we are given the baby's point of view – a pre-Oedipal and chaotic (but also extremely lyrical) perspective upon the world. This highly *regressive* sequence in the film is also one of the most beautiful ones in Pasolini's entire *opera*. In the film the moment of castration, of the Father's exercise of the Law that tragically separates the child from the Mother, is signed by a radical spatial and meteorological shift from the warm colours and lush Northern Italian climate of the Prologue (shot in soft focus) to the aridity and harshness of the Moroccan desert (in sharp focus). We lose the 'innocence' of vision only to adopt the melancholic gaze of Oedipus as he suffers along the prescribed path of his destiny, indeed until he blinds himself. (The audience shares somewhat in this blindness as the concluding sequence, the Epilogue that transfers the classical drama to the present, is shot using the distorting fish-eye lens.)

Edipo Re is a film about the disciplining of vision, and it expresses a regressive desire to return to a pre-Oedipal, ideal state of being (before language, before innocent looking hardened into a fixed point of view, we might say, in Lacanian fashion).[14] The *Trilogia* abandons this idealism, although it continues Pasolini's search for some human essence or activity that has not been rationalized or commodified by the culture of consumer capitalism. Indeed, in turning now to a discussion of various 'mannerist' aspects of these three films, we shall see how they not only reflect a world, or worlds, of innocent, uncorrupted bodies and pleasures, but also how these films, in the manner in which they address the spectator, appeal to or attempt to *resuscitate* what may be found that is still essential and uncontaminated within us. We shall suspend judgment upon this idealistic or 'nostalgic' desire for 'innocence' until the conclusion of the chapter.

Contamination, Mannerism, Ideological Pastiche

il gusto
del dolce e grande manierismo
che tocca col suo capriccio dolcemente

robusto
le radici della vita vivente: ed è
realismo.

the sensibility of the sweet and great mannerism which touches, with its
sweetly robust caprice, the roots of living life: and it is realism ...

P.P. Pasolini, *La Guinea*[15]

Although they were hailed as three films designed to entertain rather
than rebuke (as Pasolini's earlier films had tended to *rebuke* his audience),
Pasolini called his *Trilogia* his 'most ideological' project.[16] Yet, on the
surface, these films appear utterly devoid of the type of intellectual
engagement required by such films as *Uccellacci e uccellini*, *Teorema*, or
Porcile, to name only a few. While films such as these formed a reasoned
appeal to the spectators' intellect, the *Trilogia* appears to abandon the
earlier *film-saggio* (film-inquiry) political mode of filmmaking in favour
of a more subtle, but ultimately more radical, form of ideological
interpellation. In fact, to take the *Decameron* as an example, the *novelle*
often appear as a pretext, or a lure, intended to capture the attention of the
viewer in order to carry out a kind of 'subversion' of the very structure
of his point of view. As the great French 'poetic realist' filmmaker Jean
Renoir once remarked: 'If you want to persuade the public to accept a
new point of view, to share in a discovery, you have to play the part of
a prostitute, to put on a bit of make-up in order to attract ... you have
to be a little bit dishonest, you have to give something the public will
follow.'[17] That is to say: the *Trilogia* is a sugared pill (a metaphor dear
to Boccaccio [Day 8.6]): the sour taste of the active ingredient is masked
by a sweet surface. The pleasure inherent in the *novelle* themselves is
designed to carry the dose beyond the reactionary tongue, in order to
create a viewing situation in which the very form of spectating, that is,
the location of the viewing subject (a location guaranteed formally), is
put into crisis. But before proceeding further, we should describe what
exactly we mean by *subjectivity*, *ideology*, and *interpellation*. I approach
these terms by way of Lacan's re-reading of Freud's Oedipal paradigm,
and as it has been politicized by theorists such as Althusser, Heath, de
Lauretis, and others.[18]

One of the central assumptions held by post-structuralist theorists
such as these is that subjectivity must be approached as a *discursive
construct*: the subject is constituted upon the acquisition of language,

upon the acceptance of the 'I' that locates it in dialogic relations. The process of subject formation shall be described in Lacanian terms: we will subsequently see how his formulations may be appropriated by a Marxist and/or feminist position.

Ideology can be understood as the limiting, or discouraging, of a 'full' understanding of social conditions, and the way people are constituted within them. But ideology must not be considered as simply the 'imaginary' relationship to the 'world,' but also as a 'material practice' in the sense that Althusser has elaborated.[19] Ideology, he suggests, is not a set of illusions, it is not a problem of 'false consciousness.' It is the necessary condition of action within the social network. It is a material practice in that 'it exists in the behaviour of people acting according to their beliefs.'[20]

For Althusser, ideology exists in all that is 'obvious' to us, all that is considered 'common sense.' But ideology only represents partial truths, smoothing over contradictions by presenting a seemingly coherent explanation of the order of things; it is a privileging of 'unstable' discourse that reproduces the status quo or, more precisely, allows the free extension of capitalist relations of production. Althusser describes how ideological practices are reproduced by social institutions that he called 'Ideological State Apparatuses' (ISAs), the institutions that construct and maintain consent. ISAs and 'Repressive State Apparatuses' – the coercive institutions (police, judicial, military, secret services, and so on) that work by force – 'coexist' to guarantee consent.[21] ISAs include such institutions as the educational system, the family, the law, the media, and the arts. All these serve to re-present the 'myths and beliefs' consistent with dominant values, and maintain appropriate behaviour (Althusser's debt to Antonio Gramsci's writings on ideology and hegemony is obvious). Althusser explains thus how ideology 'interpellates' subjects:

I say: the category of the subject is constitutive of all ideology, but at the same time and immediately I add that *the category of the subject is only constitutive of all ideology in so far as all ideology has the function (which defines it) of 'constituting' concrete individuals as subjects.*[22]

Further:

Ideology 'acts' or 'functions' in such a way that it 'recruits' subjects among the individuals (it recruits them all), or 'transforms' the individuals into subjects (it transforms them all) by that very precise operation which I have called *interpellation* or hailing, and which can be imagined along the lines of the most commonplace everyday police (or other) hailing: 'Hey, you there!' Assuming that the theoretical scene I have imagined takes place in the street, the hailed individual will turn around. By this mere one-hundred-and-eighty-degree physical conversion, he becomes *subject*. Why? Because he has recognized that the hail was 'really' addressed to him, and that 'it was *really him* who was hailed' (and not someone else).[23]

Thus, individuals 'freely submit' to their subjection by recognizing themselves as the 'addressee' of the hailing: they recognize themselves in the way they have been recognized by others, and in the way they have been represented in the discourses of others. This is the significance of Althusser's allegory of the policeman.

In her study of cinema as a 'technology of gender,' Teresa de Lauretis insists that strategies of subjectivation must be specified as gendered (or engendering) operations, and she criticizes Althusser's representation of the subject as neuter (but actually male). In fact, she replaces Althusser's allegory of the policeman with her own allegory of the filling out of an application form: one is asked to check the *F* box or the *M* box. 'Since the very first time we put a check mark on the little square next to the *F* on the form, we have officially entered the sex-gender system, the social relations of gender, and have become engendered as women; that is to say, not only do other people consider us females, but from that moment on *we* have been representing ourselves as women.'[24] While criticizing his resistance to issues of gender and his claims to scientificity, she adopts Althusser's understanding of ideology as a practice producing subjects, and she studies the various ways classical narrative cinema interpellates, addresses, positions, or engenders male and female subjects. Although I am entirely in sympathy with most of de Lauretis's account of Althusser's theories, I would be interested in her reading of Althusser's description, found in 'Freud and Lacan' (an essay he wrote before 'Ideology and Ideological State Apparatuses'), of human culture as an ideological battlefield, or as 'a war which is continually declared in each of its sons, who, projected, deformed and rejected, are required, each by himself in solitude and against death, to take the long forced march which makes mammiferous larvae into human children, *masculine* or *feminine subjects*.'[25]

It was Lacan who actually set the coordinates for this debate in his revisionist psychoanalytic descriptions of subject formation. Lacan also sees the subject as a discursive 'construct.' That is, before entry into the Symbolic (language, culture) the child is what Freud termed an 'oceanic self':[26] having no sense of identity, unity, or what is *other* than itself. There is, during this period in the psychic life of the child, no differentiation between the child and its surroundings: the mother, the blanket, the voice, the mother's gaze, and so on. All these objects are assumed by the child to be its own 'body,' so to speak. Lacan has written that during the 'mirror stage' the child 'recognizes' itself as distinct from its surroundings, that is, from what were previously extensions of the child's body. The mirror image offers what Lacan calls an 'Ideal-I,' for it is the (mis)recognition of an 'imaginary' unified, autonomous 'I.' The 'mirror stage' also constitutes the subject in 'lack': the entry into the Symbolic 'castrates' the subject from its original 'plenitude,' its being before specular capture. 'Once the subject has entered the symbolic order its organic needs pass through the "defiles" of the network of signification and are transformed in a way which makes them thereafter impossible to satisfy.'[27] That is, this primary suture with the mirror image also marks the constitution of the unconscious, and it supplies the very possibility of future interpellations.

The subject is cut off from the primordial libidinal drives by the law of the Other, or what Lacan calls, in his famous pun, the 'nom [non] du père' (the name/no of the father). Freud's Oedipal drama, and the moment of castration, is translated into linguistic terms: the child is forced to abandon its original desire, submit to the (symbolic) father's interdiction, and forever postpone possession of the object of desire (that desire is repressed). The subject constitutes itself through speaking, but it is also spontaneously spoken: it inherits its language upon entry into the Symbolic. The primary identification with the position 'I' allows for subsequent recognition in other subject positions (he, she ...) and also allows for the subject's linguistic orientation within the system of deictic markers (here, there ...). Subjectivity, then, stems from the recognition of the self as the Ideal-I in the symbolic order, and is a matrix of subject positions.

However, the subject undergoes the same processes of articulation and disarticulation as do any linguistic 'entities.' That is, just as signifiers, in Lacan's Saussurean model, derive meaning only by differing from other signifiers, so is the identity or unity of the 'I' a product of a process of differentiation from others (the 'I' is formed in confrontation with a 'you,' and so on). In a sense, the subject exists somewhere *between* the 'I' and the 'you.' Therefore, the subject must continually re-invent itself, or re-orient itself in certain discursive operations, operations designed precisely to fulfil this recuperative service (the subject must continually locate what is other than itself). We have now come back to Althusser's appropriation of Lacan, since for him these recuperative discursive operations must be seen as ideological strategies. Indeed, his account of ideological state apparatuses is a critique of how power is exercised and guaranteed in the appropriation of those social-cultural practices that produce subjects: again, the legal apparatus, schools, the military, television, literature, cinema. And it is to cinema that we shall now turn in order to see how it may function as a 'practice producing subjects.'

Students of cinema as a 'technology of gender' or of 'subjectivation'[28] have supplied detailed examinations of how the classical style, or the 'Hollywood code,' functions to 'interpellate' the viewing subject. This process occurs through various strategies, relating to characterization, mise-en-scène, sound-track, and others. But more important to these scholars is how the viewer's gaze is captured up in various types of shot-formations. This 'specular capture,' carried out formally, constructs what is often referred to as the viewer's *identification* with the dominant viewpoint – usually that of the hero-protagonist.

In the early 1970s, many British film theorists, associated with the film journal *Screen*, came under the influence of Althusser's appropriation of Lacan and began a renewed Brechtian assault upon how classical cinema addresses the spectator, assigning him, ideologically, a prescribed point of view, and creating a 'passive' viewer incapable of critical judgment.[29] During the decade leading up to the 'radicalization' of *Screen*, film theorists also came under the influence of Godard's own Brechtian brand of subversive cinema, which made the sabotage of spectatorial expectations the first responsibility of the engaged filmmaker at odds with the 'commodification' of the 'look.' For Godard, in consumer society images are caught up, directly or indirectly, in the production of desire or demand for commodities. The 'address' of images (in Godard's films the paradigmatic images are those drawn from advertising) positions the viewer as a certain desiring subject, within a particular image repertoire (defining beauty, conformity, normalcy, and so on). The articulation of demand in the viewer operates as a kind of sexual 'taylorism,' where desire is produced in relation to certain object-commodities. As Colin McCabe writes in his study of Godard: 'Images and their production are an area of economic activity – where there is a look to be stimulated and satisfied then there is money to be made.'[30]

What McCabe calls 'dominant narrative cinema' functions on the circulation of three series of looks: the looks of the characters on the screen, the looks of the camera, and the look of the spectator.[31] The cinema of the classical style, built upon patterns of narrative that nearly always move from initial crisis to final resolution, also presents an initial incongruence of the three series of looks. This initial incongruence is necessary for its subsequent resolution, when the three looks form a single 'cathartic' look at the happy ending. 'Closure' flows from one character's look being proved 'correct,' the correct view taken on by the camera, and thus, finally, also by the spectator. The spectator's look, his 'identification' with the correct view, is (in Lacanian-Althusserian terms) the production of an illusion of unity and security in the subject; which is also the production of a consenting subject (what Pasolini would call a conformist subject) whose 'comfort' poses no threat to existing social relations.

It has been the work of feminist theorists, for the most part, that has offered such an understanding of classical cinema; and it was feminist theorists that appropriated, and translated into politicized form, Lacan's insights into subject formation.[32] Lately, de Lauretis has continued this work, insisting that the construction of subjectivity is always a gendered one. Theorists such as de Lauretis have elaborated upon the concept of 'suture'[33] to account for the economy of the looks in narrative cinema. 'Suture' names the process whereby the subject identifies with the correct view of the (usually male) protagonist (through shot-reverse-shots, subjective shots, and also simply by the lure of narrative form). The spectator is 'sewn into' the narrative, is provided an apparently stable place from which to view. In Lacanian terms, the film provides him an imaginary reflection of an individual (which he misrecognizes for himself) 'before' subjection to the Symbolic, and thus before the experience of Oedipal prohibitions. In these terms, the re-enactment of the mirror stage provides the spectator with a unified, pre-subjective self-image, where his look is not contradicted by that of an other. The classical style holds out for the viewer an illusion of non-ambiguous self-knowledge, self-centredness, where the subject's perspective is not challenged by the proximity of the look of the other. Indeed, cinema has attained the status of an Ideological State Apparatus, in Althusser's words, founded upon the occulting of other possible looks or perspectives, alternative subject positions, and it ultimately serves to prop up existing social relations through the production of a conformity of vision. It is one of the predominant institutions servicing and guaranteeing what McLuhan called the visual order of things in late modernity.

Now, to return from our theoretical excursus, I would suggest that Pasolini's 'anticlassical' or 'mannerist' cinema offers, precisely, an occasion in which the unknown possibilities of vision, and different subject positions, can take place. It is a cinema that must therefore constantly call attention to itself, to its language, and thus bring the spectator to an ironic awareness of his 'disciplined' perspective – an awareness gained by being brought 'outside' of one's self, so to speak. Pasolini's image, in contrast to the stable, centred, 'academy frame' of classical cinema, always bears within itself the 'stain' or distortion marking the 'look of the other,' and his spectator is constantly led to vacillate between possibly antithetical subject positions. The oft-noted 'antithetical' qualities of Pasolini's production[34] are designed to 'dis-locate' the spectator, subvert traditional expectations, in order to activate the viewer's capacities for critical intervention. To appropriate Althusser's observations regarding Brechtian theatre, and translate it into cinematic terms: Pasolini's brand of filmmaking attempts to 'set in motion the illusory consciousness's mythical world – develop a new consciousness in the spectator – incomplete, like any other consciousness, but moved by this incompletion itself, the distance achieved, this inexhaustible work of criticism in action; the [film] is really the production of a new spectator, an actor, who starts where the performance ends, who only starts so as to complete it, but in life.'[35]

For Pasolini, the force that drives the viewer to active interpretation of the signs of reality that surround him is the experience of 'ambiguity,' of an 'impurity' of vision:

il prodotto cristallizzato ma profondamente fluttuante di un'inconciliabile opposizione ... L'ambiguità dunque è totale: all'interno dell'opera si svolge una lotta all'ultimo sangue, una contraddizione insanabile.

the crystalized but profoundly unstable product of a unreconcilable opposition ... Ambiguity is therefore total: within the work of art there unfolds a battle to the last man, an irremediable contradiction.[36]

Pasolini remarks elsewhere:

Io cerco di creare un linguaggio che metta in crisi l'uomo medio, lo spettatore medio, nei suoi rapporti con il linguaggio dei mass-media, per esempio.

I try to create a language that would put the average person, the average spectator, into crisis in relation to the language of the mass-media, for example.[37]

As we shall see below, in turning to the issue of point of view and perspective in the *Trilogia,* one of Pasolini's overriding preoccupations was a putting into doubt of perception, a foregrounding of the types of perceptual training undergone by human beings in a consumer society dominated by technology. For Pasolini shares Walter Benjamin's views concerning the social and historical conditioning of human perception, that is, how the material basis of society conditions the perception of the collectivity. Benjamin writes: 'During long periods of history, the perception by the historical collectives changes with the changes in the historical mode of being.'[38] This is the assumption that enables Pasolini's 'pedagogical' attitude towards *all* his activities, as Golino has suggested,[39] and that underpins his approach to film as a possible apprenticeship in resistance.[40]

Discussing Pasolini in terms of mannerism is intended to highlight anticlassical elements in his films,[41] the way they veer from the restrictions of a fixed classical style. In his poetic works, this impulse can be understood in terms of an attempt to overcome 'Petrarchan' *monolinguismo*, and rediscover something of a 'Dantesque' *plurilinguismo*.[42] Mannerism also describes the qualities of pastiche or 'contamination' that characterize his texts. As Marco Vallora writes in his study of mannerist elements in Pasolini's narrative works, we find in Pasolini's work that

il linguaggio di chi scrive è attraversato (modificato e determinato) da altri linguaggi, che interagiscono e fermentano. E non soltanto a livello idiomatico, ma anche stilistico, il tessuto narrativo registra questa frizione tra differenti sotto-linguaggi, che proprio in seguito alle loro alchimie determinano il tono del racconto.

the language of the one who writes is traversed (modified and determined) by other languages that interact and ferment. And not only at the idiomatic level, but also at the stylistic level; the narrative texture traces out this friction between different sub-languages that, in accord with their alchemy, determine the tone of the story.[43]

What this form of linguistic contamination presents in Pasolini's literary works is an ironic foregrounding of the word (what the Russian Formalists isolated as the moment the poetic word calls attention to itself): the mannered qualities of Pasolini's poetry derive from the sensation of a doubling of something already said, or an echoing of the 'preformed.' The word becomes 'strange.' For Pasolini, pastiche is a strategy of poetic *straniamento*, one of 'estranging' the word from its conventional meanings and functions, of locating it within a different context, or of calling attention to the reader's 'horizon of expectations,' as Jauss has described it.[44]

Pasolini retains this poetic of contamination when he turns to film. Indeed, as we have remarked, he insists that his films are 'poetic' in the same way his written texts are, insofar as the language of his *cinema di poesia* is likewise designed to call attention to representation itself and problematizes reception.[45] And just as Pasolini's texts often have a 'recycled' quality, so will his films often present us with 'second hand' images, images with an echo-effect, so to speak. It is not so much that we find images within the image (something Godard's films are remarkable for) but that the images themselves have the feel (sometimes subtle, other times not so subtle) of past images. We might call this, along with Antonio Costa, the '*effetto dipinto*' (the 'painting effect'), and his formulations are worth some discussion at this juncture.[46]

For Costa, the *effetto dipinto* stages a confrontation between two semiotic systems or 'models of representation'; and it is nearly always 'legible as a mark of the enunciation, with an accentuation of the metalinguistic function.'[47] That is, the *effetto dipinto* calls attention to the process of the film's production and to the problems of its reception or interpretation. But what are some of the ways the painting effect may operate in a film? According to Costa, *effetto dipinto* is a term that describes any trace of the figurative model in a film: from the painted backdrops of Meliès's *Voyage dans la lune* (1902), tinted prints, to the presence of paintings within the diegesis (Vincent Minnelli's *Lust for Life* [1956]), and so on. Yet in these examples the elements drawn from the figurative model have very definite narrative functions: they are highly motivated by the diegesis, and thus the attention of the spectator is not drawn away from narrative continuity. That is, in these cases the *effetto dipinto* does not carry a metalinguistic function in the way that interests Costa the most. Indeed, Costa's attention is drawn more to those moments in certain films when the *effetto dipinto* presents a *conflict* between models of representation, a clashing of systems that draws our attention away from the diegesis and redirects it towards the enunciation. As Costa writes:

L'inquadratura evoca quindi una pittura: perché la cita esplicitamente, perché ne riproduce determinati effetti luministici, cromatici o di organizzazione spaziale, perché ne imita la staticità o la sospensione temporale o si iscrive nella logica compositiva o iconografica di uno stesso genere (per esempio, la veduta paesaggistica, o il ritratto o il decorativismo astratto).

The frame thus evokes a painting: either because the film cites it explicitly, or it reproduces determinate chromatic or lighting effects or its spatial organization, or because the film imitates the stasis or temporal suspension of the painting, or it inscribes itself in the compositional or iconographic logic of a certain genre (for example, the landscape, or the portrait, or abstract decorativism).[48]

Mannerist Tendencies in the Early Films

Pasolini ... come è noto, è un manierista, un grande manierista, forse il maggiore della nostra letteratura dopo D'Annunzio.

Alberto Moravia

Pasolini ..., as is known, is a mannerist, a great mannerist, perhaps the greatest mannerist of our literature after D'Annunzio.[49]

We find clear and excellent examples of this *effetto dipinto* in the *Trilogia della vita*. But before we describe these, it would be helpful to take a brief look at some examples taken from Pasolini's earlier films. It has been noted quite often how films such as *Accattone* and *Mamma Roma* express a frontal style when framing characters, in a manner reminiscent of the medieval iconographic tradition. Pasolini often uses the telephoto lens to flatten the image, to reduce the illusion of depth and perspective.[50]

According to Antonio Bertini, Pasolini's peculiar usage of lenses should be seen in terms of his mannerist style:

Sembra quasi che ci sia la volontà – da parte del regista – di togliere all'immagine filmica l'impressione di tridimensionalità, di profondità di campo (dovuta soprattutto all'immagine in movimento, al movimento all'interno della inquadratura) per ricondurla in un ambito figurativo e pittorico. Il richiamo a Masaccio (che ritorna spesso nelle dichiarazioni sulla sua tecnica) non è casuale. L'obiettivo viene paragonato a un pennello nelle mani di un pittore, un pennello leggero e agile che, tuttavia, ha la forza di rendere greve, massiccia la materia, con una forte accentuazione del chiaroscuro.

It seems almost as if there were the desire – on the part of the director – to subtract from the filmic image the impression of three-dimensionality, of depth of field (owed above all to the image in movement, to movement within the frame) in order to reconduct it towards a figural or pictorial context. The reference to Masaccio (found often in Pasolini's declarations concerning his technique) is not by chance. The lens is compared to the paintbrush in the hands of a painter, a light and agile paintbrush that, nevertheless, has the ability to render the material heavy, massive, with a strong accentuation of the chiaroscuro.[51]

Nevertheless, in *Accattone* and *Mamma Roma* the *effetto dipinto* is discernible mainly as a sensation, when watching the image, of something reminiscent of a long distant painterly style: that of Masaccio, Giotto, Caravaggio, and others. (Indeed, Pasolini dedicates *Mamma Roma* to the distinguished art historian Roberto Longhi, with whom, in the mid-1940s, Pasolini had begun a thesis at the University of Bologna.) However, we have a clear example of the *effetto dipinto* only when we reach *La ricotta* in 1963. This is an extremely self-reflexive film concerning a director's attempt to produce a film about Christ's Passion (the director is played, ironically, by Orson Welles, who recites lines of Pasolini's poetry – 'I am a force from the past' – when interviewed by a journalist in the film). The film is shot in black and white until we are presented with images of the Passion itself, images that are literal translations onto film of two paintings from Pontormo (1494–1556) and Rosso Fiorentino (1494–1540), shot with a telephoto lens in extremely vivid colours as found in the original works. As the *sceneggiatura* describes the scene: 'Pontormo's *Deposition* in colour, with colours that blaze *in pieno petto*. Colours? Let's call them colours.'[52] And once we leave this scene, the film returns to black and white. On the soundtrack we hear the director's frustrated voice as he tries to get all the actors into their proper positions, with the correct facial expressions, gestures, and so on. He gets particularly upset when the actors, especially the Madonna, find it difficult to remain absolutely motionless:

REGISTA (non visto) Motore!

CIACHISTA (non visto) Quattrocentoquarantadue, prima.

REGISTA (non visto) Azione!

FIGURA DI SPALLE A COLORI Maria, Maria!

REGISTA (non visto) Non così ... lo ripeta ... più rapita, più pia ...

FIGURA DI SPALLE A COLORI Maria, Maria!

REGISTA (agitato, non visto) Stop! Le ho detto che deve restare ferma. Non agiti quei bicipiti ... Ferma, ferma! Lei è la figura di una Pala d'Altare, ha capito? Ferma! Motore!

[...]

CIACHISTA Quattrocentoquarantadue, terza.

REGISTA (non visto) Azione ... Implorante, mi raccomando: e immobile,
immobile.
FIGURA DI SPALLE A COLORI Maria, Maria ...

DIRECTOR (off-screen) Camera!
CIACHISTA (off-screen) Four hundred forty-two, take one.
DIRECTOR (off-screen) Action!
FIGURE FROM BEHIND IN COLOUR Maria, Maria!
DIRECTOR (off-screen) Not that way ... repeat it ... more enraptured, more
pious ...
FIGURE FROM BEHIND IN COLOUR Maria, Maria!
DIRECTOR (agitated, off-screen) Stop! I told you that you have to stay still. You
are a figure in an altar-piece, do you understand? Still! Camera!
[...]
CIACHISTA Four hundred forty-two, take three.
DIRECTOR (off-screen) Action ... Imploring, please: and motionless, motionless.
FIGURE FROM BEHIND IN COLOUR Maria, Maria ...[53]

Eventually, the sun disappears, the proper lighting is lost, and they are
forced to postpone the take.

Just as in Fellini's *8 1/2*, where the drama is about whether the
director-protagonist will succeed in producing his film, we have in *La
ricotta* a similarly metadiscursive film (and both films were released the
same year). The drama concerns the difficulties of filmmaking itself. The
director's insistent prompting foregrounds the *process* of making a film
and, as Costa would say, detracts from the film's illusion of reality by
highlighting the 'constructedness' of the image. The effect of distancing
is further enhanced by the sudden appearance of colour within the black
and white film: we are led to ponder the nature of the emulsion on a strip
of celluloid film, and the chemical processes necessary to capture and
fix the rays of light emanating from within the camera's field of vision.
Moreover, the vividness of the colours also matches what Arnold Hauser
calls Rosso Fiorentino's 'colourist' style, in which striking colours are
used to create bizarre, uncanny effects.[54]

Furthermore, the presence of the *tableaux vivants*, fashioned quite
significantly after the mannerist paintings of Pontormo and Rosso Fiorentino, serves to stage a conflict between two semiotic models: the painterly
and the cinematic. The frustration of the director in *La ricotta* stems from
the incompatibility of these two systems of representation. Temporal
succession has been erased from the images of Pontormo and Rosso

Fiorentino, but their translation onto film, that is, into a time-based medium, foregrounds or differentiates what is essentially cinematic. As Giovanna Grignaffini would say, here painting would constitute, for the cinema, what is 'other than itself' (*altro da sè*). For her, the figurative tendency found in *auteurs* such as Pasolini, Godard, and Rohmer would represent cinema's 'other,' necessarily overcome in order for cinema to establish itself.[55]

Furthermore, we also find possible analogies between Pasolini's filmic adaptation of these mannerist paintings and certain works of the original painters. For, as Hauser notes, Pontormo often has statues (painting's *altro da sè*) within his paintings; this kind of image-within-the-image, so to speak, leads to 'a questioning of one's criteria of reality' and contributes to what is often sensed in his paintings as perceptual 'insecurity.'[56] Indeed, Pasolini appears to value these two particular 'protomannerist' painters to the extent that they express the crisis in classical Renaissance models, that is, in how they reveal what Hauser calls a moment of ideological fragmentation or alienation.[57] Indeed, for Hauser, the fact that with these artists the representation of space no longer appears to cohere within an ideal perspective, that is, the sense that the image does not understand the nature of its spectators or, therefore, how to *locate* their gaze, leads one to believe that this period witnessed a radical interrogation of the conventions of pictorial representation. But most important of all, these paintings reveal perspective itself, the coordinates of which had been worked out by artists such as Alberti and Brunelleschi during the first half of the fifteenth century, as conventional as well. As Arturo Quintavalle remarks, 'perspective is a conception of the world.'[58] Furthermore, it is interesting to note that the artists of the time identified linear perspective as a *Tuscan* convention, and as merely one system of spatial organization among many others, yet one that was being more actively 'diffused' than any others.[59] It is indeed remarkable, and worth more extended attention, that during the same period that experienced the growing hegemony of Tuscan as the peninsula's standard language, there was an analogous attempt to hegemonize what we could call the Tuscan conventions of spatial organization. Perhaps the problem of perspective should be located within ongoing studies of the *questione della lingua* – the question of Italy's national language; and it is certainly significant that Alberti was establishing parallel theories concerning the cultivation or standardization of the Tuscan vernacular along with the standardization of a perspectival system of representation. Certainly these sorts of issues were not far from Pasolini's 'Gramscian' mind when he chose these particular painters to cite in his film. We shall return to these issues during our discussion of problems of point of view in *Il fiore delle mille e una notte* further below.

However, to return to our previous discussion, the quotation of these paintings, along with the *effetto dipinto* in general as it is found in Pasolini's work, is also significant insofar as it reveals how the language of cinema has overcome other preceding languages or models, and is furthermore able partially to *contain* them. This is close to what Linda Hutcheon means by parodic quotations of preceding models; she notes how the British director Peter Greenaway's parodies of eighteenth-century painting in *The Draughtsman's Contract* serve to make this a highly 'metadiscursive' film insofar as it interrogates the codes of representation.[60] Furthermore, pastiche or stylistic and generic contamination serve to draw attention to the very problem of containment (or *framing*, as we will discuss in chapter 4: we are led to contemplate the formal system, or what Pasolini sometimes calls the *langue*, within and from which the narrative and stylistic elements draw their significance. Once this level of awareness has been attained, the remaining task, says Pasolini, is to modify the *langue* in a 'revolutionary manner': 'Voglio dire che la "*langue*" ... non si evolve solo regolarmente ... *ma può modificarsi anche rivoluzionarmente*' ('What I mean is that the *langue* ... does not evolve regularly ... *but can modify itself in a revolutionary manner as well*').[61] Indeed, *La ricotta* is saturated with a multitude of languages, its frames multilayered, and we might treat it as a prototypical example of Pasolini's style of pastiche or contamination in his films.

Only in one other film before the *Trilogia della vita* do we come upon an example of the *effetto dipinto* as it is found in *La ricotta*, and we shall only mention it here. We find towards the beginning of *Che cosa sono le nuvole?* (1967) a reproduction of Velazquez's *Las Meninas*. This painting, the topic of an influential essay by Michel Foucault,[62] presents us with an artist at his easel, staring out at the viewer. In the background of the painting we find a mirror with a reflected image of a couple not present within the image; in fact the placing of the mirror would suggest that this couple is standing in the position of the viewer. That is, the painting is *about* the place of the spectator (Foucault writes: 'we are observing ourselves being observed')[63] and about classical codes of spatial organization. Again Foucault writes: 'Perhaps there exists, in this painting by Velazquez, the representation, as it were, of Classical representation, and the definition of the space it opens up to us. And, indeed, representation undertakes to represent itself here in all its elements, with its images, the eyes to which it is offered, the faces it makes visible, the gestures that call it into being.'[64] By quoting this painting within *Che cosa sono le nuvole?*, the metadiscursivity of the cited painting is transferred to Pasolini's film, which thus becomes the representation of cinematic representation: it is Pasolini's way of standing within his own film, his Arriflex in hand, looking out from the screen onto a challenged audience.

Decameron: Pasolini's Film-Fresco

This ironic interrogation of spectatorial expectations, and of what we might call the role and function of the filmmaker, will be repeated but with even more severity in the three films that make up the *Trilogia della vita*. Indeed, in two of these films Pasolini's self-reflexivity becomes even more explicit when he plays Giotto's pupil in the *Decameron*, and Chaucer in *The Canterbury Tales*.

But of the three films that make up the *Trilogia*, the *Decameron* contains the most developed structure, and this structure is reinforced quite clearly through the presence of two reproductions of well-known paintings. As our previous chapter discussed, the film is divided into two frame-tales, the first being Ciappelletto's Tale (or the Usurer's Tale), and the second being the Artist's Tale. Their two stories are not themselves contained within any other frame-tale. Indeed, it would appear that the film's central conflict is expressed implicitly in the structural relation between Ciappelletto and Giotto's pupil: between the usurer and the artist. Judging from Pasolini's own comments on the film, as one contesting the neocapitalist commodification or reification of just about everything, one is led to view the film's structure in an allegorical manner. That is, the film stages a conflict between (a) the extension of capitalist models of exchange, based upon the abstraction of exchange-value from use-value, and (b) the 'poetic' or 'artistic' and even primitively 'religious' practice that cannot but exist as a point of resistance to the extension of this logic (according to which things become commodities and people become labour power). This opposition is not presented dialectically in the film: for Pasolini this conflict is not resolvable (it is *'insanabile,'* irremediable). There is not and perhaps may never be any way to overcome this opposition, or at least its form, once and for all. This also explains why it is that the Usurer's Tale and the Artist's Tale are not found within a frame-tale of their own. Since for Pasolini there is no dialectical *Aufhebung* of these two antithetical movements, then there is no possibility of raising oneself to a position uninfected by this dichotomy from which to survey and represent the struggle (this would hold out the possibility of a cathartic resolution of the film's central conflict: here, obviously, 'happy endings' are anathema).

This structural allegory is reinforced within the individual *novelle*, which are almost all organized around an opposition between pleasure and an institutional and/or economically motivated interdiction. That is, the structure of the individual *novelle* reflects the overall pattern of the *Decameron* itself: there is a sort of chain of resemblances in the structural world of the film. This chain of structural echoes is also found in Boccaccio's text, but there the reader is granted the possibility of a resolution of narrative oppositions since, as we discussed earlier, the experience of narrative disorder functions ultimately to 'reveal' (or actually service) the perception of an overarching order (just as is found, although far more clearly, in the *Divina Commedia*, one might add). As we mentioned, for Pasolini, no such guarantee exists.

It is in the *Decameron*, out of all the films in the *Trilogia*, where the presence of the figural model and the 'play' of the *effetto dipinto* carry a structural function. For Pasolini 'quotes' (that is, he mis-quotes or 'mix-quotes,' as we shall see) two important paintings in the film: Bruegel the Elder's *The Battle between Carnival and Lent* (1559) is embedded within the Usurer's Tale, and Giotto's *Last Judgment* (c. 1306) is placed within the Artist's Tale.[65] Yet, upon comparing Pasolini's Bruegel or Giotto to reproductions of the original paintings we see that the energies of contamination found in Pasolini's film have infected even these images. That is, in transferring Bruegel's *Battle* to the screen, he has mixed in certain elements and themes from another Bruegel image, *The Triumph of Death* (1562–3); and in Giotto's *Last Judgment*, in the very centre of the composition, we find that Pasolini has replaced Jesus sitting in judgment with the very benevolent, maternal presence of Mary with child probably taken from Giotto's *Ognissanti Madonna* (although, certainly, quite similar 'stock' images may be found in Cimabue, Duccio, Daddi, and many others; Giotto's panel painting, completed around 1310, distinguishes itself from these in its successful evocation of three-dimensional space – an evocation, by the way, *not* found in his *Last Judgment*). That is, there has been a sort of 'contagion' between two of Bruegel's paintings and between two of Giotto's. And this contagion, significant in itself, also carries a certain thematic significance. It also reveals the fate of all that enters into Pasolini's aesthetic universe: all that had been previously delimited, identified, completed, and catalogued becomes infected by ambiguity, paradox, and contradiction.[66] That is, in the stylistic world of contamination, whatever had been responsible for assigning a 'durable' meaning to signs (whatever 'linguistic institution,' as Saussure insists, or whatever ideology) is refused entry. Here previously distinct models, genres, or languages collide and interanimate one another: the very boundaries of these paintings, their frames, dissolve, and their contents blend in an allegory of unlimited contamination. To recall the Jakobsonian model, the syntagmatic and paradigmatic pressures exerted upon the signifier are not counteracted: the *ideological* counterforce is subtracted by Pasolini, as signs begin to drift and be contaminated by other signs.

Pastiche is the appearance of texts in which the nature of this 'counterforce' is brought to view, ultimately bringing about the quite radical question of whether it is possible, given the *necessity* to counteract syntagmatic or paradigmatic 'drift' (unless one is a champion of aphasia), to engage in the processes that attribute significance to things and subjects. As Pasolini has written, he is interested in revolutionary engagement within the *langue*: and as he said in an interview, 'there exist excluded, or self-excluded, people who – from the outside – are able to foresee the new structure of the world.'[67] The *Decameron* brings the spectator to experience this critical perspective of the 'excluded.' The *effetto dipinto* in the *Decameron* is an example of Pasolini's pastiche style, in the mixing of representational models and in the presence of the *preformato*; but we also see that the paintings he chooses are themselves contaminated by other paintings. Thus: contaminations within contaminations on to infinity.

This appears to me to be the most interesting way to read the presence of Bruegel and Giotto in the film, that is, from a perspective interested in a politics of form. That is not to say that at the level of theme these paintings offer nothing significant for this discussion: they do have narrative or thematic motivation, and thus do not present themselves as pure excess. Most of the *Decameron*'s tales are structured around two basic oppositions: (a) between desire/pleasure and interdiction, and (b) between 'naïveté' or 'human spirit' and money. That is, the majority of these *novelle* are structured around two basic oppositions that identify physical pleasure with naïve, and even religious, human simplicity and also identify the often institutional denial of these desires with the drive for profit. This basic 'humanist' or idealist understanding and representation of alienation under the logic of exchange as it is presented by Pasolini throughout the *Trilogia* is often attacked by those who find in it an expression of a sentimental nostalgia for a natural and un-alienated state of being. Pasolini is the first to declare that this was his intention when he made the films. Regarding the setting of the *Decameron* in particular, he remarks:

È anche per questo che ho ricostruito quel mondo come un mondo di classi popolari e sono andato a Napoli per ritrovare un rapporto autentico del popolo con la realtà, un rapporto che il popolo, quale che sia la sua ideologia, riesce a stabilire senza le distorsioni ideologiche del piccolo borghese.

It is also for this reason that I reconstructed that world as a world of popular classes and that I went to Naples in order to rediscover an authentic relationship between the people and reality, a relationship that the people, whatever its ideology, is able to establish without the ideological distortions of the petit-bourgeois.[68]

However, to return to our discussion of the *effetto dipinto* in the *Decameron*, we can see that the paintings in question, and the manner in which they interfere with one another thematically, communicate with great economy many of the narrative oppositions found in the *novelle* themselves.[69]

Let us begin with Bruegel: clearly, by representing Bruegel's *Battle between Carnival and Lent*, what the film leads us to negotiate, again, is the basic opposition between (a) the pleasure principle, and the celebration of the transgressive, desiring body, and (b) a repressive principle, designed to canalize, neutralize, or sublimate this 'carnivalesque' body (Bakhtin's analysis of the 'carnivalesque' in Rabelais comes quickly to mind).[70] (See chart 1.) As Lawton writes, the conflict centres around the 'primitive urges of Carnival and the repressive tendencies of Lent, and it is from this perspective that all the episodes in the film must be viewed.'[71] Yet Bruegel's *Battle* presents this opposition as undecided: it appears to be an even struggle with no indication of a 'victor.' However, by contaminating Bruegel's *Battle* with images from *The Triumph of Death*, Pasolini clearly communicates the corruption of carnivalesque vitality through the agents of institutionalized dogmas. And in fact this sequence ends on a particularly pessimistic note when the Christological symbol of the fish held out on the pallet in the *Battle* is replaced by a skull – the principal motif of *The Triumph of Death*. And in this manner Pasolini's anguished reaction to the 'corruption' and 'commercialization' of the human body is translated to the screen. As he remarked during a conference on sexuality and cinema in 1973, up until then he had believed in the transgressive and liberatory essence of the sexual body:

mi è sembrato che la sola realtà preservata fosse quella del corpo ... Ora, i borghesi, creatori di un nuovo tipo di civiltà, non potevano che giungere a derealizzare il corpo. Ci sono riusciti, infatti, e ne hanno fatto una maschera.

Chart 1 *Ciappelletto's Vision*

---

1. Extreme LS. Telephoto lens (flattened image); few depth indicators; little motion. Reproduction of Bruegel's *Struggle between Carnival and Lent* (3 secs.)

2. LS. Figure of Lent on wheeled pedestal; motionless (4 secs.)

3. LS. White robed monks playing in circle (4 secs.)

4. LS. Pan of acrobats tumbling (5 sec.)

5. LS. Figure sleeping next to wagon; figures playing leapfrog screen-left (5 secs.)

6. LS. Standing women; one woman seated in wooden sled (4 secs.)

7. LS. Figures, representing Carnival, seated on long wheeled barrel (2 secs.)

8. LS. Figures asleep around table (3 secs.)

9. LS. Black robed figures walking towards camera with tree-branch; men on crutches in foreground (6 secs.)

10. LS. Group of figures pulling cart with wrapped corpse, moving towards camera (6 secs.)

11. LS. Two black hooded men pushing cart full of skulls (4 secs.)

12. LS. Pan from right to left; women carrying black chair; black hooded soldiers in background (4 secs.)

13. MLS. Figure of Lent; arrival of cart with corpse behind her; pan left to right to follow cart (7 secs.)

14. MS. Hand-held camera; corpse wrapped in white gauze, in cart (5 secs.)

15. CU. Hand-held camera; Lent; great depth of field; women in middle ground; black soldiers in background (4 secs.)

16. CU. Skull on end of Lent's pole; seated women in background (5 secs.)

Total shots: 16
Average shot length: 4.5 seconds
Duration: 71 seconds

---

it seemed to me that the only surviving reality was that of the body ... Now, the bourgeoisie, creators of a new type of civilization, could not but arrive at the de-realization of the body. They have succeeded, in fact, and they have made of it a mask.[72]

The *Decameron* is the eloquent and passionate expression of this (inevitably nostalgic and utopian) anguish.

Having thus established the thematic importance of Bruegel in the Usurer's Tale, we now turn to the presence of Giotto in the Artist's

Tale. Whereas Bruegel is made to be emblematic of Ciappelletto's world, the images derived from Giotto's frescoes appear diametrically opposed to that world, and in fact present a (certainly religious and artistic) counterforce to it. In this film, the spectator is led to conceptualize a sort of moral struggle between the figures of Ciappelletto and Giotto's pupil, and we are asked to consider their allegorical significance. The film presents what Pasolini calls a 'monstrous' opposition between art and commodification in the film – 'monstrous' since insuperable. And indeed, as he writes, cinema is itself the 'guilty' medium that tries to balance out these apparently contradictory forces:

Infatti il cinema in quanto arte è impuro essendo *anche* merce; e in quanto merce è impuro essendo *anche* arte. L'ambiguità dunque è totale: all'interno dell'opera si svolge una lotta all'ultimo sangue, una contraddizione insanabile; e, in tale caso, l'ambiguità dell'opera sarebbe l'unico possibile superamento, l'unica possibile sintesi. In tutto questo però, a pensarci bene, c'è qualcosa di sbagliato. Arte e merce non possono essere due forze contraddittorie, all'interno di una stessa opera. La loro coesistenza infatti – enunciata così – non è un rapporto dialettico, ma semplicemente una mostruosità; una sirena, metà donna e metà pesce, o un ermafrodita, metà uomo e metà donna; insomma un fenomeno da baraccone. Non si può opporre arte a merce, perché i due concetti appartengono a due universi incommensurabili e diversi; e perciò non possono integrarsi, ma semplicemente se mai coesistere in un solo corpo, che è dunque un 'monstrum.'

In fact, insofar as it is art, cinema is impure being *also* commodity; and insofar as it is commodity, it is impure being *also* art. The ambiguity is thus total: within the work of art there unfolds a battle to the last man, an irremediable contradiction; and in this case the ambiguity of the work would be the only possible sublation, the only possible synthesis. However, in thinking this over, in all this there is something mistaken. Art and commodities cannot be two contradictory forces, within a single work of art. In fact, their coexistence – described in this manner – is not a dialectical relationship, but is simply a monstrosity; a siren, half-man and half-woman, that is, a phenomenon of the carnival. It is not possible to oppose art and the commodity because the two concepts pertain to two incommensurable and different universes; and for this reason they are unable to integrate themselves but perhaps they can simply coexist in one body, which is therefore a *monstrum*.[73]

And as we shall discuss further below, the reproduction of the 'mercantilist' Bruegel in Ciappelletto's vision-sequence is carried out in an extremely asymmetrical fashion by Pasolini, whereas the artist's Giottesque dream-sequence contains an extremely symmetrical structure: it would appear that, when compared, these two sequences are about the presence or absence of an organic centre, and the impact that this presence or absence will exert upon representation.

But before we explore this issue, we can see that Pasolini's reproduction of Giotto's *Last Judgment* contains thematic and structural significance quite similar to that found in the Bruegel sequence. Giotto's fresco also submits to the forces of contamination found in Pasolini's film: for as we mentioned earlier, the *Last Judgment* is made to blend with Giotto's *Ognissanti Madonna*, and in the 'mix' the central figure of Christ sitting in judgment is displaced by the benevolent figure of Mary and child. I would not be the first to note here a displacement of the paternal image of Christ carrying out the law by the image of Mary's perfect maternal love. An interpretation of this shift along Oedipal lines certainly seems legitimate given Pasolini's oft-noted 'regressive' Oedipal obsession with his own mother, and antagonism towards his father (this has become a cliché in Pasolini criticism), although I would resist such a transfer of attention onto a biographical level.[74] However, if we are willing, as Brunetta suggests,[75] to project this idea of Pasolini's own individual Oedipal anguish onto a broader area of social relations, we can read this maternal displacement as yet another image of a general resistance to the imposition of Law, or the exercising of power by the 'fathers.' It is in Pasolini's plays[76] where he most insistently projects the Oedipal struggle between father and son onto a 'mythic' conflict of dominators versus the dominated; and it is when read in this allegorical manner that any perceived Oedipal drama ceases to produce simplistic psychologistic commentary on Pasolini's work.

But the real significance of the presence of these two painterly worlds is revealed when they are compared to one another. For not only do we find a marked contrast in theme, but there is also a striking difference in the way each vision-sequence is structured. Let us first examine structure. Both sequences are of nearly identical duration, about one minute long; both contain nearly the same number of shots (Ciappelletto's vision contains sixteen, Giotto's pupil's eighteen); and both sequences have an average shot length of about one hundred frames (roughly four seconds). Furthermore, both sequences seem to be shot according to a basic formula: an extremely static establishing shot reproducing quite literally the original paintings, shot with a telephoto lens to flatten the image, followed by an analytic breakdown of this image in a montage sequence containing a great deal of camera-movement highlighting movement within the *mise en scène*. The sequence moves from stasis to motion, from long shots to close-ups, and from a flattened image to a more 'realistic' representation of depth of field. As our earlier discussion of the *effetto dipinto* indicated, we are initially asked to consider the images as the original artist intended: we are led to scan the entire image and segment it on our own in order to locate its focal point or centre of attention. That is, Pasolini calls upon our competence as viewers of paintings. We then proceed through a rather rapid montage series that calls upon an altered viewing competence: one derived from the cinematic model of representation. Here the *effetto dipinto* stages a conflict in readerly competences. Indeed, it calls attention to potentially divergent codes of representation and perception (and, ultimately, to the structured and structuring nature of perception itself).

But this is where the similarities between these two sequences end. For what is clear, given their shared 'metrical' form, is a radical dissymmetry of the Bruegel sequence as compared to the extreme symmetry found in the Giotto sequence (see chart 2). In this sequence, the image is clearly centred around the Madonna, and we are given close-ups of her face at regular intervals. The panning of the camera to the right of the Madonna, scanning the choirboys, is followed by a symmetrical panning of the camera to the left; a close-up of the boys at her feet to her right is followed by a close-up of boys at her feet to her left. Against this highly symmetrical horizontal composition is the vertical descent of the damned into Hell. The camera movement traces out the pattern of the crucifix. And the 'harmony' of the image is reinforced by the Gregorian chants on the sound-track.

The primary Giottesque image and Pasolini's cinematic version of it continually reassert the principle of their orientation and stability. Ciappelletto's vision sequence, on the contrary, offers no analogous representational centre, or organic principle according to which to orient the composition. We have none of the visual 'counterpoint' that we have described in the Giotto sequence: there is no matching of camera movement, and there is no reiteration of a central, controlling presence in the image. That is, while the figure of Lent might appear to provide such a centre, the activities of the other characters in the image, and the various peripheral episodes being carried on around her, do not appear to have anything to do with her; neither the lines of compositional force in the initial establishing shot of the image nor Pasolini's editing procedures or camera motion seem to be motivated by her guiding presence. Certainly,

Chart 2 *The Artist's Vision*

---

1. MLS. Hand-held camera. Pasolini/Giotto's pupil lying in bed, shot from feet; strong side-lighting; he suddenly awakens, stares into camera (5 secs.)

2. Extreme LS. Reproduction of Giotto's *Last Judgment*, with Christ replaced by The Ognissanti Madonna. Extremely flat image (telephoto lens); very symmetrical, static (3 secs.)

3. CU. Madonna's face against blue field; she stares into the camera (4 secs.)

4. MLS. As 1

5. LS. Boys in choir to the right of Madonna; camera pans right to scan choir (10 secs.)

6. LS. Boys in choir to the left of Madonna; camera pans left to scan choir (7 secs.)

7. MLS. Boys at feet of Madonna on her right (2 secs.)

8. MLS. Boys at feet of Madonna on her left (2 secs.)

9. ECU. Madonna staring into camera (4 secs.)

10. As 4 (3 secs.)

11. LS. Detail of Inferno section of painting; camera tilts down while panning slightly from right to left; souls are dragged to hell (3 secs.)

12. LS. Camera tilts down and continues pan left; figures descending downwards into hell (3 secs.)

13. MLS. Hand-held camera; group of wailing nuns (3 secs.)

14. As 4 (2 secs.)

15. LS. Detail of lower left portion of painting (2 secs.)

16. MS. Detail of three women standing next to Church on boy's shoulders (3 secs.)

17. MS. Church on boy's shoulders (3 secs.)

18. As 4; Pasolini/Giotto's pupil puts head on pillow, returns to sleep (5 secs.)

Total shots: 18
Average shot length: 4 seconds
Duration: 65 seconds

---

the disparities of these two sequences may have a historical explanation; clearly, as art historians have remarked, the theological and cosmological order presumed by Giotto's medieval frescoes is no longer possible in Bruegel's world-view,[77] and Bruegel is usually described as one of the first painters to organize his canvases according to modern scientific (post-Galilean) principles. The fragmentary, acentred, and episodic qualities of his paintings derive from his privileging of rationalist certainties over theological ones.[78] And the progress of art history since Giotto shows a gradual fragmentation of space along with the search for principles of representational order not linked to an ahistorical, supernatural, or irrational guarantee. Pasolini does not reproduce this progression. Indeed, it is significant that Giotto's imagery appears in the *Decameron* within the Artist's Tale that forms a response to the Usurer's Tale, with Bruegel as an emblem of that mercantilist, rationalist (and, as we discussed, allegorically neocapitalist) world. That is, Giotto's pupil, played by Pasolini himself, becomes the ironic presence of the filmmaker within the film; and the analogy thus set up between the fresco painter and the filmmaker would suggest some kind of a 'return' to the type of religious and didactic model found in pre-modern art as a response to the experience and representation of fragmentation in modernity.

On the other hand, it may be argued that Pasolini is simply presenting us with two contradictory modes of representation, and two antithetical attitudes towards the organic or edifying responsibilities of the artist, and we are left to vacillate, as he does, between the two. That is, between the rationalism and realism of Bruegel and the moralizing religious frescoes of Giotto, and the two vastly different social roles these artists conceive for themselves, we find Pasolini's own contradictory or antithetical, non-dialectical film style.[79] Also significant is how these two artists express diverse understandings of spectatorship, as we shall see more clearly in a discussion of Giotto to follow. That is, whereas Bruegel has clearly interiorized the humanist or Tuscan codification of perspective, and organizes his canvasses around an ideal individual point of view, Giotto's frescoes do not locate an individualized, organizing viewpoint. Indeed, they presume a collective viewer, and provoke a shared response to whatever (usually biblical) topic he represents. Pasolini, himself attempting to provoke a collective negotiation of sociopolitical issues while utilizing a technology born of post-Renaissance or Cartesian models of representation that resist such a collective address, is clearly presenting this contradiction as an aporia. And such a problematization of point of view or perspective is present in Pasolini's reproduction of Giotto's fresco.

What is most obvious in the image of Giotto's *Last Judgment* are the distortions in proportion of the bodies, as well as an extremely flattened image where the illusion of depth has been eliminated completely.[80] Thus, the chorus boys flanking the Madonna appear to occupy the same plane, and they appear to be hanging in space (which is characteristic of painting especially *before* Giotto, with Cimabue for example). The fresco fails to locate any single point of view, and Giotto seems to appeal to a collective audience rather than to a single viewer whose perspective would organize the composition.

In a certain sense, Giotto's fresco does not 'suture.' It retains what Pasolini calls the 'epic' address in that it addresses a collectivity rather than a subject; it retains the flavour of the collective utterance of medieval oral culture. Thus, Pasolini's representation of this image forms a rejection of the singularization and disembodiment of point of view that occurred in the Renaissance, and it is a refusal of bourgeois modes of subjectivation that depend upon such a constriction of vision (cinema being one of them, ironically). It forms an appeal to an idealized, pre-Renaissance way of seeing identified with the medieval characters of the film, and with their wholly un-bourgeois modes of comportment. The combination of this 'epic' address with the conventional perspective (and thus 'realistic' organization of space) found during the rest of the film also reproduces the 'mixed' perspective found in Boccaccio's text which, as writing, addressed an individual reader, but also idealized its audience as a collectivity (in the novel the audience is always assumed to be a group). This combination is significant insofar as Pasolini insists that his own free-indirect style 'presuppone non un destinatario, ma un coro di destinatari.'[81] Thus, the ironic identification with the fresco-painter in the film becomes even more significant.

But it is also essential to note that Giotto was involved in a series of experiments with various conflicting systems of representation. Pasolini's early mentor Roberto Longhi was one of the first art historians to note how Giotto was among the first to show an awareness of the compositional possibilities of quasi-rectilinear perspective (quasi since not yet worked out mathematically). What this offered to the painter was a new sense of depth; and as Erwin Panofsky and John White have shown, this was the actual birth of pictorial space in late-medieval painting, which involved profoundly new attitudes towards spectators: a new location of the viewer.[82] White, especially, has shown how both Giotto and Masaccio, Pasolini's favourite painters, produced frescoes containing multiple points of view.[83] He notes how their experiments with perspective indicate a certain *confusion* concerning the location of the viewer.[84] But what interested Longhi the most was that Giotto treated the apparent breakthrough in the possibilities of naturalistic composition in depth as merely one system of representation available to the artist; that is, only one amongst many others (including certain Oriental modes imported along the cultural trade routes leading through Tuscany; these modes, by the way, will be the ones Pasolini will find interesting for *Il fiore delle mille e una notte*, whose citations of Persian miniatures form what he calls a challenge to Eurocentric perspective, as we will discuss further below). Pasolini, probably influenced by the findings of his teacher, finds in Giotto an artist experimenting with various codes of representation, codes that are in competition over the location of viewers; new terms of spectatorship are beginning to be elaborated. And in paintings designed to 'convert' the audience, such as Giotto's (and Pasolini's, for that matter), this is clearly an important issue.

However, the presence of multiple perspectives in Giotto's work, with no real privilege given to one – that is, the contamination of pictorial systems that is characteristic of Giotto's work seen on the whole – has suggested to some art historians that Giotto was situated in a period of transition, when the very nature of reception or of spectating was not entirely clear. This was a period of time in which the legitimacy of traditional ways of seeing was beginning to be questioned, and modes of representation began to hybridize. In the literature of the age this development can be seen in hybrid forms such as Dante's *Vita nuova*, and indeed in Boccaccio's own *Decameron*, which forms a sort of pastiche of pre-existing genres, and which is also a text very much preoccupied with the actual physical location and spiritual conditions of its readers. These stylistic and ideological issues help to explain the motivations behind Pasolini's choice of Giotto as well as Boccaccio.

For Pasolini was, like these two, an artist working in an age of transition, a period of ideological fracture. And indeed, what has been called the post-modern hybrid or pastiche aesthetic can be seen, as Jameson suggests,[85] as a symptom of crises characteristic of late capital. Pasolini too felt himself to be engaged in battle over the imaginary of his spectator. And we should remember, in fact, that he turned from literary writing to cinema because he had lost faith in traditional genres, and was no longer confident that he understood the expectations of readers and spectators. Pasolini's ideal interlocutor no longer read books but went to the cinema: this fact obviously called for a change in technique.

Pasolini's *Decameron* is a film that attempts to capture the eye of the viewer in order to split it, as it were – the eye is taken up within a collage of recognizable visual languages, so to speak – and it is a film that mixes perspectives. But, one might object, does not montage in any given Hollywood-style film multiply or fragment perspective? Certainly it does, but it does so while maintaining point of view intact or, we might say, coherent, through a conventional organization of narrative space and time. This was shown to us, for example, by the Surrealist filmmakers especially. Pasolini contaminates conflicting or untenable points of view, but not in a surreal fashion. In the *Decameron* he often presents unlocated spaces and temporalities (recall the Prologue sequence, for example), and the episodic nature of the original text contributes to the fragmentary qualities of the film. He presents his spectator with a series of perceptual challenges, appealing ultimately to the spectator's own creative ability to form meaningful narrative links between spaces and times where perhaps none are offered. And in the reproduced Giotto fresco, we are nearly overwhelmed by a sort of baroque excess of visual information, and by distortions in proportion: it is clearly meant to be a *mirabile visione*, a miraculous and sublime vision. Such a vision, by definition – and it has become a literary commonplace since Dante's *Divina Commedia* – requires but also defies interpretation, and in fact it installs an unbridgeable gap between apprehension and comprehension. As Pasolini would say, meaning is suspended: ' "To suspend the meaning": here is a stupendous epigraph for what could be a new description of the commitment, the mandate of the writer' (*HE*, 136).

In his films, Pasolini brings the cinematic model into conflict with the painterly model, and in so doing the spectator's consciousness is made to vacillate between two diverse competences. That is, we are led to an experience of a sort of 'in-betweenness,' of indecision and ambivalence in our attempts to form meaning. And it would appear that, for Pasolini, this experience of disorientation is a necessary step in his search for an altered film language and film spectator. By putting representational codes into play, and by forcing this experience of what Barthes has called the reader's 'jouissance,'[86] that is, the moment of confusion between apprehension and comprehension (or the time it takes for us to locate the concept that might account for or rationalize an image), Pasolini produces in the spectator an awareness of the power of the code itself, and of the coded nature of phenomena. And, as our discussion of Althusser has shown, the distance from critical awareness of the organizing power of the code (or 'ideology,' in his terminology) to a theory of a radical cultural praxis is short. Or again, in the ironic contamination of conflicting models within a text, 'si opera violentamente e brutalmente, una dilacerazione, una falla, da cui irrompe l'*altra materia*' ('A rent, a breach, is effected violently and brutally on such cultured material; from it the *other* material erupts.').[87]

For Pasolini, cinema, the 'written language of reality,' reveals precisely the coded nature of our relationship to 'reality.' Indeed, it shows what the Centaur in *Medea*, in his lectures to the young Jason, calls the non-naturality of nature: 'Non c'è niente di naturale nella natura, ragazzo mio, tienilo bene in mente' ('There is nothing natural in nature, my boy, keep that well in mind'). According to Pasolini, the invention of the movie-camera/projector at the end of the last century is analogous to the invention of writing: writing gives the sign a new density, draws it away from the mouth, and presents an objective distance between signs and referents; after writing, language presents itself as an object of study, and as subject to morphological and semantic mutations. For Pasolini, writing

ha rivelato all'uomo cos'è la sua lingua orale, prima di tutto. Certamente è stato questo il primo scatto in avanti della nuova coscienza culturale umana nata dall'invenzione dell'alfabeto: la coscienza della lingua orale, o, tout court, la coscienza della lingua. Il secondo momento rivoluzionario è quello che – in polemica con De Saussure – descrive Benvenuto Terracini: ossia una maturazione del pensiero, che, se si rappresentava 'naturalmente' nella lingua orale, non si poteva che rappresentare 'coscientemente' nella lingua scritta. Infine, la lingua scritta ha rilevato e accentuato la 'linearità' della lingua (che, nell'essere solo parlata è corretta dalle intonazioni e dalla mimica).

revealed to man what his oral language is, first of all. Certainly this was the first movement forward in the new human cultural consciousness born of the invention of the alphabet: the consciousness of oral language or, *tout court*, the consciousness of language. The second revolutionary moment is the one that – in disagreement with Saussure – Benvenuto Terracini describes: that is, a maturation of thought which, if it is represented 'naturally' in oral language, could only be represented 'consciously' in written language. Ultimately, written language revealed and accentuated the 'linearity' of language (which, when it is only spoken, is corrected by intonations and by gestures).[88]

Just as any 'natural' relations between language and thought or things are made problematic with writing, so will our own 'natural' relations with the world, that is, the way we relate to people and things that surround us, be revealed as ideological relations:

Gli stessi procedimenti rivoluzionari che la lingua scritta ha portato rispetto alla lingua parlata, il cinema porterà rispetto alla realtà. Il linguaggio della realtà, fin che era naturale, era fuori dalla nostra coscienza: ora che ci appare 'scritto' attraverso il cinema, non può non richiedere una coscienza. Il linguaggio scritto della realtà, ci farà sapere prima di tutto che cos'è il linguaggio della realtà:

e finirà infine col modificare il nostro pensiero su di essa, facendo dei nostri rapporti fisici, almeno, con la realtà, dei rapporti culturali.

The same revolutionary procedures that written language produced in regard to spoken language, cinema will produce in regard to reality. The language of reality, as long as it was natural, was beyond our consciousness: now that it appears 'written' through cinema, it cannot fail to demand a consciousness. The written language of reality will cause us first of all to know what the language of reality is, and it will end up finally modifying our idea of it – at least transforming our physical relations with reality into cultural relations.[89]

Furthermore, we are clearly being invited, while watching his films, to involve ourselves within the arena where the meanings of these mutable cultural relations are being formulated. That is, in Barthes's words, we are being asked to consider 'the history of the semantic techniques by which literature [and film, in this context] imposes a meaning (even if it is an "empty" meaning) upon what it says; in short, we must have the courage to enter the "kitchen of meaning." '[90] Or simply, as Pasolini notes: 'Bisogna ideologizzare, bisogna deontologizzare' ('We must ideologize, we must de-ontologize').[91]

The type of stylistic contamination found in the *Decameron* is found throughout the *Trilogia*, and is designed to elicit an active critical consciousness in the viewer. As Pasolini will specify repeatedly, what we are being asked to consider in particular in the *Trilogia della vita* is the *conventionality* of our physical and sexual 'nature.' The body and sex, he writes, are a language, and thus subject to change:

Il rapporto sessuale è un linguaggio (ciò per quanto mi riguarda è stato chiaro ed esplicito specialmente in *Teorema*): ora i linguaggi o sistemi di segni cambiano. Il linguaggio o sistema di segni del sesso è cambiato in Italia in pochi anni, radicalmente. Io non posso essere fuori dell'evoluzione di alcuna convenzione linguistica della mia società, compresa quella sessuale. Il sesso è oggi la soddisfazione di un obbligo sociale, non un piacere contro gli obblighi sociali.

The sexual relation is a language (as far as I'm concerned, this has been clear and explicit especially in *Teorema*): now languages or sign-systems change. In Italy, the language or sign-system of sex has changed in very few years, radically. I cannot exist outside of the evolution of whatever linguistic convention of my society, including the sexual one. Today, sex is the satisfaction of a social obligation, not a pleasure against social obligations.[92]

Indeed, Pasolini makes *Salò* as an expression of his refusal of this sexual division of labour. The *Decameron* is a celebration of an ideal, pre-capitalist sexuality, when sex was still a 'compensation' for repression, and thus a resistance to repression:

... la cosa più sincera dentro di me, in quel momento, era fare un film su un sesso la cui gioiosità fosse un compenso – come infatti era – alla repressione: fenomeno che stava per finire ormai per sempre. La tolleranza di lì a poco avrebbe reso il sesso triste e ossessivo.

... for me the most sincere thing, during that time, was to make a film about a sexuality whose joyous nature was a compensation – as in fact it once was – for repression – a phenomenon that was then about to disappear forever. Soon thereafter tolerance would render sex sad and obsessive.[93]

What was not tolerated, however, was Pasolini's *Decameron*, which excited such reaction that, since its release, 152 lawsuits and four unmotivated seizure orders (subsequently revoked) have been lodged against it.[94] This reaction cannot be accounted for simply as one provoked by certain 'excessive' contents of the film. Rather, it is the manner in which thematic excess translates into formal excess (what we have been calling contamination or mannerism) that guarantees such a radical response in those groups whose security depends upon the system of subjection Pasolini so consistently attacks.

Contamination and Excess: *I racconti di Canterbury* as *una struttura da farsi*

Gli unici momenti espressivi acuti del film, sono, appunto, le *'insistenze'* delle inquadrature e dei ritmi del montaggio, il cui realismo d'impianto ... si carica attraverso la durata abnorme di un'inquadratura o di un ritmo di montaggio, fino a esplodere in una sorta di *scandalo tecnico*. Tale insistenza sui particolari, specie su certi particolari degli excursus, è una deviazione rispetto al sistema del film: è *la tentazione a fare un altro film*.

The only expressively sharp moments of the film are, precisely, the *'insistent pauses'* of the framing and of the rhythms of the editing. The programmatic realism of these devices ... is charged during the abnormal duration of a shot or of an editing rhythm until it explodes in a sort of *technical scandal*. This insistence on particulars, especially on certain details in the digressions, is a deviation in relation to the system of the film: *it is the temptation to make another film*.[95]

What most characterizes Pier Paolo Pasolini's *Trilogia della vita*, what arguably lends this tripartite work its unity, is the *insistence* of the images upon their own materiality – an insistence, furthermore, upon the *beholdenness*, or the *debt*, that Pasolini's images hold out towards past figural traditions (from which his films appear to spring). Such debts are revealed throughout the *Trilogia* in moments of what Pasolini calls 'technical scandal': when the narrative succession of the episodes that make up these films is exceeded, or ruptured, by an awareness of *style* – style partially freed from function, set adrift from clear narrative motivation, and thus potentially *useless*, excessive, and bothersome (or we might say, *heretical*, in relation to the *project* embodied in the plot).[96] It is in the essay 'Cinema di poesia' where Pasolini most clearly explains his understanding of what constitutes an excessive or 'poetic' moment in films: 'È il momento, cioè, in cui il linguaggio, seguendo un'ispirazione diversa e magari più autentica, si libera dalla funzione, e si presenta come "lingua in se stesso," stile' ('It is, in other words, the moment in which language, following a different and possibly more authentic inspiration, frees itself of function and presents itself as "language as such" – style').[97]

As we have seen, throughout the *Trilogia*, there is a recurring tension between narrative system and style; between images dominated by a communicative or referential function, and images (or elements within those images) that 'contaminate' the communication with a surplus of meaning, with a 'stain' of what Pasolini calls 'other material.' The 'free indirect' style of the *cinema di poesia* is designed precisely to call up that material, and set loose its force against the narrative film's own progress. As Pasolini remarks elsewhere in *Empirismo eretico*:

Si opera, violentemente e brutalmente, una dilacerazione, una falla, da cui irrompe *l'altra* materia, quella che compone l'oggettività, il tessuto reale delle cose, sfuggita all'intellettuale-poeta, e sfuggita anche in gran parte all'uomo.

A rent, a breach, is effected violently and brutally on such cultured material; from it the *other* material erupts which makes up the objectivity, the real texture of things – which escaped the intellectual poet and also in large part escaped man.[98]

For Pasolini, the problem of excess and contamination, and the 'liberation' of style from function, carry not only aesthetic significance, but also offer, given his insistence upon asserting a homology between narrative and social structure, an allegory of an altered society: what he might call *una società da farsi* (a society in process, or, to recall Agamben's suggestive formulation, a 'coming community').[99]

In the *Trilogia della vita* in general, contamination takes the form of an *insistence* on Medieval and Renaissance figural traditions (in the case of the first two films), as well as Persian and Rajput miniature traditions (in the last film).[100] In *I racconti di Canterbury* in particular, the paintings of Bruegel and Bosch serve as the 'subterranean' figurative models underlying the film's images, lending them a doubled quality reminiscent of the pastiche-like nature of the *Decameron*. However, here the investment in an ideologically motivated presentation of 'excess' is not accompanied by a structural complexity as found in the preceding film. The *Racconti di Canterbury* underwent four seizure orders after its release in August 1972, and was received as an assault upon *buonsenso* and upon the dignity (and abstinence) of the Franciscan Order.[101] This film is, like all of Pasolini's, a resistance to power, the 'sistema di educazione che ci divide in soggiogati e soggiogatori' (the 'system of education that divides us into subjugated and subjugators'),[102] and it carries out this resistance in ways similar to the *Decameron*. However, here the investment in an ideologically motivated presentation of 'excess' is not accompanied by the structural complexity found in the preceding film. This difference will lead certain critics to attack *Canterbury* as a weak sequel to the *Decameron*. For Sandro Petraglia, '*Decameron* è un'opera autentica. *I racconti di Canterbury* è un brutto calco divitalizzato ... Tutte le storie del primo film si sono coagulate nel secondo in una preziosa ma sottile operazione di rimasticamento' ('The *Decameron* is an authentic work. *I racconti di Canterbury* is an ugly, lifeless repetition ... All the stories of the first film coagulate in the second in a precious but subtle operation of re-mastication').[103] And Bernardo Bertolucci remarks upon its lack of inspiration (though this comment seems to account for his attitude towards the entire *Trilogia*, produced, he says, by a 'reactionary poet').[104] And while Pasolini probably would not have had too many problems with the notion of *rimasticamento* (something easily bent into a positive observation within the context of the present discussion), he would certainly have conceded a difference in tone of the second film. Indeed, if the *Decameron* celebrates 'innocent' sexuality and uncorrupted bodies, his *Canterbury* is far more cynical, dark, pessimistic, and non-humorous in its representation of these same themes. Compared to the *Decameron*, *Canterbury* certainly contains a marked lack of 'vitality,' and the landscape itself, owing also perhaps to the climate on the particular days Pasolini was shooting on location in England, appears quite dark and oppressive. It is useful to note Pasolini's own comparison of these first two films of the *Trilogia della vita*:

The world of Chaucer and Boccaccio hadn't yet experienced industrialization. There wasn't any consumer society, there weren't any assembly lines ... Chaucer stands astride two epochs. There is something medieval and gothic about him, the metaphysics of death. But often you get the feeling you are reading Shakespeare or Rabelais or Cervantes ... Chaucer still has one foot in the Middle Ages, but he is not 'of the people,' even though he took his stories from the people. He is already a bourgeois. He looks forward to the Protestant Revolution, in so far as the two were combined in Cromwell. But whereas for Boccaccio, for example, who was also a bourgeois, had a clear conscience, with Chaucer there is already a kind of unhappy feeling, an unhappy conscience. Chaucer foresees all the victories and triumphs of the bourgeoisie, but he also foresees its rotten-ness. He is a moralist but he is ironic too. Boccaccio doesn't foresee the future in this way. He catches the bourgeoisie at its moment of triumph, when it was being born.[105]

Thus, while both films are concerned with analogous issues, and are similar in structure (given the episodic nature of the original works), there is from the very beginning of the second film an impossibility of the kind of celebration of innocence and popular humour found in the *Decameron* (indeed, Pasolini remarks that 'humour is a class privilege in England').[106] Furthermore, what Petraglia calls the derivative nature of Pasolini's *Canterbury*, as a reworking of materials and themes already found in the *Decameron*, is inscribed in Pasolini's *Canterbury* itself. That is, at a certain point in the film, Chaucer, played (again ironically) by Pasolini himself, is seen studying at his desk. He is startled by a shout from his wife and he quickly, in an embarrassed gesture, hides the book he was obviously enjoying enormously beneath a pile of other books. The book is identified in a close-up as Boccaccio's *Decameron*. Thus, Chaucer's indebtedness to Boccaccio (and his 'anxiety of influence')[107] is registered in the film, and the film itself is presented as a continuation of the first film of the *Trilogia*.

What is continued is the form of contestation found in the *Decameron*. And again, what is represented thematically is excessive; but what is more important is the excessive manner in which it is represented. As Omar Calabrese remarks in his study of 'neo-baroque' elements in contemporary art, excess (a 'baroque' quality he finds characteristic of postmodern works) is always a 'destabilizing' of a given order of things, and usually 'qualsiasi azione, opera o individuo eccessivo vuole mettere in discussione un qualche ordine, magari distruggerlo o costruirne uno nuovo' ('whatever it is, an excessive work or individual wants to put some order into crisis, perhaps to destroy it or build a new one).[108] Calabrese's recuperation of the historical baroque in his studies of contemporary culture seems highly appropriate here given Pasolini's own penchant for reactivating or reanimating in his own films what were apparently superseded moments in the history of art. For, just as in the *Decameron*, in *I racconti di Canterbury* the *effetto dipinto* is put into play; and the citational nature of the film, often divorced from narrative motivation, is perceived as destabilizing moments of pure excess. There seem to be few other ways to account for the numerous allusions, to be discussed further below, to Bruegel's *Flemish Proverbs* (1559) and the rather puzzling sequence at the conclusion of the film where we are overwhelmed by the infernal imagery of Hieronymus Bosch.

Calabrese's approach to the problem of excess takes two forms: he would distinguish (a) representations of excess and (b) excess in representation.[109] That is, thematic excess as opposed to formal or stylistic excess. The strong moralistic reaction that met the *Trilogia* is caused by excess of the first order: 'obscene' representations of nudity, hetero- and homosexuality, unethical Franciscan monks, and so on.[110] However, these transgressive aspects of the *Trilogia* actually interest us relatively little in the present context; that is, unless these thematic excesses translate into stylistic excesses. In *I racconti di Canterbury*, the often transgressively erotic world of the tales is presented in a hybridized visual language: what Pasolini also calls, in a manner peculiarly appropriate for the *Trilogia*, an 'overexposed' style. Not only is there a mixing of film genres (most clearly in 'The Cook's Tale,' which forms a homage to Chaplin, with Ninetto as the Tramp – a homage that is also carried over into 'The Miller's Tale,' where we find Geraldine Chaplin as the character May), but there is also, just as in the *Decameron*, a mixing of the cinematic and painterly representational models. However, while in the *Decameron* the citations of Bruegel and Giotto have clear narrative motivation, as we mentioned, in *Canterbury* the allusions to Bruegel and Bosch, or literal citations of their paintings, do not have the same narrative legitimacy. Divorced from such motivation, they become pure excess, and, as Costa suggests, call our attention away from the narrative and towards the enunciation. The *effetto dipinto*, for Costa, stages a confrontation between two semiotic systems or 'models of representation'; and it is nearly always 'legible as a mark of the enunciation, with an accentuation of the metalinguistic function.'[111] While Costa acknowledges that the *effetto dipinto* is not always 'excessive,' in the sense we are adopting here, his own attention is drawn more to those moments in certain films when the *effetto dipinto* presents a conflict between models of representation, a clashing of systems that draws our attention away from the diegesis and redirects it towards the enunciation.

The 'neoformalist' theorist Kristin Thompson's understanding of cinematic excess helps to clarify this point further. For her, excess is 'an inevitable gap in the motivation for the physical presence of a device; the physical presence retains a perceptual interest beyond its function in the work.'[112] Something excessive calls attention only to itself, and retains no responsibility to narrative continuity: it falls outside of the causal chain of the plot. For Thompson what is always potentially excessive is the very material of the medium, or what post-structuralist theorists might call a film's *écriture*, which may threaten to break up a film's homogeneity or unity. Homogeneity or unity is the product of a coherent narrative system, which, in this style, is itself based upon conventions of continuity editing. In this style, all devices or elements within the frame must have a narrative motivation; excess must be kept to a minimum in order to avoid any interruption of narrative flow. However, the very devices that function to maintain continuity, and repress excess, by their very physical presence in any work inevitably call attention to a potential heterogeneity within that work; and there is always something present in the image that retains connotations irrelevant to the given story. As Stephen Heath writes:

Just as narrative never exhausts the image, homogeneity is always an effect of the film and not the filmic system, which is precisely the production of that homogeneity. Homogeneity is haunted by the material practice it represses and the tropes of that repression, the forms of continuity, provoke within the texture of the film the figures – the edging, the margin – of the loss by which it moves; permanent battle over the resolution of that loss on which, however, it structurally depends, mediation between image and discourse, narrative can never contain the whole film which permanently exceeds its fictions. 'Filmic system,' therefore, always means at least this: the 'system' of the film in so far as the film is the organization of the homogeneity and the material outside inscribed in the operation of that organization as its contradiction.[113]

For both Heath and Thompson, alongside any narrative film there exists another non- or even counter-diegetic film, and as critics they are both sensitive to the forces of unity and disunity at conflict in any given work.[114] Furthermore, certain unorthodox or marginal filmmakers may produce films that foreground their stylistic worlds and, according to Thompson, force the spectators to 'skid' in their interpretation of the narrative. The idea of 'skidding perception' is derived from Roland Barthes's notion of the 'third meaning' of an image (also referred to by Barthes as a 'obtuse meaning'): the materiality of the signifier (or the image) goes beyond the coherent narrative system of a film, and the image takes on a density or opacity that short-circuits or, as Barthes would say, subverts the narrative (without necessarily destroying it).[115]

What is the value of this 'skidding perception' brought about by a perception of excess? For Thompson, the spectator is forced to cope with the perceptual difficulties brought about by an experience of excess in a way that is traditionally avoided by the classical style, a style productive of passive viewing habits. In films in which style is allowed a great deal of independence from narrative functioning, as in the *Trilogia*, the perception of excess leads to a questioning of the viewing procedures necessary to decode the text. For Thompson, the value of films such as these 'rests less in their thematic material than in their ability to shift our habitual perceptions of filmic conventions through defamiliarization.'[116] And here she shows her debt to the formulations of Russian Formalism, and indeed she cites Shklovsky in particular as her source of inspiration.[117] For Shklovsky asserts, much as Pasolini will in his theories of the 'cinema of poetry,' the importance of 'prolonging' the process of perception in order to 'de-familiarize' the spectator with his usual viewing habits (what he calls in his essay on the cinema of poetry 'prose perception'):

If we start to examine the general laws of perception, we see that as perception becomes habitual, it becomes automatic ... Such habituation explains the principles by which, in ordinary speech, we leave phrases unfinished and words half expressed ... The object, perceived in the manner of prose perception, fades and does not leave even a first impression; ultimately even the essence of what it was is forgotten ... And Art exists to make one feel things, to make the stone stoney. The purpose of art is to impart the sensation of things as they are perceived, and not as they are known. The technique of art is to make objects 'unfamiliar,' to make forms difficult, to increase the difficulty and length of perception because the process of perception is an aesthetic end in itself and must be prolonged.[118]

For Thompson, 'this concentration on perceptual difficulty has ideological implications. The perceptual skills necessary for resolving the uncertainty of viewing [excess] relate to social as well as filmic practice.'[119] That is, the defamiliarization carried out in the reception of films invites us to develop a potentially altered perception of our lived environment.

Thompson's approach to excess in narrative films can provide crucial insights into Pasolini's *Canterbury*. For the importance of excess in this film appears to be two-fold: (a) as Heath would say, the material of the image, divorced from narrative motivation, exists as a force of potential rupture within the narrative system (the excesses of style present what Deleuze calls 'a foreign language in a dominant language'),[120] and thus the system's drive to maintain homogeneity is revealed in a 'sinister' manner; and (b) excess puts into crisis normal viewing habits and forces the spectator to consider altered patterns of reception. In order to understand this more clearly, it is necessary to locate moments of stylistic excess in *I racconti di Canterbury*.

We shall describe two such moments, one rather subtle and the other not very subtle at all. A subtle form of excess can be detected throughout the film insofar as the *dispositio* of elements within the frame, especially the characters and the architecture, recalls Bruegel's *Flemish Proverbs* (and, furthermore, the selection that Pasolini makes from Bruegel's episodes seems to be motivated by the lessons they contain). Indeed, the similarities between Pasolini's images and those by Bruegel lend the characters and settings a 'doubled' nature: the simple presence of one of Pasolini's Bruegelian characters is 'stained' by a sense of derivation from the still space of Bruegel's canvas; the 'time' of Pasolini's cinematic universe is infected or ruptured by an 'alien' time (what Pasolini calls an 'abnormal duration'),[121] and, indeed, the temporal succession of the film seems to fight against a threat of arrest. That is, the sequence of prosaic time of the narratives struggles against the poetic materiality that would tend, in a moment of 'technical scandal,' to impede or halt it. In a sense this is how we may understand Pasolini's belief in the 'revolutionary' or 'resistant' potential of the past (and why he is drawn throughout his career to film ancient myths and medieval narratives, and why he campaigned to save the walls of San'A, in Yemen). As Pasolini remarks:

Adesso, preferisco muovermi nel passato proprio perché ritengo che l'unica forza contestatrice del presente sia proprio il passato: è una forma aberrante ma tutti i valori che sono stati valori nei quali ci siamo formati, con tutte le loro atrocità, i loro lati negativi, sono quelli che possono mettere in crisi il presente.

Now I prefer to move through the past, precisely because I believe that the past is the only force able to contest the present: it is an aberrant form, but all the values that were the values which formed us – with all that made them atrocious, with their negative aspects – are the ones that are capable of putting the present into crisis.[122]

Pasolini contaminates the cinematic code with superseded codes of representation, since, as he believes, every language is always a metaphor of an epoch of history of society.

The 'echo-effect' brought forward by the *effetto dipinto* is clearly discerned in the film. Besides a general sense of indebtedness to Bruegel's popular and humorous imaginary, sensed from the very introduction of the film set in a thirteenth-century market near the duomo of Canterbury, there are moments when the forces of allusion and citation become the dominant forces within the text.

Indeed, we find an episode from Bruegel's painting translated literally into the film, along with its allegorical lessons, during 'The Reeve's Tale.' Two young students, Alan and John, set off to visit the Miller, who has been dealing unfairly with their school; they bring corn for the Miller to grind, and intend to watch him to make sure he performs the job without 'trickery.' Upon arrival at the Miller's home, they are met with the vision of two *derrières*, those of the Miller's wife and daughter, issuing from a single window of their home. This detail is not derived from Chaucer, but from Bruegel's *Flemish Proverbs*. As the art historian Michael Gibson explains, the significance of this episode in the painting is as follows: literally, two persons defecate from the same aperture, but the lesson contained is that these two are forced to make a virtue of necessity.[123] Within the context of Pasolini's episode, this original lesson seems quite irrelevant; in fact, the motivation for the appearance of these *culi* is not clear, although they may function as an anticipation of the events that follow involving these women and the two students. However, the image remains ambiguous. Indeed, this clear allusion to Bruegel functions to multiply possible interpretations of the episode: that is, the image's narrative function is exceeded by another content. In the film, it portends erotic engagement; in the painting, a lesson concerning survival and dignity. It is an image that stages, thus, a conflict of contexts, and it contributes to the poetic ambivalence of Pasolini's signifiers.

Yet another example of such ambivalence is found during 'The Miller's Tale.' Here, in one of the episodes where Pasolini remains fairly close to the letter of the original text, we find Nicholas 'The Gallant,' a poor student-boarder (with certain supernatural and prophetic powers) taken in by the Carpenter, warning the Carpenter to make Noah-like preparations for an impending flood. However, Nicholas's advice is only a ploy to distract the naïve *legnaiuolo* for a while so that the student could have some time in the Carpenter's wife's bed. Nicholas has the man suspend three large tubs with ropes from the ceiling of the house, one each for husband, wife, and boarder, and he advises that they should sleep in the tubs lest they be surprised by the flood. Once the water level was high enough, they would all cut the tubs loose, and survive in their tiny 'ships.' The Carpenter carries out the young man's instructions carefully and, that very night, they all retire to their tubs. Once the old man is asleep, Nicholas and the wife wander off as planned, leaving the Carpenter alone, suspended comically from the rafters. Ultimately, he is awakened by noise and, thinking it the sound of the oncoming tide, he cuts himself loose and falls to the ground sustaining a variety of injuries.

Compared to the other episodes Pasolini chooses to 'adapt' from the original, in which he often takes great liberties, this episode remains unusually faithful to Chaucer. However, as was found in 'The Reeve's Tale,' the images here seem highly overdetermined. They contain a 'surplus.' This is most evident in the precarious image of the Carpenter asleep in the hanging tub. We are again presented with a citation from the same painting by Bruegel, in which we find, near the very right-hand margin of the canvas, the image of a man hanging below the ceiling of his house in a basket that is clearly unable to carry his weight. In the painting, this appears to represent human existence caught between heaven and earth; the apparently inevitable fall and destruction of the basket signifies that one's chances of transcendence or salvation are ruined. Thus, while the allusion to Bruegel found in 'The Reeve's Tale' contained little or no narrative motivation whatsoever, here the original significance of Bruegel's image reinforces that of Chaucer and Pasolini, who present the Carpenter in an attempt to escape from a prophesied flood meant to purify the world of earthly corruption. And all three artists – Chaucer, Bruegel, and Pasolini – present this desire for salvation in a comical fashion (in Bruegel it is a theme carried over into his later paintings of the tower of Babel); however, perhaps only in Pasolini's episode is there such a strong suggestion that ascetic rituals of transcendence form pernicious strategies of mystification.

There thus seem to be definite thematic motivations for this particular allusion to Bruegel. Nevertheless, the image retains the type of doubled nature that we have been describing, although here, as we mentioned, in a rather subtle form. What we are offered is the same theme or lesson, the same image, and the same comical attitude, as represented in three different media: writing, painting, and film. But what is important is not so much the idea of continuity, or of an evolution of techniques; rather, Pasolini's film here appears to assert itself as the medium able to contain and synthesize these traditional media while never entirely overcoming them. That is, the 'surplus' that is lent to the image by the *effetto dipinto* serves as a reminder of cinema's indebtedness to that (incorporated) medium; the *effetto dipinto* constantly reminds us of an internalized but irrepressible structural 'otherness.' The excess, the echo, or the surplus found in Pasolini's images continually reiterate this form of generic indebtedness that both explains the fragmentary qualities of *Canterbury* itself and that leads ultimately to an awareness of the very processes of structuration – that is, of how the possibility of structural unity or homogeneity depends upon the repression of the history of signifying materials themselves. The excessive materiality of Pasolini's contaminated images presents what he refers to as 'una deviazione rispetto al sistema del film.'[124] In *Canterbury* Pasolini presents systemic, narrative tendencies working towards homogeneity struggling against the highly overdetermined materiality of the signifiers – a materiality that, in Stephen Heath's words, tends to rupture the organization of the text.[125] The fragmentary nature of the film derives from Pasolini's attempt to present a structure that refuses to repress its own material origins; and thus *Canterbury* may be seen as yet another example of Pasolini's habit of producing texts that tend to erase themselves, that continually put themselves into crisis: that is, *Canterbury* is 'una struttura da farsi' (a structure in the process of becoming, a 'coming structure').[126]

The notion of excess, then, allows us an insight into the allegorical significance of *I racconti di Canterbury*. For if, as many suggest, the film continues Pasolini's examination of sexuality and repression (as it is found in all three films of the *Trilogia*), it does not do so in the same manner as do the *Decameron* or *Il fiore delle mille e una notte*. For while these other films present a celebration of sexuality (and predominantly heterosexuality) as an expression of liberty, in *Canterbury* the expression of desire seems highly regulated, and bodies are under constant surveillance; indeed, for Gian Piero Brunetta, the film is closer to *Salò* than it is to the *Decameron*.[127] Moreover, sanctioned forms of sexual expression found in the film, the sense of normalcy attributed to heterosexual coupling, is gained through the repression of non-sanctioned sexualities. That is, an image (or ideology) of sexual homogeneity is produced through the identification and public obliteration of what is other. This is clearly the significance of the 'Racconto del Frate' in the film, where the energies of voyeurism of the Spy (Franco Citti) are harnessed to the official system of surveillance through the lure of financial gain.[128] The spy locates and reports homosexuals who, if they have not the appropriate amount of money to bribe the authorities, are to become the victims of public burnings. As Foucault discusses in *Discipline and Punish*, public executions such as these served to harness the power of transgression in order to strengthen the image of rule; the punishment of the excesses of sexual 'aberrants,' heretics, witches, madmen, and criminals provides the opportunity to re-produce the unity or homogeneity that these outlaws were said to threaten.[129]

Ultimately, the problem of excess in *Canterbury*, and the allegory of structuration it reveals, must be related to this political, socio-sexual commentary that forms the horrible subtext to the film (just as the unfinished, meta-documentary structure of Pasolini's *Appunti per un'Orestiade africana* forms an allegory of an African society in transition. In Pasolini, his message is not limited to what he represents; often, more importantly, it is conveyed by *how* he represents it). And we would not be the first to suggest that Pasolini's own death, and the use to which it was put by the organs of popular culture, seem sickeningly analogous to a public execution of a heretic.[130]

Canterbury is an allegory of a community or institution *da farsi*. In Sam Weber's terminology, the film provides an image of 'ambivalent demarcation': it forms a system that assumes rather than occults its relations of indebtedness, and it assumes the ambivalence inherent in its own materiality.[131] Ambivalence arises from a structure that refuses completely to efface its beholdenness to other models, although, in the very process of being formed, it must partially repress these 'originating' models. For Pasolini, as for Weber, the possibility of such an 'arrested effacement' provides an altered image of social aggregation. However, this Gramscian 'optimism of the will' found in the structural allegory seems to be betrayed by a profound 'pessimism of the intellect' found at the thematic level, and especially at the infernal conclusion of the film.

Here, the figural excesses and the palimpsest-like nature of *Canterbury* reach a sort of crescendo. With the concluding sequence, relating the prologue to 'The Summoner's Tale,' pastiche and citation become the dominant forces in the text. As recounted in Chaucer's original, the Summoner relates a story of a Friar who has a vision of Hell, in which the Friars found there are punished by being kept in Satan's 'tail.' Again, as in 'The Miller's Tale,' Pasolini remains fairly close to the letter and spirit of the original; however, his imagery recalls the infernal imaginary of Hieronymus Bosch (whose works date from the late 1400s to the early 1500s) along with Dante's *Inferno*, and certain elements from the medieval iconographic tradition:[132] his signs have, again, a hybrid nature. The organization of space and certain punishments found in *Canterbury* are highly reminiscent of those found in Bosch's *Table of Wisdom* or *The Millennium*. The posture of Satan, and the imprisoning function of his posterior, seem to be drawn from the left panel of *The Temptation of Saint Anthony*. The location of this episode would indicate a pattern shared by both *Canterbury* and the *Decameron*. For just as in the *Decameron*, the film concludes with an image of contamination. However, whereas in the previous film we find a *mirabile visione* of the Madonna (an unusually optimistic finale), *Canterbury* ends on a far more pessimistic note; indeed, the profound sense of degradation running throughout the film, and the sense of defeat offered at the conclusion, would seem to contradict the Gramscian 'optimism of the will' we have described in the film's allegory of a structure *da farsi*.

In *Canterbury*, Pasolini's brand of stylistic contamination is expressed through images that exceed their narrative or rational motivation: images that leave something outside, and thus are without a function within, the film's formal system (what Pasolini calls its *sistema grammaticale*). This excess exists as a threat to the unity of the work. But whereas films of the classical style attempt to eliminate such excess or, as Kristin Thompson and Stephen Heath have shown, 'repress' excess in order to maintain homogeneity, Pasolini refuses this model of textual and, by homology, social organization. Excess is the 'political unconscious' of dominant narrative cinema:[133] and Pasolini's film is the stylistic de-negation of this unspeakable 'other material' that erupts within the text. And thus *Canterbury* must be seen as a continuation of Pasolini's will to speak the unspeakable. That is, excess presents material that seems devoid of rational or narrative motivation within the context of the film: there is something, the Barthesian 'third meaning,' that does not belong, that remains outside but apprehendable through the fissured text, with a function that is not readily explainable. Pasolini's films call upon the spectator to begin to search for that mysterious motivation, to begin to conceptualize a function for that material. Unable to deny such material, one is forced to conceive of a perhaps utopian structure-in-process that would grant it a place and a function: a 'revolutionary' engagement within the *langue* that, for cinema, says Pasolini, 'is reality itself.'[134] Contamination then, as an ideological form of pastiche, produces in

I racconti di Canterbury an allegory of a society *da farsi* but also an ironic image of Pasolini's life as a poet of the margins.

Che un individuo, in quanto autore, reagisca al sistema costruendone un altro, mi sembra semplice e naturale; così come gli uomini, in quanto autori di storia, reagiscono alla stuttura sociale costruendone un'altra, attraverso la rivoluzione, ossia alla volontà di trasformare la struttura. Non intendo quindi parlare, secondo la critica sociologica americana, di valori e volizioni 'naturali' e ontologici: ma parlo di 'volontà rivoluzionaria' sia nell'autore in quanto creatore di un sistema stilistico individuale che contraddice il sistema grammaticale e letterario-gergale vigente, sia negli uomini in quanto sovvertitori di sistemi politici.

That an individual, as author, reacts to a system by constructing another seems to me simple and natural; in the same way in which men, as authors of history, react to a social structure by building another through revolution, that is, react to the will to transform the structure. I therefore don't want to speak, in the terms of American sociological criticism, of 'natural' and ontological values and volitions; but I am speaking of a 'revolutionary will,' both in the author as creator of an individual stylistic system that contradicts the grammatical and literary-jargon system in force, and in men as subverters of political systems.[135]

Erotic Contaminations in the Arabian Nights

I made [the *Trilogy of Life*] in order to oppose the consumerist present to a very recent past where the human body and human relations were still real, although archaic, although prehistoric, although crude; nevertheless they were real, and these films opposed this reality to the non-reality of consumer civilization.[136]

The *Arabian Nights* are a narrative model ... Unlimited narration. One thing after the other, and one inside the other, to infinity.[137]

Pasolini's *Il fiore delle mille e una notte* (*Arabian Nights*) was released in 1974, and forms the third 'chapter' of the *Trilogy of Life*. Much like the first two films of the *Trilogia*, in which Pasolini draws material from the medieval works of Boccaccio and Chaucer, *Il fiore* presents an adaptation of an important episodic model of storytelling. For Pasolini, the *Arabian Nights* in particular offers a model of 'unlimited narration' or *il narrare illimitato*. But while he insists, in an interview with Gideon Bachmann, that he made the *Trilogia* 'for the sheer joy of telling and recounting,'[138] he suggests at the same time that 'the films of the *Trilogia della vita* are the most ideological films I have ever made. Certainly *Il fiore delle mille e una notte* is not, quite obviously, a topical and directly ideological film like *Uccellacci e uccellini* or *Accattone*. Its ideology is hidden deep below the surface. It is brought out not by what is explicitly said, but by representation.'[139] Therefore, what interests us here is to attempt to describe some of the ways this ideologically engaged film is brought out from below the enjoyable surface of the *Trilogia*, to account for what we might call the 'ideological pleasure' of Pasolini's films, while focusing on *Il fiore* in particular. For Pasolini, narrative structures and visual strategies offer an image of social structures. In *Empirismo eretico* he develops a theory of a homology, or structural parallel, between models of storytelling and models of social and economic aggregation, and thus reveals an ethical dimension of style. The pleasure of the *Trilogia* is never divorced from an awareness of ideology, an awareness brought about through stylistic experimentation. Pasolini attempts to bring his spectators, collectively, to 'recognize the experiences from which the deduction of the norm is born.'[140] For Pasolini, styles of narration are always experienced as allegories of society. Ultimately, much like the two films that preceded it, Pasolini's *Il fiore* is an example of his 'genealogical' cinema, designed to reveal the historical nature of visual regimes and gesture towards new ones. He accomplishes this goal through disjunctive narrative structuration and through an experimentation with diverse styles of figuration, often bringing mutually incompatible visual codes into contact. In the process, Pasolini's films subvert the models of subjectivity presumed by conventional cinematic codes, provoking a perceptual disorientation in a spectator forced to become an active participant in, indeed a 'co-author' of, the narration.

Structural Contagion: Embedded Tales

The dark pessimism that pervades *Canterbury* is jettisoned for the last 'chapter' of the *Trilogia* della vita. *Il fiore delle mille e una notte* is perhaps Pasolini's most playful film, and some think his best. And while *Canterbury* concludes with an image of Chaucer/Pasolini and of the title insisting that 'Qui finiscono i Racconti di Canterbury raccontati per il solo piacere di raccontare' ('Here end the Canterbury Tales, told only for the pleasure of the telling'), that pleasure was a product of a dark irony, which Pasolini attributes to Chaucer's bourgeois 'guilty conscience.'[141] This guilt accompanying visual and sexual pleasure in the film is not to be found in *Il fiore*, just as it was not found in the *Decameron*.[142]

Indeed, the film seems to appeal to an infantile or even preconscious pleasure in unlimited narration, and in the 'play' of dream-work. We should remember that Scheherazade's very survival, in the frame-tale of the original text, depended upon this very pleasure: the infantile, sadistic, and redundant pleasure of King Shahryar. In Pasolini's adaptation of *Le mille e una notte*, it is the spectator that takes the place, and the pleasure, of the King; and the masochism of Scheherazade – who is not found as a character in the film, since Pasolini does not reproduce the original frame-tale – is assumed by the director himself (a bitter irony, indeed). It is interesting that none of Pasolini's readers has understood this point. It is not that the original frame-tale has simply been rejected. Rather, it has been projected out of the film itself onto the relations of cinematic or literary production: *Il fiore* is framed by the 'tale' of a director-author whose survival depends upon the pleasure he produces and the desire he excites in the cultural market-place. The film is framed by this negated image of the 'auto-lesionistic' film-director, telling his stories to put off the moment of death: but not only his own death, but that of other potential victims of his own sort. For Scheherazade narrates in order not only to save herself, but also to save those of her own gender who would have followed her as victims of the King's desire. As Naomi Greene points out, nowhere in the *Trilogia* is Pasolini's attraction to *il narrare illimitato*, or unlimited narration, given such free reign.[143] The *Arabian Nights* offers itself as the prototype of 'pure' narration: that is, of narratives that live off one another, that are embedded in one another to such an extent that it is often impossible to determine the containing tale from the contained. *Il fiore* will reproduce the image of the self-generating tales of the original text, and yet its expulsion of the original frame-tale, the story of Sheherazade, is also a function of Pasolini's refusal to trace a possible outer limit to narration within the film itself. A 'politics' of narrative framing is carried on in this film much as it was in the *Decameron*; however, here there is no unambiguous frame inscribed within the film, as there was in the *Decameron* (where the tales are framed by the stories of Ciappelletto and Giotto's pupil[144]) and in *I racconti di Canterbury* (where the motif of Chaucer/Pasolini at his desk serves as the framing device). The only tale that seems to have such a unifying function is that of Zumurrud and Nur ed Din; indeed, the enamoured Nur ed Din's search for his lost Zumurrud takes the form of an extended trajectory gag. Carried along by the momentum of his desire for reunification with his beloved, this character seems to crash through the other tales. Thus, this tale is often embedded in the very stories it embeds, as it were, 'appearing enclosed by that which he encloses,' to cite a decontextualized Dante (*Paradiso* 30.12).

Narrative Embedding in *Il fiore**

1 *Tale of Zumurrud and Nur ed Din*
   1a Tale of Harun ar-Rashid
      1aa Tale of Harun and Zeudi
1 *Zumurrud and Nur ed Din*
   2 Tale of Munis
      1 *Nur ed Din*
      2a Tale of Tagi: meets Aziz
         2b Tale of Dunya, her dream, her 'tela'
      2a Tale of Tagi and Aziz
   2 Munis and *Nur ed Din*
      1 *Nur ed Din*
      2a Tale of Tagi and Aziz
         3 Tale of Aziz, Aziza, Budur
         2b Dunya's 'tela'
         2 Tale of Munis: beggars
      2a Tale of Tagi, his desire for Dunya
      2d Tale of Shahzaman
      2e Tale of Yunan
      2a Tale of Tagi: encounter with Dunya
   2 Tale of Munis
      1 *Nur ed Din*
1 *Zumurrud and Nur ed Din*

[*Primary frame-tale (or elements found therein) italicized.]

As shown in the chart, the oft-noted Chinese box structure of the film, which Pasolini reproduces in part from the original text – a structure that presents tales within tales (potentially, as Pasolini says, on to infinity) – runs into a possible moment of confusion when the embedding tale, or some objects or characters from that tale, are found to be circulating in one or more of the embedded tales. Examples of this are found, as seen in the chart, when elements of the primary frame-tale find their way into Munis's tale; and there is Dunya's *tela*, which seems to circulate freely. The beggars are present in both Munis's and Aziz's tales. This contagion between narrative levels poses a threat to the logic of containment, and it denies the possibility of any meta-textual or, one might say, meta-historical perspective, on the margins of all stories, that could survey and account for all those stories. In a sense, history (*storia*) is subverted by stories (*storie*). That is, in this film, elements derived from the narrative's 'origins,' its initial frame, the first story (Nur ed Din and Zumurrud), erupt within the structures of the other tales that follow, introducing a potentially destabilizing temporal disjunction, and putting into doubt the continuing presence of a founding meta-structure underlying the progress of narration. Indeed, when read in this manner, again as an allegory of textual but also social structuration, *Il fiore* appears to present a parable of a 'self-framing' structure, or a structure framed from the inside, as opposed to a structure whose legitimacy is guaranteed by an externalized, 'a-historical' (extra-narrative) agency.

Pasolini's allegorical interest in *Le mille e una notte* is also found in the works of the American novelist John Barth, who appears, in this regard, to be involved in similar experiments in narrative form (he is also an author who has written eloquently on the theoretical issues of narrative framing).[145] Barth, who, like Pasolini, was drawn to the image of unlimited narration found in the *Arabian Nights*, writes in *Chimera* the story of his imagined visits and conversations with Scheherazade and her sister Dunyazadiad. The topics of their talks swing from problems of theme to those of structure. And as Barth writes, the characters 'speculated endlessly on such questions as whether a story might imaginably be framed from inside, as it were, so that the usual relation between container and contained would be reversed and paradoxically reversible – and (for my [the narrator's] benefit, I suppose) *what human state of affairs such an odd construction might usefully figure.*'[146] Elsewhere Barth himself will explain the apparent political 'usefulness' of insights gained through the study of embedded structuration. He suggests that the problem of 'tales within tales within tales,' as found in the *Arabian Nights*, puts our 'concept-structures,' and the 'cultural consensus' that frames them, into crisis; that is, he suggests, it problematizes the models of social organization and personal comportment that we attempt to emulate in structuring the stories of our lives.[147] Barth will also allude to Borges's idea that embedded stories 'appeal to us because they disturb us metaphysically. We are reminded by them, consciously or otherwise, of the next frame out: the fiction of our own lives, of which we are both the authors and the protagonists, and in which our reading of *The 1001 Nights*, say, is a story within a story.'[148]

Pasolini's film attempts to bring his spectators to this metaphysical and political-cultural awareness, in ways quite similar to those discussed by Barth. But whereas for Barth the reminder of 'the next frame out' does come to an end, at what he calls God the storyteller,[149] Pasolini's image of the *narrare infinito* allows no such delimitation – although it does call attention to how the invocation of God's presence functions. Indeed, the fact that in his film the embedded tales are often 'infected' by properties found in adjacent tales (Nur ed Din's trajectory especially between the frame and Munis's tale, Dunya's painting of the gazelles, the same beggars found in Munis's tale and then in Aziz's tale, as it is told by Tagi, who is a character in Munis's tale, and so on) provides not so much an image of textual layers ('Chinese boxes') moving outwards towards God as the ultimately arbitrary Frame, but one of a structure that turns in on itself in Moebius-strip fashion, so that the enabling 'ground' of the stories (and, allegorically, that of our histories) is conceived of as a construct of these very stories. Thus, Pasolini's film does not conform simply to an idea of Chinese boxes, which may merely function (within certain approaches to this text) as a ploy designed to delay, or worse to *conceal*, the invocation of an ultimately extra-textual or meta-historical Limit (what Roland Barthes once called 'God and his hypostases'[150] or what John Barth calls the narrating God). Pasolini's film, rather, presents an allegory of an 'eversive,' self-effacing structure where the framing agency (an author, a state, a divinity) that had been held to exist outside of that structure – since its legitimacy and authority were derived from the uncontaminated or 'disinterested' status of this agency – is found to be located firmly within that structure, and thus open to radical alteration. The text everts, like a glove pulled inside out, rendering an image of continual 'frame-replacement.' *Il fiore* thus is an allegory of a text without an author and a society without a State.

Stylistic Contagion: Embedded Pictures

Diegesis locks together the synthesis of movements in the temporal order; perspectivist representation does so in the spatial order.

Jean-Francois Lyotard[151]

This 'eversive' nature of *Il fiore* is found in the other films of the *Trilogia* as well, and it explains the ironic presence of Pasolini within his own texts in both the *Decameron* and in *I racconti di Canterbury*. And the *Trilogia* may be read as an allegory of textual and social organization given Pasolini's belief in the homological relation of textual and social ordering, derived from his study of Lucien Goldmann.[152] However, neither the *Decameron* nor *Canterbury* employ the complexity of narrative layering found in *Il fiore*, and neither of them present such contagion between individual tales themselves.

The forces of contamination that can be detected throughout Pasolini's *opera* have produced, in *Il fiore*, an image of structural contagion. However, the forces of pastiche or citation found at the level of style in most of Pasolini's work have not been excluded from this film. Nevertheless, stylistically speaking, *Il fiore* resembles the other films in the *Trilogia* very little insofar as Pasolini's visual sources are no longer the icons and masterpieces of the European tradition (except in his framing of Gaiwan the Thief's crucifixion: it seems Pasolini couldn't resist an allusion to Western representations of the Passion).[153] Rather, in this film Pasolini abandons this tradition, along with the codes peculiar to it, and draws his imagery from the art and architecture of the Orient; and, as Pasolini's scenographer Dante Ferretti remarks, Pasolini is especially intrigued by the art of Oriental miniatures.[154] Not only does Pasolini use Persian and Indian miniatures as sources for costumes, architecture, decor, and so on – all elements found within the *mise en scène* – but he will also reproduce, as much as his medium will allow, certain distortions in spatial composition as found in these miniatures.

As Gian Piero Brunetta has noted, such distortion (what he calls a 'figural disorientation' caused by 'the mutation of certain visual codes') is introduced into the film through Pasolini's adoption of Oriental figural models, and it is a sign of an altered address to the film spectator.[155] The 'mutation' Brunetta describes has its origin in the fact that the miniatures that Pasolini translates to the screen do not conform to the perceptual codes characteristic of Western art since the Renaissance. Persian art does not organize space according to a single, idealized observer whose gaze 'controls' the representation. As John White observes, generally speaking this art avoids the types of perspectival cues used in Western art since the fifteenth century: receding orthogonals are avoided, as is the Western tendency of foreshortening. The point of view is usually an approximation of a humanly untenable bird's-eye view.[156] Thus, the images often appear to suffer from a lack of spatial coherence given the absence of a single coordinating gaze.

Indeed, perceptual distortion arises with a denial of a Cartesian organization of space. This perceptual code gives rise to a specific response in spectators; it produces real, material effects within the psyches and upon the bodies of those whose vision it defines.[157] Any experimentation with the 'play' between perceptual codes at work in cinematic representation entails a denial of the various narrative and formal strategies found in dominant or classical cinema: a denial of cinema as a *reproductive* technology of subjectivation.[158] Furthermore, the presence of these 'alien' figural models within film, whose lens-system was developed out of post-Renaissance experiments in perspective and optics,[159] is part of Pasolini's attack upon the hegemonic forms of representation of the West, and ultimately an attack upon the cultural hegemony of the West as it spreads throughout the 'periphery' (in this case, particularly the Third World). As Pasolini himself remarks, in *Il fiore* 'my polemic was against the culture of the dominant Eurocentric class.'[160] And just as Pasolini celebrates the bodies and pleasures available to a pre-capitalist, non-industrialized society in the *Decameron*, in *Il fiore* he celebrates an analogous 'peasant' society, that of the Third World, with which he came to identify more and more in his own life ('I feel better there').[161] For Pasolini, it was a society still on the margins of consumer capitalism, where the bodies and imaginaries of the people had yet to be fully 'homologated' by the culture of neocapitalism.[162]

For Pasolini, non-Western societies and traditions exist as cultural 'hold-outs' providing a potential point of resistance to the cultural hegemony of the economic centre. Thus, the Persian and Rajput miniatures that he brings to life in his film should be taken as emblematic of this form of cultural resistance. They are 'visual dialects,' as it were, and their presence in the film is analogous to Pasolini's use of dialects in his other writing and films. As he insists: 'Today dialect provides a means to oppose acculturation. As always, it will be a lost battle.'[163] The use of dialect in his writing is not simply a moment of linguistic resistance. From the beginning, as we can see in his Friulian poems, the choice of dialect also manifests Pasolini's nostalgia for the peasant culture of his childhood Friuli, the primarily agrarian region whose rituals and rhythms of life accompanied his first sexual experiences and made such an indelible impression upon his poetic imagination.[164] The contamination of standard Italian and regional dialects found in his later works, inspired in part by the style of 'plurilinguism' as found in the writing of Pascoli and Gadda, is, in Pasolini's own words, 'characteristic of a collective style.'[165] Moreover, the presence of dialect reveals a nostalgia both for a non-industrial society and non-bourgeois models of sexuality.

Pasolini carries these poetic tendencies over into his films. In *Il fiore* we have an analogous mixture of a 'standard,' classical cinematic language (that is, the editing procedures of the continuity system) and visual 'sub-languages' functioning within the conventional cinematic code. These 'sub-languages' form an internal contestation of the standardized code they inhabit: Pasolini might call them a 'poetic' contestation of the 'cinema of prose' (the term he used to denote the classical style). The film is an *ibrido linguistico* (or 'linguistic hybrid') that, as Pasolini remarks concerning poetry, 'is always a product of a moral hybrid – I almost said historical hybrid.'[166] Just as his early poems in the Friulian dialect formed a linguistic resistance to the standardizing culture of Fascism in the early 1940s,[167] the contamination of visual languages characteristic of *Il fiore*, in its mixture of Western and Oriental pictorial models, is a manifestation of an analogous resistance to what he called in his *Lettere luterane* the 'angolo visuale' (or 'visual angle') of the conformist or even neo-Fascist majority.[168] Regional dialects and visual subcultures serve as functions of Pasolini's search for counter-traditions and counter-sexualities.

Cinematic Codes and Spectatorship

In *Il fiore*, Pasolini creates an alien language within a dominant language. The narrative presents tales within tales, tales that are at times embedded within what they embed. As we mentioned above, the film (as an allegory of a nearly impossible structuration) comments upon the 'dis-interested' framing agencies that are presumed to provide the 'ground' for the stories that combine into histories (the stories of the protagonists within the film and the protagonists watching it). Embedded tales thus present a continual delaying of the invocation of that 'ground' which could provide structural guarantee, as well as a principle of unity or identity. That is, embedded tales as an eternal deferral of the exercise of power: Scheherazade's narratives as a technique of delay is prototypical for Pasolini's 'embedded pictures.' The motif of enframing is carried over into the visual material as well. As Pasolini remarked concerning the 'narrare illimitato,' outside the limits of one story there begins another ad infinitum. For Borges, this problem led to an existential or metaphysical dis-ease; for Barth it brought him to contemplate God.

Embedded pictures in *Il fiore* bring one to a similar dis-ease concerning the referential nature of images, and a contemplation of the coded nature of reality itself. The contamination of diverse forms of visual space in the film brings the spectator to contemplate the nature of the organization of real space, and to call into question the agency and interests that oversee the 'composition' of what we might call the lived space of the 'world picture.' According to Marco Vallora, it is Pasolini's 'mannerist' aesthetic that reveals the coded nature of reality: reality as the product of 'layers' of languages, 'embedded' languages, struggling over objects and people. As he writes: 'Nature, that is, is already artifice, culture, spectacle; anything elementary or primary no longer exists; all things refer to a preexisting code, art descends into life ... Reality presents itself as art or, better, it is already art; cultivated references are "natural," not simply imposed by the poet's own culture.'[169]

Pasolini's theory of cognitive codes, as it is found in *Empirismo eretico*, presents precisely this idea of eternal deferral of any ultimate 'underlying code' or *codice sottostante*.[170] This is made clearest during his response to Umberto Eco's critique of Pasolini's insistence that the 'Code of Reality' and the 'Code of Cinema' are identical. For Eco, Pasolini's formulations suffer from a methodological 'dilettantism' (a 'semiological naïveté') in its theory of codes that, suggests Eco, reduces cultural facts (the objects of representation) to natural phenomena.[171] Eco insists that a semiological theory of codes performs the opposite: it studies the facts of nature in order to reveal them as cultural phenomena.[172] This is a rather strange criticism given Pasolini's insistence upon the necessity to render all 'natural' relations to our physical surroundings as cultural relations. In his argument with Eco he insists that 'all of my chaotic pages concerning this problem ... *tend to bring Semiology towards the definitive culturalization of nature* (I have often repeated that a General Semiology of reality would be a philosophy that interprets reality as a language).'[173] The *Semiologia Generale*, which is Pasolini's form of filmmaking itself, thus refuses to acknowledge any existence of a *codice sottostante* (which he insists Eco presumes, and which is the source of Eco's resistance to Pasolini's formulations), a 'grounding' code that would enable any discourse that refers itself to that underlying code for its authority to assert itself as dogma: '*Non vorrei cioè che avesse nessun valore nessun dogma*' ('I would not want it to have any value or dogma').[174] Pasolini's cinema presents itself as a *semiologia generale* that reveals reality as a Language from which subjects and objects (what he calls the *paroles* of the Code) derive their meaning. And the narrative structure and stylistic contamination found in *Il fiore* provide one of the most effective examples of such a radical semiology (put into action in the moment of its reception) that, 'making all of living into a speaking,'[175] renders the 'object' a social relation – and therefore open to renegotiation – and the subject available to an altered 'suture.' As Pasolini remarks: 'Sometimes I ask myself (without the least anxiety) if by chance this *Trilogia* to which I am giving myself body and soul (like an exile who lives in a marvelous foreign country) is not a form of political disengagement and ... indifference. But I know intimately that my recent works are political precisely because they do not want to be so ... The interruption of meaning is not only more honest, it is more universal than the meaning itself.'[176]

Pasolini's theory of codes as developed in *Empirismo eretico* is intended to enable a radical cultural politics: it 'suspends' or 'interrupts' the meanings of things and individuals, and opens them to different articulations.[177] In *Il fiore* Pasolini brings two antithetical 'visual spaces' into contact in a hybridized film style that manifests an *ibrido morale* (or 'moral hybrid'). Jacqueline Rose's discussion of Black filmmaking and visual regimes helps us to understand this moral conundrum as both a necessity and a refusal of identification within prescribed psychic and visual regimes. This ambivalence can only be presented by constructing an alien language within the dominant one or, as Rose suggests, through a 'collision' of two forms of visual space: 'It seems that the sexual and political identification, what is both a necessity and a refusal of identification within the available visual and psychic parameters, can only be represented in the two forms of visual space.'[178] This collision translates the filmmaker's ambivalence into filmic techniques that 'deconstruct the positionality of the spectator as controller of the field of vision.'[179] As we mentioned, Pasolini carries out this form of deconstruction in *Il fiore* through a contamination of two figural traditions, containing two diverse approaches to the viewer. The cinematic 'suture,' built into and presumed by the photographic technology itself, is short-circuited from within by the 'contagious' presence of another figural tradition, another 'visual space,' which tends to subvert that suture and call upon an altered response in the spectator. This 'alien space' in the film is embedded within what Stephen Heath identifies as the 'Quattrocento space' presumed by the humanist codification of perspective. This code, which provides the ideological conditions and subjective disposition for the technical development of the camera, is the perceptual rule that underpins what Pasolini calls the bourgeois *angolo visuale* or world-view that continues to establish its hegemony. As Francastel writes, during the development of this code of perspective by artists such as Alberti and Brunelleschi, 'It was a question for a society in process of total transformation of a space in accordance with its actions and its dreams ... It is men who create the space in which they move and express themselves. Spaces are born and die like societies; they live, they have a history. In the fifteenth century, the human societies of Western Europe organized, in the material and intellectual senses of the term, a space completely different from that of the preceding generations; with their technical superiority, they progressively imposed that space over the planet.'[180]

Pasolini's radical interrogation of forms of spectating, or what we might call his search for a new erotics of spectating, as it is found throughout the *Trilogia*, is clearly what motivates his choice of certain Persian and Indian representations of specifically erotic theme for *Il fiore*: representations that provide an inherent resistance to the imposition of bourgeois space, as described by Francastel. For example, the highly (or even violently) metaphorical representation of Aziz and Budur's lovemaking and the rather undefined spatial organization of the frame present an ideal example of the 'alien' presence of another figural tradition, which itself beckons an altered sexual 'language' (as Pasolini would call it). It would appear that Pasolini's source for this representation of Aziz and Budur was the seventeenth-century Rajput miniature (as reproduced in the illustrations, after p. ix), although he left no documentation to support this claim. Clearly, for the Western observer, who can merely read the image literally, it seems rather shocking in its violent representation of lovemaking. Or perhaps the only resonance it contains for us is with the classical theme of sex as a 'hunt' – and in the miniature tradition the comparison of sex to a tiger hunt was a topos. Nevertheless, even at the thematic level, the image calls upon a visual literacy, and a sexual imaginary, that we as Westerners do not share: it is opaque, and this opacity is not lacking in the film's *riscrittura* of this miniature.

The difficulty we encounter as spectators in interpreting this image is also entirely appropriate given its situation within this particular episode. For throughout the tale, Aziz is constantly being baffled by the strange object-language that Budur uses to communicate with Aziz (a language in which banal, recognizable objects are given mysterious significance by an unknown, and apparently female, code) and he is continually running to Aziza for her competence in such language. In the end it appears that the real drama of the story is taking place between Aziza and Budur, with Aziz as the naïve vehicle of their cryptic messages (and his very incompetence in their language will cost him dearly). The difficulties we have as spectators of the scene between Aziz and Budur seem to be Pasolini's way of having us share in Aziz's drama of mis-reading. Pasolini invites his spectators to suspend habitual patterns of reading or reception, just as Aziz does, and consider other possibilities of interpretation.

But besides these thematic difficulties, we can see that something of the original's spatial organization (or 'distortion') has found its way into the film. As can be seen in the original miniature, the artist's abilities in foreshortening seem to us to be rather limited. The image presents at least two conflicting viewpoints, as revealed most clearly by the mats upon which the lovers are resting. The one on the left appears to locate the point of view high above the figures, with the mat existing, logically, on the same plane as the underlying rug. The mat beneath the character on the right, however, is seen from a much lower point of view, apparently very near to the floor, and thus the plane of the mat and the plane of the rug intersect, presenting a geometrical contradiction or distortion. The rug itself is not foreshortened while the figures are, and the resulting lack of any sense of verticality in the wall or horizontality of the floor destroys any possible illusion of depth that could have been provided by the figures themselves. The distortion of the image arises from its lack of a single organizing point of view that would unify the pictorial space and lend it 'firmness.' Its spatial 'incoherence' derives from compositional procedures not ordered according to European codifications of perspective.

Some of this incoherence finds its way into Pasolini's film. Along with the metaphorical and transgressive contents of this image, Pasolini's filmic translation of it captures some of the original's formal inconsistency (although, as we mentioned, the camera-based technology of the film would largely disallow the kind of radical disjunctions in point of view found in the miniature). We can see that the lack of receding orthogonals in the architecture enclosing Aziz and Budur detracts from the image's sense of depth; and the only real indication of such depth is offered by the slight movements and the foreshortening of the figures themselves, who are surrounded in a relatively undefined space of the tent. Relatively speaking, this frame contains an unusually small number of spatial cues that would lend the image an illusion of depth. It is a frame, that is, in which two visual spaces collide: the first derived from another aesthetic tradition, that of the miniature; and the second, the spatial organization imposed by film, which is the technical expression of Western codes of vision and spatial organization, the mechanical guarantee of their reproduction. Furthermore, this technology shrouds its codic operations within a discourse of naturalistic or realistic reproduction.

The 'alien language' of the Persian pictorial tradition found within the dominant language of the cinema is deployed by Pasolini precisely to contest this ideology of technical reproduction: it is the presence of a visual subculture that exists as a moment of rupture within the rationalizing hegemony of Western forms of spatial and cultural organization – a hegemony of a mode of production, insists Pasolini, that is spreading into and colonizing other non-European or Third World traditions and cultures. It is a mode of production that 'not only produces commodities, but also social relations, humanity.'[181]

Furthermore, as found in Pasolini's use of regional dialects in his writing, these visual subcultures not only form a resistant front to that cultural and economic hegemony (what he calls the new power of 'consumerism'), but also to its moral attitudes towards bodies and sexuality. For Pasolini finds in the Oriental erotic miniatures a correlation between (a) an apparent structural incoherence or representational disorder and (b) images of less constrained sexuality. The manner in which these images fail to offer an individualized, privileged point of view is the formal expression of another, perhaps less restrictive, attitude towards sexuality. That is, a certain lack of 'firmness' or rigidity in form seems to translate into a sense of flexibility in matters of pleasure, almost as if the absolute logical fixity of the location of point of view in bourgeois art somehow was a correlate of a fettering bourgeois code of personal, sexual comportment.

Conclusion: *Trilogia* as Auto-Lesionistic Cinema

The rationalization of perspective in the Renaissance is accompanied by a parallel rationalization of human comportment or by what Pasolini calls an anthropological modification of human bodies. The entire *Trilogia della vita* is one massive reaction to this modification of the language of human bodies that has 'traumatized' Pasolini.[182] In bourgeois society, sexuality and pleasure satisfy 'a social obligation'[183] and are betrayed by guilt. The *Trilogia* is an attempt to represent an image of sexuality untouched by this guilt, and pleasure as something 'against social obligations.'[184] This is found in the 'innocent' bodies of the *Decameron* and the sense of sexual *play* in *Il fiore* (while *Canterbury* appears as an exception here, given its presentation of generally corrupted and instrumentalized expressions of desire).[185] As Pasolini writes concerning these films: 'I made them in order to oppose the consumerist present to a very recent past where the human body and human relations were still real, although archaic, although prehistoric, although crude; nevertheless they were real, and these films opposed this reality to the non-reality of consumer civilization.'[186]

The comparative innocence he projects onto medieval society and the ideal of pleasures unladen by guilt or bourgeois morality he detects in Third World societies constitutes a reaction to the pressures of rationalization that have imposed a certain visual order and uniformity of space. Cinema (and later television), as a mass medium, is the most developed technology subtending this visual order. Therefore, 'cinema of contestation' may seem to be a contradiction in terms, since it is the technical expression of the hegemony of this order. Franco Fortini, for example, claims that Pasolini's 'turn' to film made him complicitous with that hegemony: he was compromised by the medium itself.[187] In another context, Adorno and Eisler, likewise, see the cinema as a technology responsible for a rationalization of the eye: 'The eye has adapted to bourgeois rationality and ultimately to a highly industrialized order by accustoming itself to interpreting reality, a priori, as a world of objects, basically as a world of commodities.'[188]

Yet for Pasolini, in the first place, a *refusal* to engage in the 'audio-visual technique,' so powerful in contemporary cultural formation, would render one complicitous. Imperative, however, is an ironic or 'heretical' use of the technology, a self-reflexive and necessarily 'auto-lesionistic' form of filmmaking, as Pasolini insists.[189] As he writes in the poem 'Progetto per opere future':

Bisogna deludere. Saltare sulle braci
come martiri arrostiti e ridicoli: la via
della Verità passa anche attraverso i più orrendi
luoghi dell'estetismo, dell'isteria,
del rifacimento folle erudito.

It is necessary to frustrate people, to throw oneself upon the coals like roasted and ridiculous martyrs: the avenue of Truth often passes through the most horrendous places of aestheticism, of hysteria, of crazy, erudite re-makes.[190]

The *Trilogia della vita* subverts the traditional language of cinema which, in the words of American filmmaker Stan Brakhage, proposes 'a form of sight which is aggressive and which seeks to make of any landscape a piece of real estate.'[191] And it carries out this subversion in spite of the medium itself, in a self-deconstructing manner. Pasolini's cinema offers a genealogy of the modern visual order, gives it a history, and he does so through adaptations of pre-modern and non-Western texts, and through what he describes in his essay 'Cinema of Poetry' as a 'poetic' style that reveals 'another film,' the stylistic-expressive film that manifests the 'pre-grammatical,' or 'oneiric' basis of a cinematic language, a language that is 'extremely crude, almost animal.'[192] It is this other film, a 'hypnotic monster' lurking below the logical surface of 'the prosaic language of narrative' (and threatening to disrupt this communicative language) that Pasolini's *cinema di poesia* celebrates.[193] It pushes its spectators to a renewed involvement in 'subconscious life' in order to reveal how 'the truth is not to be found in a single dream, but in many dreams' ('La verità non sta in un solo sogno, ma in molti sogni'), as the prefacing title to *Il fiore* announces.

In the *Trilogia* Pasolini adopts a mannerist style designed to tear cinema away from its 'naturalist' or realist ideology as a technology of reproduction, and he calls attention to the relation between camera and physical reality as a cultural relation: 'we must fight to the end, therefore, to demystify the "innocence of technique."'[194] Furthermore, through a contamination of styles, genres, and visual traditions, found throughout the *Trilogia*, Pasolini attempts to remind his viewers of preceding ways of seeing and thus intervening in the world (the compositional strategy of pastiche is maintained in the *Decameron*, where intertextual references are to Giotto, Masaccio, and Bruegel, and in *I racconti di Canterbury*, where we find citations from the medieval iconographic tradition, and from Bruegel and Bosch). What he calls, in a very Bakhtinian fashion, his 'translinguistic research' provides the source for stylistic contamination in a work that injects what he refers to in 'Progetto per opere future' as an 'ancient figurativity in the flank of the new generation.'[195] This abrasive stylistic offensive, or *delusione* ('bisogna deludere'), is carried out by way of an often parodic recuperation of the past. In the process, Pasolini attempts to evoke a cultural memory in the spectator, to force a conflict between memory and perception, and to thus raise him or her to a position from which to critically judge the present – a present, that is, located in a society of forgetfulness, since the commodity and memory are at war with one another, since the ideal consumer would have no memory at all.[196] Indeed, in the poem 'La poesia della tradizione,' Pasolini accuses the 'unfortunate generation' of May 1968 of being fooled into making a virtue of forgetfulness in their refusal of the bourgeois cultural canon:

I libri, i vecchi libri passarano sotto i tuoi occhi
come oggetti di un vecchio nemico
sentisti l'obbligo di non cedere ...
venisti al mondo, che è grande eppure così semplice,
e vi trovasti chi rideva della tradizione,
e tu prendesti alla lettera

tale ironia fintamente ribalda,
erigendo barriere giovanili
contro la classe dominante del passato.

The books, the old books pass before your eyes
like the objects of an old enemy
you felt the need to resist ...
you came into the world, which is huge yet so simple
and there you found those who laughed at tradition,
and you took this falsely rebellious irony literally
erecting youthful barriers against
the dominant class of the past.[197]

This 'generazione sfortunata' failed to understand that their 'disobe-dience' was naive obedience:

e così capirai di aver servito il mondo
contro cui con zelo 'portasti avanti la lotta':
era esso che voleva gettar discredito sopra
la storia – la sua;
era esso che voleva far piazza pulita
del passato – il suo.

in this way you will understand to have served the world
against which you 'carried on the struggle' with such zeal:
it was the world that wanted to toss out
its own discredited history;   .
it was the world that wanted
to sweep out its own past.[198]

For Pasolini, this forgetfulness was yet another requirement of gov-ernability: memory provides the potential basis for resistance to the continual anthropological, ideological, and geographical mutations of the present. The refusal of 'tradition' is an example of what Pasolini sees as the obedient disobedience of the new radicalism of the sixties and seventies, and led him in theory to reject militants and *autonomisti* as reactionaries of the Left.

Pasolini's work explores literary and figural traditions in an attempt to construct a 'counter-memory,' to keep his spectator from fully 'adapting' to the 'atrocious' and 'repressive' present. As he remarks, the *Trilogia* was not a typical film of political denunciation, however; he made it 'with such a violent love for the "lost time," to be a denunciation not of some particular human condition but a denunciation of the entire present (necessarily permissive). Now we are inside the present, at this point to an irreversible degree: we have adapted ourselves to it. Our memory is getting ever worse. We are experiencing, therefore, that which happens today, the repression of the tolerant power, which, of all repressions, is the most atrocious.'[199]

In the cinema, the production of a 'counter-memory,' capable of pushing us 'outside' of this present, entails what we have described as transgressing the conventions of filmic representation, recalling historically superseded representational models, mixing visual 'dialects,' so to speak, with the standard language of cinema: he sets loose a *vecchia figuratività* in the flank of this unfortunate generation. This is a style of contamination (or *plurilinguismo*) that is found throughout Pasolini's entire *opera*, lending them its coherence across the variety of media and genres he adopted throughout his life. And as Jonathan Crary writes, concerning Walter Benjamin and regimes of looking, filmmakers especially must counter the 'redundancies of representation' found in standard cinematic fare, or what Pasolini called the cinema of prose: 'That kind of redundancy of representation, with its accompanying inhibition and impoverishment of memory, was what Benjamin saw as the standardization of perception.'[200] What was necessary was to locate 'the moment when a conscious rift occurred between memory and perception, a moment in which memory had the capacity to rebuild the object of perception' (ibid.). Pasolini's cinema is designed to do just this: to call attention to the process of perception in order to defamiliarize spectators with traditional habits of viewing. And, indeed, he calls upon a new *spettatore da farsi* (an incomplete spectator, in the process of becoming), 'in such a way that every spectator would be called upon to choose and to criticize, that is *to be co-author*, instead of being a wretch that sees and hears, all the more repressed the more he is adulated.'[201] By presenting us with his 'translinguistic research' in the *Trilogia*, Pasolini invites us to become such 'co-authors' of the infinite sequence shot of reality (reality that is nothing but 'cinema in nature'): the 'magma without amalgam' of the *Trilogia della vita*.

> gioisco come si gioiesce seminando,
> col fervore che opera mescolanze di materie
> inconciliabili, magmi senza amalgama, quando
> la vita è limone o rosa d'aprile.

I rejoice as one rejoices sowing,
with the fervour that operates mixtures of
irreconcilable materials, magmas without amalgam, when
life is lemon or april rose.[202]

3

Pasolini's Ironic Recantation:
The 'Abiura dalla *Trilogia della vita*'

Io abiuro dalla 'Trilogia della vita,' benché non mi penta di averla fatta.
Non posso infatti negare la sincerità e la necessità che mi hanno spinto alla
rappresentazione dei corpi e del loro simbolo culminante, il sesso.

I recant the *Trilogia della vita* though I do not regret having made it. In fact,
I cannot deny the sincerity and the necessity that pushed me to the
representation of bodies and their symbol, sex.[1]

If the *Trilogia della vita* is concerned with a force of the past capable
of displacing the present – capable, that is, of preventing a complete
'adaptation' to the present – then Pasolini's 'Abiura' (abjuration or
recantation) seems rather dramatic in its assertion of the impossibility
of this very project. For in this short recantation, written while he
was working on *Salò* and just months before his murder in November
1975, Pasolini appears to admit a sort of 'defeat': he will concede to
his critics that his nostalgia for a lost sexual innocence, a time before
repression, was idealistic and unrealistic. Furthermore, he 'disowns' his
works for the way they had become 'instruments' of 'false tolerance' and
the hypocritical movement towards 'sexual liberation.'[2] However, the
essay is not devoid of Pasolini's usual irony, although few are willing
to note it. Indeed, the ease with which this document was accepted by
his critics remarks less upon its 'reasonableness' than it does upon the
compromised and compromising character of most of its readers. And
furthermore, if the 'Abiura' is read as an ironic or even parodic *recantatio*
(as we shall see, much like those of Boccaccio and Chaucer before

him), then the real object of his scorn is not only the *Trilogia* but the spectators who have turned it into a celebration of sexual liberation and democratic tolerance. But perhaps, in the end, the abjuration serves more to focus and intensify, rather than abandon, the ideological messages of the *Trilogia*. Indeed, Pasolini's recantation of these films might function most importantly as rhetorical protection of these messages, produced to screen them from the censorship that so often threatened their circulation.

'Abiura' of Instrumentalized *Trilogia*

In this short essay, written with extreme economy, Pasolini bemoans the way his films had been 'co-opted' by the 'forces of progress in the Fifties and Sixties.'[3] This period is characterized by a movement towards greater sexual 'liberation' and 'expression'; that is, towards a more 'tolerant' and apparently less repressive society. Pasolini is not the only writer who detects below the surface of this apparently popular movement a latently pernicious strategy of even greater repression. Indeed, he asserts, along with Michel Foucault,[4] that the 'tolerance' being celebrated was 'false,' and that the political Left had surreptitiously been made into the instrument of this falsity. In Foucault's terminology, the Left had become complicit in making sexuality an instrument of government, insofar as one's identity was identified with one's gender and sexual preferences, and these systems of categories make individuals into objects of self-surveillance.[5] The 'Abiura' revolts against these very 'progressive' forces – even if apparently sympathetic with his project – to the extent that they harness his films to this 'hypocritical' ideological project, and to the extent that they reveal the Left as being under the control of those in power.

As we have observed, one of Pasolini's principal aims in making the *Trilogia* was a celebration of sexuality as a force untouched by 'social obligations': it was the last 'un-alienated' zone of human activity, since the body and its rhythms and appetites were apparently not subject to cultural modification. However, this belief in the innocence of the body, as it was projected onto medieval and Third World societies, gave way to Pasolini's pessimistic observations of how sexuality and the body were a language, and therefore open to mutations: 'Ora tutto si è rovesciato' ('now everything has been overturned').[6] What the *Trilogia* revealed was how the body itself had undergone an 'anthropological change,' and had become 'corrupted' by power:

anche la 'realtà' dei corpi innocenti è stata violata, manipolata, manomessa dal potere consumistico: anzi, tale violenza sui corpi è diventato il dato più macroscopico della nuova epoca umana ... Le vite sessuali private (come la mia) hanno subito il trauma sia della falsa tolleranza che della degradazione corporea, e ciò che nelle fantasie sessuale era dolore e gioia, è divenuto suicida delusione, informe accidia.

even the 'reality' of innocent bodies has been violated, manipulated, submitted to consumerist power: or rather, this violence on bodies has become the most macroscopic datum of the new human epoch ... Private sexual life (such as my own) has undergone both the trauma of false tolerance and of corporal degradation; and in sexual fantasies what was once pain and joy has become suicidal disappointment, formless sloth.[7]

In other words, the irrepressible world of bodies and pleasures in these films, and their ideological messages, had been betrayed and neutralized by a society of tolerance and an ever more pernicious form of culture producing self-policing subjects.

However, Pasolini addresses his critics directly, and insists that his recantation is not offered for the reasons they presume. The critics he addresses are not only those on the Right, who reacted to certain moral transgressions in the films, but more importantly those on the Left who attacked these films for a lack of engagement. These critics will not be satisfied by this *abiura*: in fact, it presents an even more intense and focused ideological critique than did the films, and it holds the 'doveri' of the Left partly responsible for the 'degradation' he here describes:

Non si sono accorti che la degenerazione è avvenuta proprio attraverso una falsificazione dei loro valori. Ed ora essi hanno l'aria di essere soddisfatti! Di trovare che la società italiana è *indubbiamente* migliorata, cioè è divenuta più democratica, più tollerante, più moderna ecc. Non si accorgono della valanga di delitti che sommerge l'Italia ... Non si accorgono che in Italia c'è addirittura il coprifuoco, che la notte è deserta e sinistra come nei più neri secoli del passato ... Non si accorgono che la liberalizzazione sessuale anzichè dare leggerezza e felicità ai giovani e ai ragazzi, li ha resi infelici, chiusi, e di conseguenza stupidamente presuntuosi e aggressivi: ma di ciò addirittura non vogliono occuparsene, perché non gliene importa niente dei giovani e dei ragazzi.

They did not realize that the degeneration took place through a falsification of their own values. And now they have the air of being satisfied! To find that

Italian society has *doubtless* improved, that is, has become more democratic, more tolerant, more modern, etc. They remain unaware of the flood of crimes that are submerging Italy ... They are unaware that in Italy there is even a curfew, that the night is deserted and sinister as in the darkest centuries of the past ... They do not understand that, instead of giving lightness and happiness to young people, sexual liberation has rendered them unhappy, closed and, consequently, stupidly arrogant and aggressive: but indeed they do not want to bother themselves with this, because they don't give a damn about young people.[8]

Clearly, the recantation takes the Left as its object of scorn at least as much as it does the *Trilogia della vita*. In fact, it is the *fault* of these forces of 'progress' and 'liberation' that his films have become the instruments of the corporal and cultural 'degradation' of the Italian people. For Pasolini, the fact that Italy was still a largely underdeveloped nation led him to believe before the *Trilogia* that this degradation had not yet spread throughout Italy, as it had in France and in other 'developed countries' where 'ormai i giochi sono fatti da un pezzo. E' un pezzo che il popolo antropologicamente non esiste più' ('the game has been up for quite awhile. It has been quite a while since the people anthropologically no longer exists').[9] And thus his *Trilogia*, with its carnivalesque celebration of people still on the margins of bourgeois society, and its attempt to prevent a complete adaptation to the present, seems to be abandoned for lack of an audience.

Indeed, the *abiura*, writes Pasolini, 'mi conduce all'addattamento' ('leads me to adaptation').[10] The instrumentalization of his films, and the way the past he explored was immediately fetishized by pornographic filmmakers who produced films capitalizing upon Pasolini's 'transgressions,' led Pasolini to review his beliefs in the 'revolutionary' potential embedded in the past.

Dunque io mi sto addattando alla degradazione e sto accettando l'inaccettabile. Manovro per risistemare la mia vita. Sto dimenticando com'erano *prima* le cose. Le amate facce di ieri comminciano a ingiallire. Mi è davanti – pian piano senza piu alternative – il presente.

Therefore, I am adapting myself to the degradation, and I am accepting the unacceptable. I am manoeuvring to reorganize my life. I am forgetting how things were *before*. The beloved faces of yesterday are beginning to fade. I am – slowly and without alternatives – confronted with the present.[11]

The Irony of the 'Abiura'

The inspiration and prime mover of everything Pasolini writes is antithesis ...
Antithesis can be found at all levels of his writings ... including even his most
preferred rhetorical figure, that subspecies of oxymoron called syneciosis in
ancient rhetoric, by which one affirms two contrary attributes of the same
object.[12]

While it is essential to read the 'Abiura' literally, and gather its important
ideological message, it must not be read only on this level. The essay
has traditionally been taken only at face value: readers typically accept
Pasolini's gesture as a straightforward recantation, the fruit of a rational
process of *autocoscienza*. This reading supposes that Pasolini has here
abandoned his 'poetic' of contamination in writing the essay. Indeed, the
essay was written for his weekly column in the *Corriere della sera*. That is,
it pertains, at first glance, to a journalistic or editorial genre of writing:
a genre held to be non-poetic or, better, purely communicative. All of
Pasolini's journalistic essays, collected in *Le belle bandiere*, *Scritti corsari*,
and the *Lettere luterane*, belong to a genre that is traditionally dominated
by this communicative function, where the 'verticality' of the language
(the 'play' of connotations along the paradigmatic axis of discourse in
the Jakobsonian model) is subordinated to the demands of persuasion.
Therefore, it is a genre of writing, unlike poetry, where the attention of
the reader is not drawn to a consideration of the enunciation: the reader's
horizon of expectations does not permit such meta-textual sensitivity
even if it were intended by the writer.

This genre, to which the 'Abiura' appears to belong, conditions its reading to such an extent that precisely such a 'meta-literary' or potentially
ironic sensitivity has tended to be overlooked in preceding readings of
this essay.[13] This is slightly surprising, given Pasolini's penchant for
transgressing codes of reception and conventions of genre, something he
carries out, with absolute coherence, in every project he ever engaged: be
it a poem, novel, journal (*Officina*, *Nuovi argomenti*), or film. Why is it to
be assumed, then, that he abandons such an attitude when he writes for
newspapers? It should not be: just as it should not surprise us when we
read one of his poems where allusions to Ungaretti, Leopardi, Shelley,
or Dante exist beside diatribes against the Italian Communist party,[14] or
where, in *La ricotta*, Christ's Passion is re-enacted as the film crew in the
diegesis dances the Twist to blaring American rock and roll. Indeed, it is
this 'spirit' or aesthetic of contamination, which I have been describing

throughout the present work, that provides Pasolini's *opera* its very unity – albeit a paradoxical one. There is no reason to believe that this spirit is not carried over into his journalistic essays, written, I would suggest, *en poète*.

This view, as I will show, is supported by the fact that the 'Abiura' functions as the conclusion of the *Trilogia della vita*: it is the last word, the moment of closure. However, this closure is highly ambivalent, if we can call it closure at all. It is marked by an unexpected irony. That is, as an example of verbal irony, it carries a *double meaning* (which we will call, after Capellanus, a *duplicem sententiam*) of which the writer is conscious, but the reader is unconscious: one thing is said, but a different and antithetical – but parallel – meaning is intended. The source of this irony is found in the fact that Pasolini's 'Abiura' follows rhetorical conventions of *apologia, reprobatio*, or *recantatio* dating from Ovid, but rendered commonplace during the scholastic tradition, and conventions already drawn upon by both Boccaccio and Chaucer *qua* conventions. That is, the 'Abiura,' like the texts of the *Trilogia della vita*, is born of a *riscrittura*. It calls upon what Pasolini refers to as the reader's 'philological fervour' in his preface to the *Scritti corsari*: a fervour, he suggests, produced in the reader's absolutely essential task of relating Pasolini's journalistic essays to his other literary, cinematic, and especially poetic works and, beyond these, to the works of other writers. In this intertextual 'fervour' the reader is more responsible than usual, he remarks, in the establishment of the text's structure or unity, if one can be located at all.[15] Thus, it appears certain that Pasolini presumed that the readers of his newspaper pieces would be sensitive to far more than simply what was being communicated: there was also the question of style.

The irony of the 'Abiura' is undeniable, I would suggest, given the fact that two of the original novels that Pasolini adapts in the *Trilogia* contain either a recantation or a defensive response to critics.[16] Moreover, the defences that Boccaccio and Chaucer provide are themselves not devoid of irony. Thus, the 'Abiura' appears to be an example of Pasolini being 'faithful' in his adaptation of those original texts. And just as both Boccaccio and Chaucer address their 'apologies' to those in power, and rather rhetorically distance themselves from their often transgressive material in order to protect it, so does Pasolini's recantation have a similarly rhetorical ring to it. As so often in his work, dominated (as Fortini has remarked) by the rhetorical figures of oxymoron or syneciosis, Pasolini communicates two antithetical messages at once.

Boccaccio's Strategies of Defence

Boccaccio's response to his critics, found first in the 'Introduction' to Day 4 and finally in the 'Conclusione dell'autore,' does not take the form of a recantation, and he does not admit of any error in his ways. However, he does open his 'Conclusione' in a defensive tone, insisting that the 'liberties' he has taken in the work are sanctioned by 'la divina grazia.'[17] Furthermore, he likens his own work to certain parallels in religious painting and literature in order to protect his text from the 'riprensione' of Church officials.[18] And in both the 'Conclusione' and the 'Introduction' to Day 4, Boccaccio insists that he is only a scribe, reporting the stories he has overheard in the past, and therefore not responsible for their 'invention.'[19]

However, Boccaccio does not only defend his work's thematic novelties. His 'assalitori'[20] are also upset by the popular genres he adopts, the language he uses, and his writing in prose.[21] He defends himself by asserting that his 'istilo umillissimo e rimesso'[22] is suited to his audience (it is a matter of *convenientia*): and the fact that he writes for women is his ultimate defence from any charges of stylistic unorthodoxies. However, Boccaccio does adopt a rhetoric of concession several times in the 'Conclusione,' as a tactic to forestall censure. And just before giving thanks to God for having 'helped' him to reach his 'desiderato fine,' Boccaccio concedes:

Confesso nondimeno le cose di questo mondo non avere stabilità alcuna, ma sempre essere in mutamento, e così potrebbe della mia lingua essere intervenuto.[23]

I confess, however, that the things of this world have no stability, but are subject to constant change, and this may well have happened to my tongue.

That is, the 'errors' found in his text are not his responsibility, but are the products of history itself, of the mutable nature of all worldly things.

Running throughout Boccaccio's self-defence, however, is a definite sense that his humble conclusion is purely rhetorical, certainly not intended to be taken entirely seriously, and simply fulfils one of the conventions of medieval – especially ecclesiastical – literature: the apologetic act of humility that denies such an earthly endeavour as writing any lasting importance.

Furthermore, it is clear that in the 'Conclusione' Boccaccio repeats a gesture that had become a *topos* in the Middle Ages: the *reprobatio amoris* as it is found in Ovid's *Ars amatoria* and later in the last book of Andreas

Capellanus's *De amore* (concerning the highly ironic 'rejection' of love and of the entire *De amore* itself) – both works that had wide circulation, in Latin and in the vernacular, at the time of the *Decameron*'s composition.[24] The Ovidian motif of *reprobatio* became a commonplace especially in literature concerning love or related 'obscene' topics, and it clearly acted as a model for Cappellanus. Moreover, Boccaccio continually demonstrates an indebtedness to both Ovid and Cappellanus (among other treatments of love).[25] The ironic tone found in Ovid and Capellanus, where the *reprobatio* almost certainly performs as a defence against censure,[26] is carried over into the defence against possible criticisms found in Boccaccio's 'Proemio,' the 'Introduction' to Day 4, and the 'Conclusione dell'autore.'

However, the defence takes on a peculiarly confessional tone as well. Here, as demonstrated in the passage cited above ('Confesso nondimeno ...'), the verb *confessare* provides one of the keys to an understanding of the rhetorical strategies of the 'Conclusione.' That is, Boccaccio here clearly links his defence to apologetic formulae found in manuals of confession. Such penitential manuals were of two types in the Middle Ages: the first provided formulae to adopt within the organization of the mass; the second type of manual was intended for individual, private penance.[27] These manuals often contained elaborate classifications of sins, and the manner appropriate for their confession. As Olive Sayce has shown, among the variety of sins often contained in these manuals, references to the sinfulness of secular poetry are often found.[28] Clearly, Boccaccio's 'confessional' tone must be linked to this rhetorical tradition.

Boccaccio appears to concede to the Pauline injunction according to which all that is written that is not morally and spiritually edifying must be retracted. The formula, as reproduced in Romans 15:4, is as follows: 'Quaecumque enim scripta sunt, ad nostram doctrinam scripta sunt'; or in 2 Tim. 3:16: 'omnis scriptura divinitus inspirata utilis est ad docendum.' This formula, often found in ecclesiastical writing as a strategy to condemn all secular literature, is alluded to in the language Boccaccio adopts in the 'Conclusione'; and while he ostensibly displays an agreement with this formulation, he extends the notion of what is *utile* beyond the strictly *scriptural* boundaries of the idea of *doctrina*. In defending his *novelle* against any possible 'corrupt' reception (which would be no fault of his own), Boccaccio writes:

Quali libri, quali parole, quali lettere son più sante, più degne, più reverende che quelle della divina Scrittura? E sì sono egli stati assai che, quelle perversamente intendendo, sé ed altrui a perdizione hanno tratto. Ciascuna cosa in se medesima è buona ad alcuna cosa, e male adoperata può essere nociva di molte; e così dico delle mie novelle. Chi vorrà da quelle malvagio consiglio o malvagia operazione trarre, elle nol vieteranno ad alcuno, se forse in sé l'hanno, e torte e tirate fìeno ad averlo; e chi *utilità* e frutto ne vorrà, elle nol negheranno, né sarà mai che altro che *utili* ed oneste sien dette o tenute, se a que' tempi o a quelle persone si leggeranno per cui e pe' quali state son raccontate. (678; emphasis mine)

What other books, what other words, what other letters, are more sacred, more reputable, more worthy of reverence, than those of the Holy Scriptures? And yet there have been many who, by perversely construing them, have led themselves and others to perdition. All things have their own special purpose, but when they are wrongly used a great deal of harm may result, and the same applies to my stories. If anyone should want to extract evil counsel from these tales, or fashion an evil design, there is nothing to prevent him, provided he twists and distorts them sufficiently to find the thing he is seeking. And if anyone should study them for the usefulness and profit they may bring to him, he will not be disappointed. Nor will they ever be thought of or described as anything but useful and seemly, if they are read at the proper time by the people for whom they were written.

Boccaccio here takes up once again the claim that he will furnish his readers with *utile consiglio* ('useful advice') as suggested in the 'Proemio': his *novelle* shall be *utili* and shall contribute to the moral rectitude (or *onestà*) of the melancholic ladies who figure as the text's readers.

Thus, the confessional rhetoric of recantation, which here combines with the Pauline topos we have described as it was employed by Boccaccio, performs a very complex operation: (a) it repeats a conventional commonplace, found often in both secular and religious material, of penitential epilogue; (b) it concedes, to a certain degree, to ecclesiastical dogma, though in a superficial fashion; but (c) it also explodes that dogma in the process by extending the limits of traditional ecclesiastical categories, thus opening a cultural space for secular literature. As Lucia Marino asserts, 'it is clear that we find boldly extended here the limits of what any other contemporary humanist would have countenanced as "proper" literature.'[29] The 'double nature' of Boccaccio's defensive language is designed precisely to gain cultural legitimacy by conceding to the very forces that question that legitimacy – forces, that is, that ultimately control the mechanism of legitimation. He will advance significantly and retreat slightly in order better to secure the newly captured territory.

This project (we might call it proto-humanist in nature, in partial agreement with Marino) of legitimating such a secular literature is theorized again later in Boccaccio's *De Genealogia Deorum*, where he devotes the fourteenth book to an *apologia* of secular literature. Furthermore, the titles to his chapters often reveal the novelty of the positions Boccaccio is willing to take: vi, 'Poesim esse utilem facultatem'; ix, 'Composuisse fabulas apparet utile potius quam damnosum'; xviii, 'Non esse exitiale crimen libros legere poetarum.'[30] Throughout these examples, the notion of *utilità* is central, and openly polemical.

Thus, Boccaccio's epilogue carries out an extremely complex operation: rhetorically, he reproduces traditional topoi of closure (usually, as in the *Decameron*, a repetition of motifs already traced out in the prologue), including requests for divine intervention in the fortunes of both text and author, an address to the reader, a denunciation of the mutable nature of all wordly things – including language itself – an invocation of God's grace, and finally a reiteration of the title of the book. All that is excluded from Boccaccio's epilogue, and something traditionally found within such closings, is a mentioning of the author's name – usually, as in Chaucer, one of the very last elements present in a work's conclusion. Such adherence to literary commonplaces already suggests a high level of irony, or even satire, in such allusions to and compliance with these ideologically charged compositional patterns. The genius of the 'Conclusione dell'autore' is found in the manner in which he both submits to the authority of the Church and redefines, in the process of transgressing, institutionalized notions of doctrine and *utilità*, thus effectively defending the *novelle* and carving out a place for literature in the vernacular. As we shall see, the 'double nature' of Boccaccio's defensive conclusion (similar to the 'duplicem sententiam' Capellanus claims in his own retraction)[31] will be reproduced by both Chaucer and Pasolini at the end of their own 'vernacular' works.

Chaucer's *Retracciouns*

Now pray I to yow alle that heren this litel tretis or reden it, that if ther be any thing in it that liketh them, that therof thay may thanke oure Lord Jhesu Crist, of whom procedith alle witte and al goodnes; and if ther be eny thing that displesith them, I pray them that thay arette it to the defaulte of myn unconnying, and not to my wille, that wolde fayn have sayd better if I hadde connying; for the book saith, al that is writen for oure doctrine is writen, and that is myn entent. Wherefore I beseke yow mekely for the mercy of God that ye praye for me, that God have mercy on me and forgeve me my giltes, and nameliche of my translacciouns and editying in worldly vanitees, whiche I revoke in my retracciouns.[32]

The 'double nature' of Chaucer's now infamous 'Retracciouns,' as he called them, is attested to by the degree of uncertainty found in critical accounts of it. Indeed, the critical tradition reveals an ongoing argument over whether Chaucer wrote his 'Retractions' with sincere penitence as a man nearing death (and thus absolutely devoid of the irony found throughout the rest of the *Canterbury Tales*). Others question whether it is merely ironic, playful, or simply rhetorically conventional. Some note a certain degree of doubt as to whether Chaucer even wrote it at all, or wonder if it wasn't supplied later by a monk-scribe.[33]

As John Gardner remarks, 'the question of just what to do with the Retraction has nagged Chaucer criticism for centuries.'[34] For William Lawrence, Chaucer here provides a 'huddled and inconsistent' retraction, a 'final cry of penitence and remorse': 'Like any poor sinner, he could only cry *mea culpa*! ... Let us hope that it brought him peace of mind in the end, but let us rejoice that it came no sooner!'[35] Peter Elbow insists that here Chaucer abandons irony, since it poses a danger to 'full participation in life'; the danger he sees is in gaining experience 'only in surrogate ways, in books or dreams or writing. I can not help guessing that the joke, like so many in Chaucer, is not just a joke.'[36] Pat Pinsent claims that the question is simply undecidable,[37] but for Derek Brewer, the 'Retraction' stages a 'disastrous victory' for 'the severest aspect of ecclesiastical culture.'[38]

However, there are those who radically differ with these views regarding the sincerity of the 'Retractions.' Indeed, Nevill Coghill recalls how Chaucer ironically recants his *The Legend of Good Women*:

> Forced to recant our cant, if we have wit,
> Our recantation will have cant in it.

For Coghill, Chaucer here demonstrates how he 'toed the party line,' but 'decided to toe it to an inward and ironical tune of his own.'[39] He suggests that the conclusion of the *Canterbury Tales* should be read with this precedent in mind.

However, by far the most compelling accounts of the 'Retractions' insist upon its *conventional* nature, thus resisting post-Romantic impulses to read autobiographical significance into the conclusion – impulses characteristic of many of the positions reviewed above. Kemp Malone suggests that Chaucer 'followed a familiar and deeply rooted medieval literary convention, that of the religious ending,' and he reminds his readers of the similar penitential conclusion found in *Troilus and Criseyde* and in Dante's *Paradiso*.[40] For both Laura Kendrick and Olive Sayce, it has been necessary to recognize the Romantic anachronisms that distort many of the most recent approaches to Chaucer: approaches that would fail to recognize how, for a medieval writer such as Chaucer (and Boccaccio for that matter), the importance of autobiographical material in their texts was minimal, and was far outweighed by the demands of established compositional procedures.[41] For Kendrick, the 'Retractions' would be an example of how Chaucer 'playfully' conforms to rhetorical formulae throughout the *Canterbury Tales* – indeed, perhaps the 'Retractions' provides the clearest example of this tendency.[42]

Sayce argues most convincingly against the possibility that Chaucer's 'Retractions' are sincere. Providing numerous examples of ecclesiastical and secular models of abjuration and *reprobatio* (including Matthieu de Vendôme's *Ars Versificatoria*, penitential manuals, St Augustine's *Retractationes*, French treatises concerning love almost certainly modelled upon Capellanus, and examples from Boccaccio himself), of which Chaucer was almost certainly aware, Sayce clearly locates the 'Retractions' within a rhetorical tradition shared by both Chaucer and Boccaccio as *European* writers (united by the cosmopolitan koiné offered by Latin).[43] Her findings suggest to her that in the 'Retractions,' 'Chaucer is not expressing a conventionally pious attitude, as has often been claimed, but rather ... he is viewing the problem with ironic and humorous detachment.'[44]

For Sayce, Chaucer, like Boccaccio before him, adopted a rhetoric of concession to conclude his polemical, and certainly often morally transgressive, text in order to defend it from possible attacks from the Church: 'Why did medieval poets in such number repent of their worldly works? It can only be explained as a consequence of the relative insecurity of secular literature in the face of a strong opposing tradition.'[45] Her philological sensitivity to Chaucer's allusions to literary precedents allows Sayce insight into what is only an apparent contradiction in tone between the 'Retractions' and the rest of the *Canterbury Tales*, and she thus provides a response to those critics whose only option is to claim its sincerity: 'In English mediaeval literature it is an erratic block, but viewed against a European tradition, it falls into place as a widely used commonplace.'[46]

Just as we found in Boccaccio, Chaucer's penitential conclusion is forced to attempt to secure a cultural place for secular literature (especially his own) while simultaneously appearing to submit to the very forces working to deny the legitimacy of such a literature. Thus a contradiction: the *Canterbury Tales* exist as a testament to the growth and independence of secular literature, yet in his repentance of the 'worldly vanitees'[47] expressed in the text, Chaucer reproduces the traditional condemnation of it, and adequates himself to established *doctrina*. This *duplicem sententiam*, as Capellanus called it in his own abjuration, reveals what Sayce calls 'a complexity of meaning, which forbids a straightforward reading as an expression of sincere repentance ... Thematically, it reflects the tension between traditional ecclesiastical teaching and the growing autonomy of secular literature. Far from being a personal confession of literary sin, it is a conventional motif which is used as a vehicle for the expression of opposing aesthetic standpoints. By means of irony and humour Chaucer presents the problem in all its complexity.'[48]

Pasolini's Re-written Recantation

Just as in the defensive recantations found in both Boccaccio and Chaucer, in Pasolini's 'Abiura dalla *Trilogia della vita*' nothing is simply abjured – at least not for the most obvious reasons. Pasolini's 'Abiura' must be viewed as an ironic, meta-literary re-enactment of Boccaccio's 'Conclusione' and Chaucer's 'Retractions.' Thus, as Sayce might say, one must be attentive to the 'complexity of meaning' produced by the intertextual play of Pasolini's *riscrittura* of the ultimately Ovidian topos of the *reprobatio amoris*.

Pasolini clearly links himself to Chaucer's 'Retractions' when he misquotes him in the concluding title of *I racconti di Canterbury*; and in the 'Abiura dalla *Trilogia della vita*' he will recant the errors of his films for historical reasons very similar to those Boccaccio mentions. Chaucer's concluding lines read: 'Here ends the book of the *Tales of Canterbury* compiled by Geoffrey Chaucer, on whose soul Jhesu Crist have mercy. Amen.' The concluding scene in the film presents Chaucer, played by Pasolini, writing the last page of the *Tales*. We are given a close-up of the page, which reads, 'Qui finiscono i Racconti di Canterbury raccontati per il solo piacere di raccontare' ('Here end the Canterbury Tales, told only for the pleasure of the telling'). A close-up of Chaucer/Pasolini's face shows him uttering the final, and suddenly hilariously parodic, 'Amen.'

The parody is present in Pasolini's subversion of the religious rhetoric of the original: Pasolini replaces Chaucer's deferential language, intended as a double-edged acknowledgment of the authority of the Church, with a hedonistic and almost profaning insistence upon the pleasure of narration: 'Qui finiscono i *Racconti* di Canterbury, *raccontati* per il solo *piacere* di *raccontare*.' The repetition of the word *raccontare* in its verbal and nominal forms is intended to insist upon the *ontological* claims Pasolini is making for his understanding of narrative: he celebrates an ontology of narrative that displaces the divine origins supposed by Church doctrine. This is the subversion carried out in his parodic citation of Chaucer's last words.

Where Chaucer ostensibly defers to what Deleuze would call the 'powers of the true' as the source of his legitimacy, and to guarantee his fiction with institutional sanction, Pasolini presents the storyteller as one who denies institutionalized truths that would make his stories into fictions. As Deleuze writes, the storyteller is the *creator of truth*: and as we discussed in relation to Pasolini's *Decameron*, these films present an attempt to 'rediscover the pure and simple storytelling function,' which is free from the 'model of truth': 'What is opposed to fiction is not the real: it is not the truth which is always that of the masters or colonizers; it is the story-telling function of the poor, in so far as it gives the false the power which makes it into a memory, a legend, a monster.'[49] This is the subversive significance of Pasolini's parodic citation of Chaucer, where he displaces completely any deference (albeit empty of real significance in the original) to the 'true' and insists upon the *piacere di raccontare*. Pasolini's *Trilogia* takes back the storytelling function. He refutes the institutionalized discourses that deny the storyteller his ontological function as the 'creator of truth' – discourses, that is, that strip the artist of his mandate. What is this mandate? It is to locate 'una coralità, insomma, d'ascolto e di riconoscimento delle esperienze da cui è nata la deduzione della norma' ('a chorus listening to and recognizing the experiences from which the deduction of the norm is born').[50] The subversion of institutionalized discourse carried out by Pasolini's ironic 'Amen' at the end of his *Canterbury* is necessary in order to free his stories from the 'powers of the true' which make his films into fictions: in order that his storytelling can become a memory, 'and memory is the invention of a people.'[51] As Pasolini concludes his essay on the *cinema di poesia*, in this manner he reascribes 'ai poeti una funzione tardo-umanistica: il mito e la coscienza tecnica della forma' ('to the poets a late humanistic function: The myth and the technical consciousness of form').[52]

It is in an effort to reestablish and protect this mandate as it is expressed in the *Trilogia* that he writes the 'Abiura.' It is a recantation, that is, that recants actually quite little, yet may satisfy the critics and the censors long enough for his films to circulate (given the fact that his films were often the targets of extreme suppression, as we discussed in the preceding chapter). And, indeed, after his legal experiences with the *Trilogia*, Pasolini learned that a public recantation might be the only way to defend his works, and their messages, from this sort of suppression. As he remarks in a self-interview in March 1975, 'È vero, *Salò* sarà un film "crudele," talmente crudele che (suppongo) dovrò per forza distanziarmene, fingere di non crederci e giocare un po' in modo agghiacciante.'[53] The manner in which he makes this remark would indicate that he had long considered the rhetoric of recantation as a means of defence, and there is no reason to believe that the 'Abiura dalla *Trilogia della vita*' is not an example of such a defensive rhetoric. As it happened, whether or not he would have written another ironic *recantatio* of his last film is unknown, given his death in November 1975, soon after the completion of *Salò*. Clearly, however, the 'Abiura' functions as a screen designed on one level to postpone the moment of suppression, as well as, on another level, to prevent the type of instrumentalization that he describes as a partial neutralization of the *Trilogia*'s project of recollection.

Furthermore, it is important to note that Pasolini had already carried out an abjuration, which opened the fifteen-year period dominated by a confidence in the poetic language of the *cinema di poesia* as the new vernacular of the popular masses. As he will write in a poem he composed in the early sixties, but published only in 1980:

Dicevo no alle mie origini piccolo borghesi, voltavo le spalle a tutto ciò che fa italiano, protestavo, ingenuamente, inscenando un'abiura che, nel momento di umiliarmi e castrarmi, mi esaltava.

I said no to my petit-bourgeois origins, I turned my back on everything Italian, I protested, naïvely, staging an abjuration that, while it humiliated and castrated me, exalted me.[54]

As we remarked in the opening chapter, Pasolini abandoned the novel and switched to film as an attempt to escape from his own nationality: it was a gesture, for Pasolini, of self-exile. In response to an interviewer's question, Pasolini once remarked:

Sa perché ho fatto del cinema? Perché non ne potevo più della lingua orale e anche di quella scritta. Perché volevo ripudiare con la lingua il Paese da cui sono stato le centinaia di volte sul punto di fuggire.

Do you know why I made films? Because I couldn't stand oral and even written language any more. Because, along with the language, I wanted to repudiate the country I was so close to fleeing from so many hundreds of times.[55]

Furthermore:

Nel confronto con la poesia scritta che è sempre definita da una serie di limiti storici nazionali, il cinema rappresenta un linguaggio transnazionale e la sua scelta in questo momento ha anche il significato di un'abiura della lingua italiana, e assieme, un po' alla volta, della sua letteratura e di 'tutto ciò che fa italiano.'

Compared to written poetry, which is always defined by a series of historical, national limits, cinema represents a transnational language, and my choice [to make films] has the additional meaning of an abjuration of the Italian language and also, little by little, of Italian literature and 'everything Italian.'[56]

The first *abiura* pushes Pasolini into a linguistic exile, designed to allow him a position from which to survey the linguistic and medialogical currents traversing the peninsula (and it is an exile quite similar to that which offered Dante his historical perspective and critical insights into the linguistic conditions of medieval Italy as reflected in the *De vulgari eloquentia*).[57] It is during the period of his cinematic 'exile' that Pasolini locates technology as a source of mutations in the national language, but also as a vehicle of linguistic homogenization – something he perceived especially around the industrialized centres in Northern Italy – observations initially rejected but eventually accepted by many philologists, including Maria Corti.[58] Indeed, Pasolini's switch to cinema must be seen not only as a gesture of self-exile, but also as an attempt to remain engaged within newly hegemonic communication technologies.

While the first *abiura* signals the beginning of his cinematic activities, and the celebration of his optimistic views concerning the 'revolutionary potential' of an engaged form of filmmaking, the second 'Abiura dalla *Trilogia della vita*' seems to signal their close. However, this capitulation, this 'adaptation to the present' that Pasolini ostensibly offers in the 'Abiura,' is only apparent. For, if anything, after the *Trilogia* Pasolini's critique of the type of 'neutralization' of bodies and pleasures carried out by consumer culture gains in intensity, both in the 'Abiura' where he fully states his thesis in relation to the *Trilogia*, and in *Salò* (his last finished film) and in *Porno-Teo-Kolossal* (Pasolini's unfinished screenplay, to be considered his last film project).

Indeed, the function of the 'Abiura,' just as those we have described in Boccaccio and Chaucer before him, is highly complex: it both repeats the nostalgic and optimistic view of sexual liberty expressed in the *Trilogia* but also reproduces the very sort of rationalistic condemnation of such a nostalgia as expressed by his detractors: here is, once again, the *duplicem sententiam* we have found to be characteristic of the rhetoric of recantation. And clearly, one of the functions of this 'doubled' point of view in Pasolini's 'Abiura' is to defend his work from official censure – to provide a protective screen through a rhetoric of concession – and thus to secure the survival and continuing circulation both of his films and of the type of *cinema di poesia* that produced them. This strategy of defence is doubly ironic, given the nature of the original retractions as found in Boccaccio and Chaucer.

Conclusion

In conclusion, the 'Abiura' locates Pasolini in a long history of innovators (but also heretics and dissidents) forced, in one way or another, to offer a public recantation of their transgressive works. It must be read as the ironic 'Conclusione dell'autore' for the entire *Trilogia*. It presents Pasolini in line, after Boccaccio and Chaucer, as an author working within a new medium, in a new style, and addressing an altered spectator, on the frontier between one epoch and another: between modernity and 'la nuova preistoria.' We find combined in the rewritten recantation two apparently antithetical positions: an abjuration of how his films had been instrumentalized by the forces of false tolerance, and a recantation of an irrational or even utopian nostalgia for a lost innocence; at the same time, however, Pasolini yet again *stages* a theatrical *abiura* 'che, nel momento di umiliarmi e castrarmi, mi esaltava.'[59] This *duplicem sententiam*, the juggling of parallel and antithetical messages, is one of the defining features of Pasolini's 'monstrous' and 'autolesionistic' style – a style found in varying degrees of intensity throughout his *opera*, including his journalistic and theoretical essays composed *en poète*. It is a style in which the line of demarcation separating complicity and transgression is never entirely clear, since it is continually shifting as determined by the location of the 'line of fire,' of which Pasolini never lost sight. It is this ambivalence, found so clearly in the 'Abiura,' that was often criticized in Pasolini, given the fluidity of his position. But this fluidity, this *leggerezza* ('lightness') as the poet Sium might say in *Il fiore delle mille e una notte*, is only a function of his engagement within the cultural wars of position peculiar to late modernity: a fluidity that jars with rigidified stances taken up by not only the traditional institutions of the Left, but also by the new social movements proliferating following 1968 – a rigidity that, for both these social forces, was an index of defeat. Pasolini's 'Abiura' maintains, in its very structure, in the 'philological fervour' it sets loose in the moment of its reception, the aesthetic of contamination that produced his other films, novels, poems, and essays. It is yet another example of Pasolini's practice of *autonegazione* ('self-negation'), 'grazie a cui l'arte può riuscire in qualche modo a negare ciò che la nega.'[60]

4

Framing Boccaccio: Pasolini's Adaptation of the *Decameron*

Pasolini's *schermo eloquio*: The New Vernacular

In 1970, when Pasolini turned to filming the *Decameron*, it appeared to many that he was abandoning his earlier brand of socially engaged cinema. Pasolini had become known for a style of filmmaking that challenged cinematic and narrative conventions. Moreover, his was a cinema that was often hostile towards its own spectators and towards the general conditions of cinematic reception.[1] Pasolini's *Decameron* attracted immediate criticism for its accessibility from among the élite audience of avant-garde films, spectators whose élitist consumerism, for Pasolini, was merely a pretentious copy of the consumerism of the popular audiences. Before the *Decameron*, Pasolini's openly (and, many say, naïvely) subversive attitude produced films such as *Accattone* (1961), *Mamma Roma* (1962), *La ricotta* (1962–3), *Uccellacci e uccellini* (1965–6), all films dealing with the same socio-economic stratum (the Roman sub-proletariat) that had populated his first two novels of the 1950s (*Una vita violenta* and *Ragazzi di vita*), and a class to which Pasolini, during this period, had transferred his optimism concerning social change. Pasolini's critique of the Italian bourgeoisie gained its most aggressive and some suggest most effective expression in his combination film-novel *Teorema* (1968),[2] the last film that he would make that directly depicted the corruption and hypocrisy of the postwar bourgeoisie. Nevertheless, all of his films (indeed, his entire corpus of literary, critical, and filmic works), whether directly or indirectly, in his realistic films or in his allegorical adaptations of ancient myth (*Edipo Re* [1967], *Medea* [1969], *Appunti per un'Orestiade africana* [1968]) or medieval texts (the *Trilogia della vita*), form a passionate indictment of the bourgeoisie and of the impact that its culture and economic structure have had on those who must serve its interests.

It is in this sense that Pasolini insisted that he made films as a 'victim' or, better, as a martyr, refusing to simply live according to the instinct of 'self-preservation' within a society which would thereby co-opt him. He assumes this role for what he presumed to be the benefit of other victims:

Si può allora dire che ogni infrazione del codice – operazione necessaria all'invenzione stilistica – è un'infrazione alla Conservazione: e quindi è l'esibizione di un atto autolesionistico: per cui qualcosa di tragico e di ignoto è scelto al posto di qualcosa di quotidiano e di noto (la vita). Vorrei accentuare la parola ezibizione. La vocazione alle piaghe del martirio che l'autore fa a se stesso nel momento in cui trasgredisce l'istinto di conservarsi, sostituendolo con quello di perdersi – non ha senso se non è resa esplicita al massimo: se non è appunto esibita. In ogni autore, nell'atto di inventare, la libertà si presenta come esibizione della perdita masochistica di qualcosa di certo. Egli nell'atto inventivo, necessariamente scandaloso, si espone – e proprio alla lettera – agli altri: allo scandalo appunto, al ridicolo, alla riprovazione, al senso di diversità, e perché no?, all'ammirazione, sia pure un po' sospetta. C'è insomma il 'piacere' che si ha in ogni attuazione del desiderio di dolore e di morte.[3]

One can then say that every infraction of the code – an operation necessary for stylistic invention – is an infraction of self-preservation, and therefore it is the exhibition of an autolesionistic act: through which something tragic and unknown is chosen in the place of something quotidian and known (life). I would like to stress the word exhibition. The author's dedication of himself to the wounds of martyrdom in the very moment in which he transgresses against the instinct of self-preservation, substituting for it that of self-destruction, does not make sense if it is not made as explicit as possible; if, as I was saying, it isn't exhibited. In every author, in the act of invention, freedom presents itself as a masochistic loss of something certain. In the necessarily scandalous act of inventing he exposes himself, literally, to others; precisely to scandal, to ridicule, to reproach, to the feeling of difference, and – why not? – to admiration, even if it is somewhat questionable. There is, in short, the 'pleasure' that one has in every fulfillment of the desire for pain and death.

It should not be assumed, however, that his films are simply self-indulgent and narcissistic (though they may be, and perhaps often are). Rather, Pasolini's very real marginalization within his society, and his persecution at the hands of those in power,[4] translates into a body of poems, novels, films, plays, and essays that are an open accusation not only against those who are in power, but also against those who would seek it.

Thus, when Pasolini turns to adapt Boccaccio's *Decameron*, with the stated purpose of storytelling 'for the sheer joy of telling and recounting,'[5] many breathed a sigh of relief: Pier Paolo had decided to entertain. Others, more sensitive to the irony of the statement (since Boccaccio makes a similar claim in the preface to his book), understood that Pasolini's message had simply taken on a new guise: indeed, for the most sensitive readers of Pasolini's film[6] the portrayal of a late-medieval Italian society in ideological and economic crisis, as found in the *Decameron*, becomes an allegory of late-capitalist society. For Pasolini understood his own society and culture as undergoing rapid changes, following the Second World War, especially. These included changes in the economic structure of a country coming into line with the demands of the global economy of late capitalism (the so-called Economic Boom); changes in speech caused by the intensified influence of mass media (radio, cinema, and subsequently television) and technology; changes in literary genres and fashion; and also mutations in attitudes towards sexuality and the body, and regulations concerning social comportment.

Pasolini found in Boccaccio's description of his fourteen-century society a representation of a crisis quite analogous to that of the late-modern era as Pasolini understood it. Boccaccio offers an image of a late-medieval Italian society in its movement away from what can loosely be defined as a feudal and aristocratic economic and epistemological organization that had preceded it. Furthermore, he presents an image of the cultural practices (as we shall discuss, storytelling in particular) that he would prescribe to console and restore those suffering from the subjective contradictions brought to the surface during this period of transition.

As we shall see in detail, Boccaccio figures (in an allegorical fashion) the organic crisis of his society by way of the Great Plague of 1348, a plague that wiped out a large percentage of the Italian population and seemed to stand the world upon its head. Boccaccio presents a world in need of reconstruction, and he understands that he has a role to play in this process of reconstruction. As Joy Potter writes, the *Decameron* was composed 'to reaffirm some of the newer customs and ethical codes that better reflected and influenced the prevailing society of the time.'[7] The *Decameron* appears to prescribe specific practices for restoring those individuals (figured, as we will discuss, by women readers of the text or the youths of the *brigata* in the text) who are experiencing the contradictory subjective effects of such a crisis: the most significant restorative practice prescribed by Boccaccio (based on the authority of medical treatises) is the telling of stories, and the reading of literature in the vernacular.[8]

Pasolini accepts Boccaccio's sociological analysis as it is couched in the rhetorical description of the Plague: 'I believe that the plague was simply a residue from the Middle Ages. What was important was that a new world was emerging all around Boccaccio.'[9] Moreover, he shares the medieval writer's drive to engage himself culturally as a sort of cartographer of the social (much as Dante had done before him).[10] Nevertheless, Pasolini cannot share Boccaccio's restorative literary impulse, since the social class that he spoke for did not succeed, until quite late, in asserting its hegemony, as it did, Pasolini notes, in seventeenth-century England and eighteenth-century France.[11] Rather, he will confront a text that exists as a monument to the birth of the Italian bourgeoisie (or to a bourgeois *Weltanschauung*), a class, indeed, whose emblematic literary form is the novel,[12] and a class that has come, six hundred years later, to develop cinema as yet another ideological instrument. Furthermore, he will use this text, ironically, to try to tear cinema away from the bourgeoisie, which has lost its ascendency as a historical force. To tear the *Decameron* from the bourgeoisie, which can no longer reflect itself in the carnivalesque vitality of the text, and to hold out the humorous, desacralizing, innocent, and playful figures found in the text as mirror images of the modern sub-proletariat: this is Pasolini's heretical 'betrayal' of the original. It is a 'betrayal' that nevertheless allows whatever was 'liberating' about the *Decameron*, its celebration of play, humour, and human creativity, to survive and to maintain its force. Moreover, just as Boccaccio needed, as a Florentine writer, to adopt and cultivate the vernacular as the discourse associated with the world of the mercantile class he represents in his text (as opposed to the dominant 'literary' language of Latin), likewise Pasolini must adopt and cultivate the audiovisual language of the cinema associated with the proletarian class he would represent: Boccaccio's 'volgare eloquentia' is matched by Pasolini's *schermo eloquio*.

Thus, both texts may be seen as expressive of societies in transition; both authors interrogate their own responsibilities as intellectuals; and both cultivate the medium best suited to their respective sociocultural projects. As Antonio Gramsci notes, periods of transition and literary-philosophical interrogations of language (the centuries-old 'questione della lingua' in Italy) engender one another:

Ogni volta che affiora, in un modo o nell'altro, la questione della lingua, significa che si sta imponendo una serie di altri problemi: la formazione e l'allargamento della classe dirigente, la necessità di stabilire rapporti più intimi e sicuri tra i gruppi dirigenti e la massa popolare-nazionale, cioè di riorganizzare l'egemonia culturale.

In one way or another, whenever the language question arises, it means that a series of other problems is imposing itself: the formation and broadening of the ruling class, the need to establish more intimate and secure relations between the ruling groups and the national-popular masses – that is, to reorganize cultural hegemony.[13]

Theories of Adaptation

Before setting about to describe Pasolini's adaptation and the significance of such an endeavour in detail, it is necessary to come to grips more clearly with the quite troublesome notion of adaptation from a Pasolinian perspective. The problem of cinematic adaptation will interest us not in terms of how a specific film such as the *Decameron* 'respects' or remains 'faithful' to its 'original.' Rather we will treat adaptation as a privileged operation expressing far vaster issues of social and cultural change and renewal. For indeed, adaptation locates the dialectic of cultural innovation and conservation, expressing both an aggressive and antagonistic attitude towards the 'original' as well as an attitude of 'filial respect' or even devotion. Indeed, Pasolini might characterize the problem in terms of the dialectic of fathers and sons. The very term 'adaptation' carries within itself the sense of 'filial' servitude, of sacrificing one's rights momentarily in the service of the 'father,' the original (adaptation as Oedipal drama, we might say).[14] Hence, following this logic, the traditional discourses of critics concerned with the 'fidelity' of a particular adaptation, with their demands of obsequiousness and respect; and hence the reactions of cinéastes who, in order to assert the autonomy of their medium, insist that they carry no debt towards literary precedents, and indeed that it is literature, now impoverished and ransacking other media in search of replenishment, that has become dependent upon cinema. This problematic has given rise to various studies concerning 'cinematic' elements in such authors as D'Annunzio and Pirandello,[15] in futurist and neorealist literature,[16] and there is a growing number of studies of the general issue of the relationship of cinema and literature.[17]

In one of the most significant early approaches to the problem, Sergei Eisenstein expresses an interesting variation on the first position. He insists that D.W. Griffith found examples of montage in Dickens (along with lap-dissolves, close-ups, pans, and so forth).[18] This essay can be read as an example of how an innovator tries to legitimate and protect his innovations (always perceived as an attack upon conventional and thus authoritative modes of expression) by re-finding them in canonical works. This position is both abject and strategic – or, more precisely, strategically abject: it may be the only way to guide a work that may express a critical or oppositional attitude through the inquisitive structures of official culture and good taste. (Eisenstein's attitude is certainly and understandably defensive, since the Soviet Union under Stalin could not tolerate the type of critical cinema that had earlier produced *Battleship Potemkin* [1925]. And probably the worst fear amongst the Stalinists was that Eisenstein would actually carry out the adaptation of Marx's *Das Kapital* that he had promised in the 1920s).[19]

When Pasolini sets out to film the *Trilogia della vita*, an adaptation of three canonical texts, he partakes, to a certain extent, of this type of strategic abjection. His choice of texts at least guarantees him a certain legitimacy, a cultural sanction (something Pasolini certainly could never take for granted).[20] This project also assured him a certain currency and distribution since it was *terra cognita* for the popular audience. The canonical status of the original would function as a 'screen,' so to speak, to protect the stylistic innovations and, what Pasolini might call, the 'heretical' meanings of the adaptations from censure. As we have seen in a preceding chapter, Pasolini's 'Abiura dalla *Trilogia della vita*,' his rhetorical recantation of these works, functions in a similarly protective manner).

At the same time, Pasolini opens himself up for even greater reaction on the part of official culture than he was long accustomed to for precisely these same reasons. Any form of adaptation of these particular texts would be viewed as aberrant, unfaithful, and as an insult to the originals by those individuals and institutions whose role it is to police the canon.[21] Pasolini's interest in these literary icons is unwelcome insofar as he contaminates the sphere of traditional literature with the shadowy energies of an 'avant-garde' sensibility (nowadays Peter Greenaway's televisual adaptation of Dante's *Inferno* is held suspect for similar reasons).[22] Yet what provokes most discomfort is not the fact that Pasolini's style is critical of established views of literature and of the significance of these texts in particular, but rather that he conforms neither to the traditional image of the artist or scholar nor to the transgressive figure of the avant-garde artist; that is, he refuses to locate himself in the *ghetto* or *lager* of sanctioned oppositional culture since 'l'eccessiva trasgressione del codice finisce per crearne una specie di rimpianto' ('excessive transgression against the code ends up producing a sort of nostalgia for it').[23] Pasolini refuses to position himself on one or the other 'side' of the 'line of fire' that marks the limit of the representable, seeking out, rather, 'il momento della lotta, quello in cui si muore' ('the moment of the battle, the one in which one dies'). This is imperative, he insists, since

solo nell'attimo in cui si combatte (cioè si inventa, applicando la propria libertà di morire in barba alla Conservazione), solo nell'attimo in cui si è a tu per tu con la regola da infrangere ... si può sfiorare la rivelazione della verità, o della totalità, o insomma di qualcosa di concreto.[24]

only in the instant of combat (that is, of invention, enforcing one's freedom to die in the teeth of self-preservation), only in the instant when one is face to face with the rule to be broken ... can one touch the revelation of truth, of the totality, or, in short, of something concrete. (*HE*, 274)

Moreover, I would suggest that, in addition to Pasolini's rationale for his choice to translate the *Decameron* to the screen, the very idea of adaptation contained within itself, in the conflicting of culturally hegemonic genres, the form of broader social disputes. The *Trilogia della vita* reveals adaptation as the site of conflict between a preceding hegemonic and *national* literary culture expressing the interests and values of a certain reactive economic class (the bourgeoisie) and a competing audiovisual culture expressing the hegemonic impulses and alternative, *transnational* world-view of an ascendent economic class (broadly identified as the industrial proletariat or *classe subalterna*). The increasing domination of audiovisual culture in Italy was indicative of a change in the composition of the national-popular audience, as well as yet another sign, for Pasolini, of an even greater extension of the culture of neocapitalism that had been 'spreading,' as it were, since the days of Liberation at the end of the Fascist *ventennio nero*.[25] Pasolini's own decision to devote himself mainly to cinema was made, after a career as poet and novelist, once he concluded that if he were to adopt the role of the committed intellectual as he had found described in the writings of Antonio Gramsci (Pasolini's political and, let's not forget, philological mentor, along with Contini), then he would have to adopt the medium that afforded a maximum of popular circulation.

Thus, in the case of the *Decameron*, Pasolini will use the Italian bourgeoisie's foundational text to attack this class from within. But, after all, this is precisely what Boccaccio did originally in the *Decameron*. He wrote a *summa* of the oral and written culture preceding him, a culture identified with a certain (feudal, aristocratic, clerical) organization of knowledge, in order to overcome it, exhaust it, appropriate it – all this carried out while maintaining the classical image of the serene, aristocratic *brigata* within the structuring *cornice* of the text.[26]

Pasolini's adaptation of the *Decameron* is, then, a 'betrayal' of the original, but not in the usual sense. It suggests that, between fidelity and treason, *tertium datur*: adaptation as 'contamination' of original and imitation, a sort of non-dialectical pastiche of elements of both. For, in fact, Pasolini does not betray the spirit of the stories themselves (the pleasure of the telling and reception of them; their celebration of the carnivalesque, humorous, and corporeal as is found already in Boccaccio). As he remarked: 'Yes, I did not simply want to film the book. I wanted to do an original work in which I would keep the structure of Boccaccio's stories, which pleased me greatly – the plots in all their beauty and vitality, their marvelous vitality.'[27] Indeed, one might suggest, in contrast to the views of Boccaccio scholars[28] that many of the tales in Pasolini's film remain quite 'faithful' to the original (the stories of Masetto, Caterina, and Riccardo, for example). What is indeed betrayed, however, is the organization of the tales, their disposition within the coordinating narrative *cornice* or frame-tale, as we shall see. Moreover, Pasolini populates his film not with examples of energetic proto-bourgeois characters as found in Boccaccio, but rather with images of the modern, Neapolitan proletariat. Thus, Pasolini states, while celebrating the spirit and 'marvelous vitality' of Boccaccio's characters, that 'they were members of the rising bourgeoisie, which was proclaiming new values in opposition to the feudal clerical values. They were full of joy and vitality precisely because they were revolutionaries. The bourgeoisie in Italy today is horrible, debased, decadent. Therefore, I transposed the locale to that of the Neapolitan lumpen proletariat. That is why you did not find the characters of Boccaccio, because I reduced each to a schemata and then filled them out with the reality of Naples, of a sub-proletarian world, and not a bourgeois one.'[29] In this transposition, Boccaccio's Tuscan is supplanted by the Neapolitan dialect. But what is important to understand, as Millicent Marcus as well has pointed out, is that Pasolini's *Decameron* should not be evaluated as an adaptation subordinate to the original, but as a critical reading of Boccaccio's text, a devotedly antagonistic, as it were, cinematic *imitatio* of the original.[30]

Boccaccio's *Decameron*: The *cornice*

Boccaccio's novel is composed of one hundred tales, or *novelle*, recounted in ten days (ten *novelle* per day) by a group of aristocratic Florentine youths (the *brigata*). The *brigata*, composed of seven young women and three young men, has fled the city and taken up residence in the countryside in order to escape the effects of the Great Plague of 1348 that was ravaging Florence. The plague, described in great detail in the Introduction to the text (and a description not based, primarily, on historical observation but on literary precedents),[31] functions as a pretext for the removal of these youths to the countryside. There they will attempt to isolate themselves from the pestilent world, and compose themselves as a 'micro-society' (or *piccol popolo*, small nation, as it is called in Boccaccio [Day 2.10, p. 176]), with a highly regulated set of self-imposed rules concerning comportment, alimentation, spiritual observance, leisure time, and recreation.

The principal form of recreation for the *brigata* is the telling of stories, the daily ritualistic gathering of the youths who will each, in turn, tell a tale of their choice according to the topic of the day. Each day the group elects a new leader (identified as the *principale, reina*, or *re*) whose principal responsibility is to determine the topic of the day (or, we could say, the leader imposes a 'frame' upon the tales), thus delimiting the possibilities of narration. This 'authorial' function is marked by the leader's wearing of the laurel crown.[32] The Queen or King also will take on the secondary job of organizing the events and activities of the day. But what is most important according to the present perspective is to indicate that Boccaccio offers an image of a self-regulating society, which articulates its own rules of comportment, and in which power is identified with, or is derived from, the delimitation of the sayable, the act of imposing a frame upon the field of narrative possibilities: an act of exclusion.

It is necessary, moreover, to see that this act of exclusion is a function of the brigata's seclusion: the brigata's self-exclusion within the encircling walls of an aristocratic garden in the Tuscan countryside[33] and its self-imposed organization of daily life, are the defensive, paranoiac strategies of a community whose integrity depends upon the exclusion of what is outside – elements associated with the plague, tainted with an infection that, as the Introduction illustrates, causes the breakdown of social organization. The image of the paranoiac architecture of the garden in the text – with walls that secure its 'tamed' and 'perfectly arranged' interior from external threats – is matched with a parallel and analogous paranoiac structuring or framing of the tales. Filomena, upon being crowned Queen of the second day, remarks:

Carissime compagne, quantunque Pampinea, per sua cortesia più che per mia virtù, m'abbia di voi tutti fatta reina, non sono io per ciò disposta nella forma del nostro vivere dovere solamente il mio giudicio seguire, ma col mio il vostro insieme ... È il vero che quello che Pampinea non potè fare, per lo esser tardi eletta al reggimento, io il voglio cominciare a fare, cioè a ristrignere dentro ad alcun termine quello di che dobbiamo novellare e davanti mostrarlovi, acciò che ciascuno abbia spazio di poter pensare ad alcuna bella novella sopra la data proposta contare. (Day 1.10, p. 82)

Dearest companions, albeit Paminea, more out of kindness of heart than for any merit of my own, has made me your queen, I do not intend, in shaping the manner in which we should comport ourselves, merely to follow my personal judgment, but rather to blend my judgment with yours ... I do however wish to initiate a practice which Pampinea, because she was elected late as our queen, was unable to introduce: namely to restrict the matter of our storytelling within some fixed limit which will be defined for you in advance, so that each of us will have time to prepare a good story on the subject prescribed.

It is certainly significant that Boccaccio's narration of the activities and storytelling of this group is commonly referred to as the frame-tale (or *cornice*) within which the hundred *novelle* are embedded. That is, just as the King or Queen of the *brigata* enframes the discursive possibilities of the group, and this is shown to be an act of power (in which something will necessarily be excluded), and somehow a function of a defensive community, Boccaccio likewise imposes a frame upon the *novelle*, dictates the logic of their montage within the totality of the text, as is his authorial responsibility. (It is also significant that the verb used to describe the delimitation of the daily topic, *ristrignere* [to tighten, limit, reduce, or restrict] is also the verb used to describe the architecture of the Valley of Women [Day 6, conclusion, p. 413].) And just as the *brigata* organizes its day around the telling of stories, the daily re-creation of the group (storytelling, which thus functions much like a social rite),[34] so does Boccaccio, in the 'Proemio' and in the 'Conclusione dell'autore,' insist that he writes for the benefit of female readers suffering the quite debilitating effects of melancholy. As we shall discuss, Boccaccio offers reading as a form of therapy for melancholic women, that is, as a means of capturing and neutralizing their illicit desires. Reading thus appears as a form of social recuperation of potentially transgressive energies of 'unstable' members of society.

The *Decameron* itself was offered by Boccaccio to take part in those social, recreational operations designed to lend cultural stability to a society prey to external elements that threaten its composure.[35] The 'virtuous' activity of reading combats the potentially destructive *fortuna* allegorized in the text as the plague.[36] The image of the regulative function of storytelling, which we have here ascribed to Boccaccio's text, is simply a reflection of that which is found in the *cornice* of the *Decameron* itself. As Barberi Squarotti writes, the pleasure of the telling of stories 'will indeed be that of the *novelle*, but as an example of a reconstituted world, functioning in an exemplary manner according to its laws ... It is not yet pure enjoyment of art for art's sake, nor is it a call for a hedonistic conception of art as entertainment and escape. The pleasure will thus be that of seeing how an order is reconstituted, how the human world is recomposed, how it is restored in an exemplary manner in this group to offer an example of ethical, civil, social law that guides and tempers even pleasure, joy, games – it distinguished them, chooses them.'[37]

Interesting in this regard is the function of Dioneo within the frame-tale. Indeed, as we shall see, the very possibility of order and stability for this *piccolo popolo* is dependent upon the transgressions of this member of the community. When Filomena asserts that the *principale's* primary responsibility as leader is the legislative delimitation of the topic of the storytelling ('a ristrignere dentro ad alcun termine quello di che dobbiamo novellare' [Day 1, conclusion, p. 82]), Dioneo is the only one to object:

Madonna, come tutti questi altri hanno detto, così dico io sommamente esser piacevole e commendabile l'ordine dato da voi; ma di spezial grazia vi chieggio un dono, il quale voglio che mi sia confermato per infino a tanto che la nostra compagnia durerà, il quale è questo: che io a questa legge non sia costretto di dover dire novella secondo la proposta data, se io non vorrò, ma quale più di dire mi piacerà. E acciò che alcun non creda che io questa grazia voglia sì come uomo che delle novelle non abbia alle mani, infino da ora son contento d'esser sempre l'ultimo che ragioni. (Day 1, conclusion, pp. 82–3)

My lady, like all the others, I too say that the rule you have given us is highly attractive and laudable. But I would ask you to grant me a special privilege, which I wish to have conferred upon me for as long as our company shall last, namely, that whenever I feel so inclined, I may be exempted from this law obliging us to conform to the subject agreed, and to tell whatever story I please. But so that none shall think I desire this favour because I have but a poor supply of stories, I will say at once that I am willing always to be the last person to speak.

Dioneo adopts the structural function of the transgressor, the one un-bound by the laws of the group, precisely to maintain the integrity and stability of their small community. Dioneo reveals that the exercise of the law, indeed the very possibility of legislation or rule-making within a society, is dependent upon the transgression that legitimates it. While the threat of the plague confers legitimacy upon the austere ordering of their daily lives, Dioneo's acts of transgression, carried out with the unani-mous consent of the others, guarantee the *ristringimento* of the *brigata*. As Foucault might say, Dioneo's transgressions of the law are entertained by the company since transgression always leads to the reinstatement of the limit: 'The limit and transgression depend on each other for whatever density of being they possess: a limit could not exist if it were abso-lutely uncrossable and, reciprocally, transgression would be pointless if it merely crossed a limit composed of illusions and shadows.'[38]

Dioneo's disobedience not only allows for but is also necessitated by the fine-tuning, over the ten days, of the rules. His predictable unpredictability is essential for the smooth functioning of the community, and indeed the sometimes obscene nature of his *novelle* (Alibech, to cite only one example) functions to ensure the chastity of the *brigata* insofar as the stories may produce erotic energies in the listener but only in order to exhaust them, neutralize them, and ensure that each member returns that night 'each to his own room' (as they do, Boccaccio makes sure to report, at the end of each day). In this manner, Dioneo's stories maintain the moral fabric of the *brigata*; the improprieties of his bawdy tales maintain the propriety, the virtue, of each member's conduct and thus the integrity of the community. Barberi Squarotti, in defining 'the character of exemplarity of the group's comportment,' notes

the totality of the legislative intervention that, precisely, determines even Dioneo's irregularity, his anarchy, his independence from the common rules, which are made to depend upon the rules themselves; in this manner the general form of the group appears to be defined by an irregularity of norms such that unforeseen surprises are not excluded, nor is the novelty of an act set beyond the previsions of the rule. Anarchy – as in the entire ordering of Western society (and literature), after the crisis of feudal institutions and the initial constitution of bourgeois forms – is admitted as a form and manifestation that is actually calculated by legislation; it is the element outside the rules that the rules themselves foresee and, thus, absorb.[39]

Indeed, in the Conclusion of Day Six, Dioneo insists that the obscenity of his tales is a function of his obedience ('essendo io stato ubbidiente a tutti'): in fact, the group's *onestà* ('honesty' or 'chastity'), he says, has been assured by the very obscenity of his storytelling, and he links this his social function to their collective efforts to escape the plague. Having established the topic of the day (tales concerning the *beffe*, tricks, played by husbands upon their wives), Dioneo turns to the ladies in particular and states:

Donne, io conosco ciò che io ho imposto non meno che facciate voi, e da imporlo non mi potè istòrre quello che voi mi volete mostrare, pensando che il tempo è tale che, guardandosi e gli uomini e le donne d'operar disonestamente, ogni ragionar è conceduto. Or non sapete voi che, per la perversità di questa stagione, gli giudici hanno lasciati i tribunali, le leggi, così le divine come le umane, tacciono, e ampia licenzia per conservar la vita è conceduta a ciascuno? Per che, se alquanto s'allarga la vostra onestà nel favellare, non per dovere con le opere mai alcuna cosa sconcia seguire, ma per dare diletto a voi e ad altrui, non veggo con che argomento da concedere vi possa nello avvenire riprendere alcuno. (Day 6.10, p. 412)

Ladies, I know as well as you do that the theme I have prescribed is a delicate one to handle; but I am not to be deterred by your objections, for I believe that the times we live in permit all subjects to be freely discussed, provided that men and women take care to do no wrong. Are you not aware that because of the chaos of the present age, the judges have deserted the courts, the laws of God and man are in abeyance, and everyone is given ample licence to preserve his life as best he may. This being so, if you go slightly beyond the bounds of decorum in your conversation, with the object, not of behaving improperly but of giving pleasure to yourselves and to others, I do not see how anyone in the future can have cause to condemn you for it.

Interesting to note as well is how, in the conclusion of Day Eight, Emilia likens the condition of the *brigata* to labouring oxen, weary of the yoke. That is, the group is growing tired of following its own rigid set of rules, and like the oxen, she remarks, they would more readily resume their 'labours' were they allowed a day in which their narration was not 'restrained':

E per ciò quello che domane seguendo il vostro dilettevole ragionare sia da dire, non intendo di ristrignervi sotto alcuna spezialità, ma voglio che ciascun secondo che gli piace ragioni, fermamente tenendo che la varietà delle cose che si diranno non meno graziosa ne fia che l'avere pur d'una parlato; e così avendo fatto, chi appresso di me nel reame verrà, sí come più forti, con maggior sicurtà ne potrà nelle usate leggi ristrignere. (Day 8.10, p. 548)

Accordingly, when we resume our storytelling on the morrow, I do not propose to confine you to any particular topic; on the contrary, I desire that each of us should speak on whatever subject he chooses, it being my firm conviction that we shall find it no less rewarding to hear a variety of themes discussed than if we had restricted ourselves to one alone. Moreover, by doing as I have suggested, we shall all recruit our strength, and thus my successor will feel more justified in forcing us to observe our customary rule.

Here, as with Dioneo, release from conventions serves to better secure them. In the world constructed in the *Decameron* – and in keeping with our idea of the *brigata* as an image of a well-ordered society, a *piccol popolo* – a limited period of relaxation of the rule functions as a guarantee of the persistence of the rule (which may be one of the essential functions of carnival and the literary carnivalesque,[40] as well as of the comic,[41] insofar as both may carry out an overturning of established hierarchies, codes of behaviour, or conventions, within the time and space sanctioned them by the authority they ultimately serve).

The Reader of the *Decameron*

Having thus established, in the *cornice*, a linkage between (1) the production and reception of illicit or 'pleasurable' discourse and (2) the maintenance of a given social order and, as Emilia remarks, division of labour (of the *brigata*), we are better able to understand how Boccaccio, in the Epilogue of his work, can defend the many 'liberties' that he takes in his storytelling as ultimately contributing to the health and virtue of his readers – depending upon the character of the reader ('avendo riguardo allo ascoltatore' ['Conclusione,' 674]). That is, depending upon how these stories are 'used,' they will be deemed the products of either a 'venomous' tongue ('mala lingua e velenosa' [676]) or of a 'sweet' tongue ('la più dolce del mondo' [ibid.]). These stories 'scritte per cacciar la malinconia delle femine' ('written to dispel the melancholy of women'), can poison or heal. They can function like the perilous *libro-galeotto* found in Canto 5 of Dante's *Inferno* (and referred to in the text's subtitle, *Prencipe Galeotto*), simply provoking illicit desires and thus forms of destructive behaviour in its readers (thus Dante's condemnation of Francesca's adultery as a product of this type of literature), or these stories can be collected and organized within a frame-tale that presents the moral and social benefits of this type of storytelling for its model community. Further, the virtue and cohesion of this community is seen to actually gain from – and indeed depend upon – such transgressions carried out in discourse.

The function that the stories have for the youths of the *brigata* is the same function that the *Decameron* will have for its readers. To adopt Teresa de Lauretis's terminology, Boccaccio's vernacular text will become a technology of gender.[42] The plague figures this society in crisis, in a period of transition when the principles around which people's moral and spiritual life was to be organized were put into doubt, and previous ethics of comportment were no longer compelling. It is, as Petronio describes it, a society that had lost its *telos* (in spite of Dante's attempts to relocate it in the *Divina Commedia*).[43] It is no accident that Boccaccio locates women as those members of society who, because of their marginalization (or, as he writes, because they cannot travel freely, hunt, play sports, gamble, fish, or involve themselves in business, as men do [Proemio, p. 26]), and because of their exclusion, have no relief from 'melancholy thoughts.' The term 'melancholy' here becomes a sort of catch-all term that functions to medicalize or psychologize their feelings of dissatisfaction as the excluded or enclosed [*ristrette*] members of their society). In order to 'console' them, to 'divert' their minds from their suffering (and to keep their minds from avenues of escape, presumably), Boccaccio would offer them *nuovi ragionamenti* that would dislodge the *focoso disio*.

Esse dentro a' dilicati petti, temendo e vergognando, tengono l'amorose fiamme nascose, le quali quanto più di forza abbian che le palesi coloro il sanno che l'hanno provato e provano; e oltre a ciò, *ristrette* da' voleri, da' piaceri, da' comandamenti de' padri, delle madri, de' fratelli e de' mariti, il più del tempo nel piccolo circuito delle loro camere *racchiuse* dimorano, e quasi oziose sedendosi, volendo e non volendo in una medesima ora, seco rivolgono diversi pensieri, li quali non è possibile che sempre sieno allegri. E se per quegli alcuna *malinconia*, mossa da *focoso disio*, sopravviene nelle lor menti, in quelle conviene che con grave noia si dimori, se da *nuovi ragionamenti* non è rimossa: senza che elle sono molto men forti che gli uomini a sostenere. (Proemio, 26; emphases mine)

For the ladies, out of fear or shame, conceal the flames of passion within their fragile breasts, and a hidden love is far more potent than one which is worn on the sleeve, as everyone knows who has had experience of these matters. Moreover they are forced to follow the whims, fancies and dictates of their fathers, mothers, brothers and husbands, so that they spend most of their time cooped up within the narrow confines of their rooms, where they sit in apparent idleness, wishing one thing and at the same time wishing its opposite, and reflecting on various matters, which cannot possibly always be pleasant to contemplate. And if, in the course of their meditations, their minds should be invaded by melancholy arising out of the flames of longing, it will inevitably take root there and make them suffer greatly, unless it be dislodged by new interests. Besides which, their powers of endurance are considerably weaker than those that men possess.

The *nuovi ragionamenti* that would console these readers are, obviously, the tales of the *Decameron*:

Nelle quali novelle, piacevoli e aspri casi d'amore e altri fortunosi avvenimenti si vedranno, così ne' moderni tempi avvenuti come negli antichi; delle quali le già dette donne, che quelle leggeranno, parimente diletto delle sollazzevoli cose in quelle mostrate e utile consiglio potranno pigliare, in quanto potranno cognoscere quello che sia da fuggire e che sia similmente da seguitare; le quali cose senza passamento di noia non credo che possano intervenire. Il che se avviene, che voglia Iddio che così sia, ad Amore ne rendano grazie, il quale, liberandomi da' suoi legami, m'ha conceduto il potere a' loro piaceri. (Proemio, 27; emphasis mine)

In these tales will be found a variety of love adventures, bitter as well as pleasing, and other exciting incidents, which took place in both ancient and modern times. In reading them, the aforesaid ladies will be able to derive, not only pleasure from the entertaining matters therein set forth, but also some useful advice. For they will learn to recognize what should be avoided and likewise what should be pursued, and these things can only lead, in my opinion, to the removal of their affliction. If this should happen (and may God grant that it should), let them give thanks to love, which, in freeing me from its bonds, has granted me the power of making provision for their pleasures.

Boccaccio's text will be *utile*, I would suggest, insofar as it will actually provoke the excessive desires of the readers in order to channel and neutralize them; in order, in the end, to restrain (*ristrignere*) these readers and relocate them within the gendered spaces and activities that form the basis of social order. (And we see that the same verb, *ristrignere*, is used to describe the delimitation of the daily topic, the characteristics of Dioneo's *spezial grazia* – his special liberty from the rules – the architectural symmetry of the Valley of Women, and the conditions of the women readers of the text: the text thus makes explicit a certain connection between the establishment of order and the exclusion or restriction of elements of potential destabilization.) Furthermore, these tales will be useful in their configuration or disposition within a frame, a *cornice*, that organizes them into a kind of itinerary, leading from the excesses of the sinful Ciappeletto to the virtue of Griselda, and from the formlessness and licence of the individual tales to their enframing within a coherent structure (that is, a structure born, as mentioned, from the drive to restrict the free-play of narrative possibilities).

Thus, Boccaccio offers an image of literature in the vernacular born of a regulatory impulse, as a technology of gender or a ritual of subjectivation. As we have seen, the *brigata* is his allegory of a self-managing society, composed of subjects who keep themselves under constant self-surveillance. It is an image of the late-medieval city, as Lewis Mumford describes it: a city in which 'external control had now become internal control, involving self-regulation and self-discipline.'[44] The fact that Pampinea proposes, upon the prompting of Dioneo, that their lives be organized around the telling of stories implies a new interest in the possible regulating or therapeutic functions of narratives, of reading in the vernacular. As Costa-Lima writes, the private reading of moralizing fiction in the late Middle Ages works as a means to 'control the imaginary,' to stabilize subjectivity in a society undergoing radical sociocultural transformations at the end of the age of feudalism.[45] Boccaccio's *Decameron* is a text born of this type of 'civilizing' project.

Pasolini's *Decameron*

Now, in turning to an account of Pasolini's *Decameron*, it will occur to some readers that this long description of Boccaccio's framing-tale is not particularly essential, given the fact that Pasolini rejects this type of narrative framing, and its location of the reader, in his adaptation of the text. However, Pasolini does replace the *cornice* of the novel with his own sort of frame-tale – and when it comes to adaptations of literary texts, the director's exclusions are potentially as significant as his inclusions. Indeed, what will be the focus of our attention, once we have carried out a brief account of the structure of Pasolini's *Decameron*, is the reason behind Pasolini's rejection of Boccaccio's structuring *cornice*, and thus a possible explanation of the manner in which Pasolini will try to frame the narratives in his own film, and the significance of that process.

By far the most detailed account of the structure and intertextuality of Pasolini's film (including its allusions to the late-medieval and Renaissance figural traditions) has been furnished by Ben Lawton. He has segmented the film in such a manner as to show how it is composed of ten episodes derived from Boccaccio's text, along with ten episodes provided by Pasolini. Although I find Lawton's view of the film's structure generally valid, I would note that the tales of Pasolini's invention do not carry the same weight as Boccaccio's in the film; they function rather as framing narratives in which Boccaccio's *novelle* will be embedded.

Pasolini's film is divided into two parts. Part 1 contains the following episodes from the original: the *novelle* of Andreuccio (Day 2.5); the Abbess (Day 9.2); Masetto of Lamporecchio (Day 3.1); Peronella (Day 7.2); and Ciappelletto (Day 1.1). Part 2 contains the tales of Giotto and Forese (Day 6.5); Ricciardo and Caterina (Day 5.4); Lisabetta and the pot of basil (Day 4.5); Compare Pietro, Gemmata, and Don Gianni (Day 9.10); and Meuccio and Tingoccio (Day 7.10). Pasolini also filmed the *novella* of Alibech (Day 3.10), but did not include it in the final version.[46]

Lawton provides a numerological reading of Pasolini's film, revealing how both texts are structured around the number ten:

[Pasolini's] film contains ten episodes taken from Boccaccio's text and ten original episodes. Divided into two parts, the film includes five of Boccaccio's *novelle* in each part. Furthermore, we find three Pasolini episodes in Part I and seven Pasolini episodes in Part II, respectively, the number of days of storytelling into which the two parts of Boccaccio's *Decameron* are divided by the author's appearance, and also the number of male and female narrators in the original. The total number of Pasolini episodes, like the total of those borrowed from Boccaccio, equals the number of days of storytelling in the text.[47]

This numerological coherence, though, is partially the product of Lawton's own (albeit quite interesting) segmentation of the work.[48] One could object, however, that Pasolini's episodes consist in the interspersing over the two parts of the film of what are actually only two tales (of

Ciappelletto and of Giotto's disciple) that function as framing tales, which Lawton does note, for Boccaccio's stories. Furthermore, in his charting of the film's structure, Lawton distinguishes a seventh Pasolinian episode ('a view of revelry at the peasant wedding') from the ninth episode of Boccaccio (Day 9.10), whereas in the film the wedding retains an essential narrative function within the Boccaccian episode – although I would grant Lawton that the wedding is not an element found in the original text. Furthermore, I would suggest that there are also significant overlappings of the framing stories and the framed: Ciappelletto in part 1 is an element of both frame and framed, as is Giotto's disciple in part 2.

Perhaps the clear differentiation of the episodes as found in Lawton's reading is the product of an analysis that, in its search for textual unity and numerological coherence found in the original, tends to impose that unity upon the adaptation. Another reading might suggest that Pasolini is playing upon the very opposition of container and contained (this is especially evident when we are given an image of Ciappelletto listening to a public reading of the *Decameron*). Instead of imposing a *cornice* upon the episodes from without, Pasolini uses elements found within the Boccaccian episodes to frame them (with certain changes: Giotto becomes Giotto's pupil); Ciappelletto, the eversive figure par excellence, frames himself, as it were (that is, he both 'frames' himself as a saint in the episode of Day 1.1, and his image is used by Pasolini throughout part 1 as a frame for the episodes of this section of the film). As indicated by the figure of eversion, an inside becomes an outside in Moebius-strip fashion. The opposition of interior and exterior, framed and enframing, is deconstructed – and so, in a sense, might be Lawton's reading, based as it is on the possibility of establishing such an opposition. But we have also seen that Boccaccio's *cornice* itself reveals social and textual coherence to be founded upon this very opposition.

Pasolini does not simply abandon the frame. He replaces the Boccaccian *cornice*, and the image of framing as an operation of exclusion and opposition (the plagued outside as opposed to the inside secured by and for the *brigata*), with the figures of Ciappelletto (the Forger) and Giotto's disciple (the Artist, played, ironically indeed, by Pasolini himself). An explanation of this substitution is in order since the coherence and unity of Boccaccio's *Decameron* was a product of the *cornice* – textual unity thus being revealed, as discussed earlier, as a product of certain mechanisms of exclusion and a logic of opposition. Pasolini, who is producing his film in a social order itself founded upon exclusion and opposition, and himself a victim of social mechanisms of exclusion and marginalization, cannot but reject these principles of textual and also social structuration. (And we shall see how these issues concerning narrative framing relate to Pasolini's substitution of the Neapolitan dialect for Boccaccio's Tuscan.)

Re-framing Boccaccio: The Forger and the Artist

The story of Ser Cepparello – the first story of the first day of the *Decameron*, and as narrated in the frame-tale of part 1 of Pasolini's film – identifies with great economy the central preoccupations of Boccaccio's entire text: problems of language, subjectivity, fiction, and textual and social coherence. These semiotic concerns rebound onto analogous issues of money, usury, and the mercantilist economy. The very issue of Cepparello's, or Ciappelletto's, proper name signals a preoccupation with the referential or communicative capacities of language, as well as the ontological status of the objects or referents presumed to motivate that language: Cepparello

piccolo di persona era e molto assetatuzzo, non sappiendo li Franceschi che si volesse dir Cepparello, credendo che 'cappello' cioè 'ghirlanda,' secondo il loro volgare a dir venisse, per ciò che piccola era, come dicemmo, non Ciappello ma Ciappelletto il chiamavano; e per Ciappelletto era conosciuto per tutto, là dove pochi per Ser Cepparello il conoscieno.' (Day 1.1, p. 47)

was short in stature and used to dress very neatly, and the French, who did not know the meaning of the word Cepparello, thinking that it signified *chapel*, which in their language means 'garland,' and because as we have said he was a little man, used to call him, not Ciappello, but Ciappelletto: and everywhere in that part of the world, where few people knew him as Ser Cepparello, he was known as Ciappelletto.

Ciappelletto's uncertain or 'infirm' character matches the uncertainty of his own name. Indeed, the story is founded upon – albeit an ironic foundation – the cognitive uncertainty resulting from Ciappelletto's very existence as an uncertain sign. 'Infirm' is meant in Aristotle's sense: he does not remain similar to what he was. This 'vice,' as it is called in the *Nichomachean Ethics*, makes him the perfect candidate to carry out the project, given him by Musciatto Franzesi, of recuperating loans – with interest, obviously. As Gilles Deleuze might say, he possesses the power of the false.[49]

Musciatto himself is one who has a similar infirmity. He has risen from the merchant class and attained noble status, having acquired an enormous fortune as a merchant in France ('Ragionasi adunque che, essendo Musciatto Franzesi di richissimo e gran mercatante in Francia cavalier divenuto' [46]). He exists between classes but, more important, he puts into doubt in the reader's mind the very basis of class divisions, the sources of nobility, and could reveal as illegitimate existing social stratifications.

Moreover, the uncertain identities, so to speak, of Ciappelletto and Franzesi appear to be the prerequisites of the business they conduct and of the mercantile economy of which they are the cutting edge: they are requirements of the 'ragion di mercatura.'[50] The transactions of all the participants in this story, except the priest-confessor, involve the lending or changing of money, the charging of interest: usury, a practice where money, obviously, is not identical to itself, literal, denotative; for if this were so then loans would supply no gains for lenders.[51] This practice, furthermore, as Marx describes it in *Capital*, presupposes the abstraction of money from products or use-values. That is, usury entails a distancing of currency from the values it once was supposed to reflect.[52] To repeat, money does not reflect the value, the essence, of any object or use-value that would stabilize it (it treats the objects of exchange as commodities). Once this abstraction has occurred, that which determines the value of currency (exchange value) becomes seemingly mysterious, open to speculation (or, better, the value of currency is determined by 'speculation'). Yet the ultimately indeterminate nature of money is obviously what enables usury, and the regulation of rates of exchange and interest becomes an issue involving a variety of institutions (in the Middle Ages even the Church became involved in such affairs).[53]

Boccaccio's first *novella*, which is concerned primarily with problems of language (lying, truth, fiction), figured by way of the forged confession of the moribund Ciappelletto and thus revealing the power of the false, is prefaced with this analogous problem of money and usury.[54] Such matters also affect questions of law: for we are informed that Ciappelletto is also, besides a great blasphemer, liar, murderer, and sodomite, a false witness:

Testimonianze false con sommo diletto diceva, richiesto e non richiesto; e dandosi a quei tempi in Francia a' saramenti grandissima fede, non curandosi fargli falsi, tante quistioni malvagiamente vincea, a quante a giurare di dire il vero sopra la sua fede era chiamato. (p. 47)

He would take great delight in giving false testimony, whether asked for it or not. In those days great reliance was placed in France upon sworn declarations, and since he had no scruples about swearing falsely, he used to win, by these nefarious means, every case in which he was required to swear upon his faith to tell the truth.

Pasolini's film opens with a sequence (whose symmetry and placement suggest that it forms a sort of Proemio of the film, an allegorical 'idea dell'opera') in which a figure who will later be identified as Ciappelletto is seen violently and fatally beating one of his victims whom he has confined in a sack at his feet. Once the victim shows no sign of life, Ciappelletto puts the sack over his shoulder, walks to the edge of a cliff and throws the body over with a look of great satisfaction. Pasolini then cuts directly to the story of Andreuccio of Perugia. Upon completion of this story, we are again offered an image of Ciappelletto listening to a Neapolitan storyteller reading the *Decameron* to an audience of Neapolitans. Ciappelletto here picks the pockets of the listeners, rapt in concentration (in a sort of allegory of spectatorship in consumer society that recalls Bresson's *Pickpocket*), and offers the money to a young boy in exchange for sexual favours. Then follow the stories of Masetto in the Convent (Day 3.1) and Peronella (Day 7.2). We are subsequently given the *novella* of Ciappelletto, which basically follows the structure of Boccaccio's original: from the hiring of Ciappelletto by Musciatto to his faked confession and the subsequent attribution of sainthood based upon the forged testimony. Indeed, as in the original tale, the *fratelli usurai* (the money-lending brothers) are seen to gain in reputation through their association with him.

What we see in the figure of Ciappelletto is how his apparently transgressive, hypocritical, blasphemous lies concerning his moral fibre function, in the end, to prop up the institutional hegemony of the Church he appears to revile (although in so doing, Ciappelletto reveals this institution to be founded upon a lie). For, upon Ciappelletto's falsified confession (lending him a forged virtue), he is sainted (and the *novella* does, as is often noted, parody hagiography), and all of Burgundy appears to throw itself into a celebration of everything Christian. Not only that, but his confession ensures the continuation of business-as-usual at the house of the money-lending brothers. In the end, a mercantilist economy is seen to depend upon the very instability of currency and subjectivity, and the Church profits from the abstraction of the sign from the referent. As with Dioneo's transgressions in the *cornice*, Ciappelletto's disobedience ultimately serves the rule.

The usual gloss on Boccaccio's Ciappelletto indicates the author's presumed moral condemnation of Ciappelletto for his misuse of language, for a misappropriation of rhetorical persuasion (and thus a possible echo of Dante's condemnation of Ulysses in the *Inferno* for similar rhetorical sins). Or the tale is read in terms of the comic structure of the *Decameron*: the text moves from vice to virtue, from Ciappelletto (Day 1.1) to Griselda (Day 10.10), from the dark wood of the Plague and Ciappelletto's lies to the serenity of the Tuscan Hills and the happy ending of virtuous devotion (the analogy with the *Divina Commedia* is inevitable). The explanation is thus that Boccaccio condemns Ciappelletto as a blasphemer, usurer, forger, and liar. For Ciappelletto, meaning is a consequence of the demands of the moment and the expectations of the listeners: a consequence of the context, and not of reference to an extra-discursive *res*. Ciappelletto is a rhetorical pragmatist or, as Pasolini might suggest, a character who lives the filmmaker's cinematic philosophy:

Ho da tempo l'ambizione di scrivere una 'Filosofia' del cinema, consistente nel rovesciamento del nominalismo: non 'nomina sunt res' ma 'res sunt nomina.' Se c'è una decifrazione della realtà ci deve essere a fortiori una cifrazione; se c'è un decifratore, un cifratore.[55]

For some time now I have wanted to write a 'Philosophy' of cinema, consisting in the overturning of nominalism: not 'nomina sunt res' but 'res sunt nomina.' If reality is to be decoded, there must of necessity be an encoder; if there is a decoder there must be an encoder. (*HE*, 255-6)

But Pasolini's cinematic 'reading' of Boccaccio does not take the form of a moral condemnation of Ciappelletto (and perhaps even Boccaccio's text isn't as moralistic as it would appear). In the film, just as in the novel, Ciappelletto's lying and forgeries are a function of greed (his own and that of his employer). However, he is also sainted – and part 1 ends with an image of the people's devotion to this new saint, and the profit that the Church gains from his example. There is, certainly, a condemnation of Ciappelletto in Pasolini (he refers to him as 'the delinquent or "social bandit"').[56] But it does not derive from the character's lying (nor, as Lawton remarks, from the suggestion that 'he has not understood anything' – the accusation Lawton attributes to Ciappelletto's first victim;[57] whereas it seems to me that Ciappelletto has understood everything, and all too well). Rather, Pasolini's condemnation of this character derives from the use to which language is put, to the instrumentalization of the powers of the false for the benefit of those *potenti* who dominate and exploit the people (the merchants and the Church are seen to collude in this instrumentalization). This lesson also figures Pasolini's utter rejection of the function of Dioneo, as we have described it.

For Pasolini, Ciappelletto reveals how the meaning of signs or identities is a product of the frame of reference that organizes the context in which these signs or identities are embedded. Ciappelletto is the equivocal signifier par excellence, the 'mercenary sign' who will be whatever his instinct for self-preservation dictates: for Musciatto he is a usurer, for the Church he is a saint. He will change, chameleon-like, with any change of setting, and will support himself on the returns that he receives from his exercise of the power of the false. Ciappelletto is a figure of pastiche (his very 'improper' name is the product of the collaged French words for *cappello* and *ghirlanda*);[58] he is a collage or, in more cinematic terms, a 'montage' of all these various identities (and, since he claims no 'property,' he does not experience the diversity of the roles he adopts or the discourses he inhabits as a contradiction). And for Pasolini, the 'regola di mercatura' is pastiche – but pastiche is also the only possibility of contesting that rule.

Pasolini's character resembles Deleuze's notion (found in his reading of Pasolini's concept of the free-indirect style of the 'cinema of poetry') of the Forger, one who 'provokes undecideable alternatives and inexplicable differences between the true and the false.'[59] The Forger reveals as false traditional notions of narrative whose linearity and unity depend upon the oppositional logic of inside and outside, subjective and objective; narrative that depends upon a subject supposed to know (an omniscient narrator, perhaps), but also upon causality, coherence of character, and 'proper names' that all form the basis of the 'form of the true' (and thus Pasolini's critique, as found in *Uccellacci e uccellini*, of neorealist cinema). As Deleuze writes: 'Contrary to the form of the true which is unifying and tends to the identification of a character (his discovery or simple coherence), the power of the false cannot be separated from an irreducible multiplicity. "I is an other" ["Je est un autre"] has replaced Ego = Ego.'[60]

But, most important, the Forger reveals how, as Nietzsche wrote, even 'the truthful man ends up realizing that he has never stopped lying,'[61] and thus the narrative of history (or the history of narrative) appears as the product of a 'chain of forgers': 'if the forger reveals something, it is the existence behind him of another forger.'[62] For Deleuze, it was the *Nouvelle Vague*, the film movement associated with Godard, Truffaut, and Resnais, among others, that showed how 'description stops presupposing a reality and narration stops referring to a form of the true.' These filmmakers 'broke with the form of the true to replace it by the powers of life, cinematographic powers considered to be more profound.'[63] Deleuze thus identifies the power of the false with the idea of montage. For Pasolini, it was not Nietzsche but Boccaccio's *Decameron*, with its perhaps emblematic character Ciappelletto, that showed him these 'powers of the false,' and the act of narration, of framing, as a will to power.

But Pasolini cannot so easily identify this power with 'the powers of life,' as Deleuze writes (though there would be no disagreement between them on this point). That is, the powers of the false may be exercised for both constructive, life-affirming purposes, or for destructive, life-negating purposes (Nietzsche's 'active' or 'passive' nihilism). Pasolini's Ciappelletto is not an abomination on account of his lying, but rather for his 'unethical' lying, as it were, for the way he lends himself to the forces of domination, and for the way the powers of the false are utilized to construct and maintain the hegemony of dominant social institutions. Ciappelletto's actions force his spectators to consider an ethics of the 'false.' And insofar as Pasolini's own role as filmmaker is revealed as the role of the Forger as well (which will become clearer in our discussion of the character of Giotto's disciple), we are led to ponder an ethics of montage, the essence of cinema itself. As Deleuze writes:

But what we are saying about the character is also valid in the second place, and in particular, for the filmmaker himself ... [Filmmakers] must become others, with their characters, at the same time as their characters must become others themselves ... The Ego=Ego form of identity (or its degenerate form, them=them) ceases to be valid for the characters and for the filmmaker, in the real as well as in the fiction. What allows itself to be glimpsed instead, by profound degrees, is Rimbaud's 'I is an other' ... 'I is an other' is the formation of a story which simulates, of a simulation of a story or of a story of simulation which deposes the form of the truthful. (152–3)

The episodes in part 1 of Pasolini's film are framed within Ciappelletto's narrative (from assassin to saint), a narrative that we have shown as an allegory of the powers of the frame itself, and of how identities or signs draw their significance from their arrangement (montage) within a frame of reference or discourse that establishes the logic of their linkages (thus Pasolini's famous, and heretical, identification of the language of cinema with the language of reality).[64] But he also ironically and simultaneously shows the inability to enframe once and for all and the act of enframing as a function of a will to mastery, at once enabled by the powers of the false, but also disabled by these same powers insofar as any frame is revealed as a construct (a 'forgery') and thus open to human intervention and transformation. Pasolini's principal aggression towards Boccaccio, his critique, is expressed in his rejection of the *cornice* and of the will to power that it contains.[65] Pasolini substitutes it with the discourse of the Forger.

But Ciappelletto's 'passive nihilism' is only one side of the issue, an image of the negating and destructive capacities of the powers of the false. Part 2 of the film will be framed within the narrative of another figure of the Forger: the Artist/Filmmaker. The Boccaccian episodes of the last part of the film are embedded within the story of Giotto's 'best disciple' (a character of Pasolini's invention, though his story is roughly based upon the tale of Giotto and Forese da Rabatta [Day 6.5]). This character is played by Pasolini himself (in the *Canterbury Tales* Pasolini will play the character of Chaucer, and for similar self-reflexive reasons). Pasolini draws the following analogy between himself and this character: 'I played the part of a North Italian [painter], from the historical Italy, who comes down to Naples in order to paint frescoes ... on the Walls of the Church of Santa Chiara. And I myself am – in actual fact – a writer from the North of Italy, from the historical part of Italy, who goes to Naples to make a realistic film. There is thus an analogy between the character and the author-writer. Thus we have a work within a work. That is to say, there is a critical detachment that was not part of my original intentions.'[66] We must therefore view Giotto's disciple's activities as an allegory of Pasolini's filmmaking, and as a potential key to the explanation of his intentions for his film.

The artist in the film, like Ciappelletto, presents a critique of framing, in fact a subversion of the frame. He thus serves as a very ironic framing device indeed. Furthermore, like the liar, the artist's activities depend upon the manipulation of illusion and persuasion of the spectator: both partake of the powers of the false. But the artist in Pasolini's film does not exercise this power according to the instinct for self-preservation that, as Pasolini's writes, helps us to be 'lovingly attached' to the life that has been afforded us. In the film he does not occupy a detached position that would afford him mastery over the elements he depicts, and thus he will not present the spectator with the illusion of such mastery (whereas Boccaccio's *cornice* is precisely the mastery of its contents for the benefit of the female readers who thus gain 'self-control').

The fresco that this artist is painting takes the form of a triptych, each panel contained (*ristretto*) within three different frames. Ben Lawton describes the significance of the architectonics of the triptych: 'It is an incomplete triptych, composed of a gothic, heaven directed arch in the first panel, an anthropological rectangle whose top line is perfectly horizontal in the second panel, and a third panel which is completely blank. Pasolini, the artistic descendant of Boccaccio and Giotto, has taken a step forward through an imaginary retrieval of the past.'[67] Lawton notes how the architecture of these frames expresses the world-view of the Middle Ages, and the Renaissance (and, I would add, the Enlightenment), but, as far as the last unframed panel is concerned, he offers no reading except that Pasolini 'has no simple answers for the future; thus the blank third panel.'[68] Unfortunately, Lawton does not indicate what types of questions have, as he suggests, been left unanswered. Furthermore, it could be argued that Pasolini's decision not to 'answer,' not to finish the triptych, the silence of the third panel, is precisely the form of an 'answer.'

I am in complete agreement with Lawton's interpretation of the first two panels: the gothic frame whose verticality reflects the medieval cosmology, the shape of the Christian episteme; the rectangle mirrors the horizontal 'framing' mentality of the Age of Reason, the age announced by Boccaccio's novel (and both Lawton and Marcus draw an analogy between the rectangular panel and the cinematic frame).[69] But his explanation of the third panel leaves one a bit unsatisfied. For, if the forms of the first two panels trace the medieval and modern epistemes, how does the frameless third panel indicate a break with the modern? And how does its ambiguous framing, the artist's unwillingness or inability to impose a definite frame that would establish the coordinates of perspective, suggest a 'post-modern' era in which representation itself has fallen into crisis (without God or Reason or even History as guarantees of narration or representation, the assurance of the 'form of the true')? Moreover, following the analogy that Pasolini draws between himself and the artist, how does this offer an 'answer' to the questions that the blank panel raises?

At the very end of the film, Pasolini/Giotto's pupil stands before the triptych with its blank third panel, while his assistants toast his success, and he remarks:

Ma ... Io mi domando ... perché realizzare un'opera, quando è così bello sognarla soltanto?

But ... I wonder ... why complete a work when it is so beautiful simply to dream it?[70]

The triptych as allegory of paradigmatic shifts from the Middle Ages to modernity reveals the movement from closed to open systems, from closed narrative to the very impossibility of narrative closure. That is, the panel traces out a transition from the theocentric narrative system of Dante to the enframed narrative of Boccaccio, to the unreliable structuring of Pasolini's film itself. We move from the image of the author as prophet (Dante) to the author as rational, creative, and *utile* (Boccaccio) to the author as *'pasticheur'* (Pasolini): 'I'd like to say that you can see my *pasticheur* nature in the cinema, as in the other forms (*pasticheur* by passion, that is, not by calculation').[71] The transition from closed to open system also involves an activation of the reader. To adopt Barthes's terminology, there is a movement from the passive reader of the 'readerly' texts to the activated reader of the 'writerly' text, what Umberto Eco calls the polyvalent 'opera aperta.'[72]

Pasolini's *riscrittura* of Boccaccio's text, with its rejection of the *cornice* and the latter's substitution with the discourse of the Forger/Artist, forms a critique of the 'readerly' qualities of the model. Pasolini's precarious frame-tales function much like the untrustworthy narrators found in the films and novels (or 'anti-novels') of his (post-modern) contemporaries: the films of Antonioni, Resnais, Godard; the novels of Calvino, Gadda, Malerba, Robbe-Grillet, and Duras, to name only a few.[73] The novelists in particular call into question the omniscience of the narrator as emblem of the author as creative centre and origin of classical realist narratives in order to 'un-conceal' the polyphony or intertextuality of writing, and in order to reanimate the reader, to reveal reading as the active 'performance' of the text.[74] Reading appears not as the passive reception of the author's intended meanings but rather as a process productive of meaning. Hence, texts such as Calvino's *Se una notte d'inverno un viaggiatore*, which appears as an open challenge to its readers, and forms the practical expression of the theories of Barthes, which call for the 'death of the author,' since

the writer can only imitate a gesture that is always anterior, never original. His only power is to mix writings, to counter the ones with the others, in such a way as never to rest on any of them ... Once the Author is removed, the claim to decipher a text becomes quite futile. To give an Author is to impose a limit on the text, to furnish it with a final signified, to close the writing ... In the multiplicity of writing, everything is to be *disentangled*, nothing deciphered; the structure can be followed, 'run' (like the thread of a stocking) at every point and at every level, but there is nothing beneath; the space of writing is to be ranged over, not pierced; writing ceaselessly posits meanings ceaselessly to evaporate it, carrying out a systematic exemption of meaning. In precisely this way literature (it would be better from now on to say writing), by refusing to assign a 'secret,' an ultimate meaning, to the text (and to the world as text), liberates what may be called an anti-theological activity, an activity that is truly revolutionary since to refuse to fix meaning is, in the end, to refuse God and his hypostases – reason, science, law.[75]

Pasolini's *riscrittura* of the *Decameron* performs such a 'mixture of writings.' We find elements from Boccaccio, obviously, but also from the medieval and Renaissance figural traditions (Giotto, Bruegel), as well as modern elements introduced by Pasolini's 'contamination' of the style of the original. It is a text that foregrounds rather than conceals this intertextuality, and thus presents itself with all those qualities characteristic of the post-modern aesthetic of the open-ended and indeterminate.[76] Its style is characterized by pastiche, drawing attention to the play of its assemblage (its 'montage'), all in order to activate the spectator's capacity to 'write,' imagine, and 'dream' its conclusion, as the artist's remark in the film suggests.

Indeed, Pasolini's rejection of Boccaccio's *cornice* is primarily a rejection of how that text addresses the reader, or how it locates its reader. For, as we discussed earlier, the reading of the *Decameron* formed part of a therepeutic régime designed to 'console' melancholic women. It was a text that invited its readers to locate themselves in their 'proper places,' to occupy the perspective that the text offers them, and to identify thus with the hegemonic way of seeing.

As an Althusserian reading would suggest, this is the ideological operation of the *Decameron*. Its readers are being invited to identify with the manner in which they are addressed or 'interpellated,'[77] to accept freely their 'subjection' to the address, and to construct themselves as subjects of the address. The text's intelligibility, the 'obviousness' of its meanings, carries the price of this, the reader's subjection. Pasolini's film forms a critique of this type of literature and the brand of narrative cinema (the 'cinema of prose') to which it gave rise. Pasolini works within a style designed to subvert such ideological operations, operations that Heath among others describes in terms of narrative 'suture.'[78]

Pasolini develops the 'free indirect-style' of the 'cinema of poetry' in order to abdicate the author function.[79] The free-indirect style, he writes, is the style of the *pasticheur* who 'plays' with languages (with the 'found objects' of language), who mixes styles. Pasolini creates collages of linguistic and figural fragments. His is an aesthetic of 'contamination,' which Pasolini likens to the collage aesthetic of the twentieth-century avant-gardists, thus linking his own interrogation of codes of representation with that carried out by the Cubists, Surrealists, and 'Pop' artists.[80] The type of collage aesthetics associated with these movements experimented in the multiplication of perspective, and deconstructed codes and conventions of representation, or frames of reference, and in so doing attempted to subvert the mechanisms of ideological interpellation. They carried this out, in part, by attempting to unleash the repressed contents of the unconscious. Surrealist filmmakers in particular showed Pasolini that the language of cinema resembles dreamwork, or, to parody Lacan, that the unconscious is structured like a film.[81]

In fact, for Pasolini, the free-indirect style frees

le possibilità espressive compresse dalla tradizionale convenzione narrativa, in una specie di ritorno alle origini: fino a ritrovare nei mezzi tecnici del cinema l'originaria qualità onirica, barbarica, irregolare, aggressiva, visionaria.[82]

the expressive possibilities compressed by the traditional narrative convention through a sort of return to the origins until the original oneiric, barbaric, irregular, aggressive, visionary quality of cinema is found through its technical devices. (*HE*, 178)

Just as the language of the unconscious is a fragmented language of 'contamination,' involving the free-play of signifiers, the visual language of the cinema of poetry is

estremamente rozza, quasi animale. Tanto la mimica e la realtà bruta quanto i sogni e i meccanismi della memoria, sono fatti quasi preumani, o ai limiti dell'umano: comunque programmaticali e addirittura premorfologici (i sogni avvengono al livello dell'inconscio, e così i meccanismi mnemonici: la mimica è segno di estrema elementarietà civile, ecc.). *Lo strumento linguistico su cui si impianta il cinema è dunque di tipo irrazionalistico.*[83]

extremely crude, almost animal-like. As with gestures and brute reality, so dreams and the processes of our memory are almost prehuman events, or on the border of what is human. In any case, they are programmatical and even premorphological (dreams take place on the level of the unconscious, as do the mnemonic processes; gestures are an indication of an extremely elementary stage of civilization, etc.). *The linguistic instrument on which film is predicated is, therefore, of an irrational type.* (*HE*, 169–70)

As a language predicated upon the operations of the unconscious ('untamed thought'), that is, beholden to a realm of repressed desires and excluded perspectives, rather than upon a rational *langue*,[84] the cinema of poetry attempts to release its spectators from the confinements of the rational structures they inhabit. This involves, thus, a pluralization of perspective. The free indirect, Pasolini explains,

presuppone non un destinatario, ma un coro di destinatari: una coralità, insomma, d'ascolto e di riconoscimento delle esperienze da cui è nata la deduzione della norma. Anzi, la coralità è tale da assumere la massima rilevanza, a scapito dell'esperienza testimoniata. Cioè: l'esperienza che detta le norme è significativa solo in quanto è corale, condivisa da un'intera categoria di persone (stava già per sfuggirmi l'espressione 'da una classe sociale').[85]

doesn't presuppose an addressee but a chorus of addressees – in short, a chorus listening to and recognizing the experiences from which the deduction of the norm is born. Indeed, the chorus is such as to assume the greatest relevance, to the detriment of the experience witnessed. That is, the experience that establishes the norms is meaningful only in that it is choral, shared by a whole category of people. (The expression 'by a social class' almost slipped out.) (*HE*, 79)

Pasolini describes this as the 'epic' and 'inchoative' function of the free-indirect style, which consists in exciting 'sentimenti simpatetici in altre persone che non solo hanno fatto esperienze simili, ma che non hanno nemmeno la possibilità di pensare, per sé, esperienze diverse' ('sympathetic sentiments in other people who not only have had similar experiences but who don't even have the possibility of thinking for themselves of different experiences').[86] The 'pluralization' of the spectator, what we also described as the activation of the reader, functions by way of the 'choral' or 'epic' address of the cinema of poetry, and by way of Pasolini's abdication of the conventional author function, and its narrative stand-ins. What Pasolini will do, however, is attempt to resuscitate the collective dimension of storytelling, and constitute a 'chorality' (*coralità*) of spectators, in spite of the individualization of point of view presumed by the filmic technology itself. As we have discussed in the previous chapter, this is carried out by means of a contamination of visual languages, through the staging of a conflict between competing figural models. This strategy of *contamination* is an index of Pasolini's ambivalent feelings towards the technological basis of cinema.

Pasolini does not fail to include his 'ambivalence' in his adaptation of Boccaccio's text, but not only because he is thus more 'faithful' to the original (since Boccaccio was writing during a time when writing in the vernacular was still a highly suspicious technique). Rather, Pasolini's *Decameron*, made in the free-indirect style of the cinema of poetry (shot 'more than ever in my own style'),[87] itself exists on the 'cusp' between two competing cultural modes: between, on the one hand, the written culture of the modern, bourgeois era (from the Renaissance to the twentieth century), with the novel form as its cultural emblem, and, on the other hand, a new audiovisual culture expressing a new orality or, as Walter Ong has called it, the 'secondary orality' of post-modernity.[88]

Thus, both Boccaccio's text and Pasolini's adaptation express analogous concerns over mutations in their respective symbolic 'markets.' The cinema of poetry, in its multiplication of addressees and its reanimation of the spectator as active participant in the telling of stories harks back to a time when, in the words of Paul Zumthor, the listener's 'whole body, not only his visual and auditory faculties, was engaged in the reception of the text.'[89] Pasolini's *Decameron*, in its celebration of bodies and sexuality, and in its language predicated upon the 'irrational,' the 'oneiric,' the 'barbaric,' and the 'sacred,' attempts to challenge forth a bodily response in the spectator, to reactivate what Zumthor calls the 'latent eroticism' of the reception of texts.[90] To paraphrase Heath, it is a film that 'makes the body.'[91]

Moreover, as we discussed, Pasolini's frame-tale, with the figures of the Forger/Artist, revealed the fixing or assigning of meaning to be a product of the 'powers of the false.' As Deleuze writes, 'What the artist is, is the creator of truth, because truth is not to be achieved, formed, or reproduced; it has to be created.'[92] Such a formulation, writes Deleuze, demands the deconstruction of the opposition of subject and object that underlies and guarantees the 'form of the true' and the cinema of prose that subscribes to it. Deleuze describes how it is Pasolini's cinema of poetry, and the free-indirect style, that perform precisely this deconstruction,[93] and he indicates that such a deconstructive approach is essential in order to 'rediscover the pure and simple storytelling function,' which is free from the 'model of truth': 'What is opposed to fiction is not the real; it is not the truth which is always that of the masters or colonizers; it is the story-telling function of the poor, in so far as it gives the false the power which makes it into a memory, a legend, a monster.'[94]

Thus, when Pasolini suggests that, in the *Trilogia della vita*, he wanted 'to tell, to recount, for the sheer joy of telling and recounting, for the creation of narrative myths, away from ideology,'[95] he was not, as mentioned at the beginning of this chapter, abdicating his cinema of 'engagement.' Rather, he wished to return the storytelling function to the people, to return to the collective, participatory reception of stories that cinema as a mass medium could ideally afford. While Boccaccio's text harnesses storytelling to social and ideological reproduction ('consolation' and *utile consiglio*), Pasolini's film presents storytelling as the 'production of collective utterances capable of raising misery to a strange positivity, the invention of a people.'[96] Storytelling, as Deleuze describes it, is the speech act with 'many heads,' it is memory, 'and memory is invention of a people ... The speech act must create itself as a foreign language in a dominant language, precisely in order to express an impossibility of living under domination.'[97] As Pasolini writes, the free-indirect style of the cinema of poetry locates 'a chorus listening to and recognizing the experiences from which the deduction of the norm is born.'[98] Pasolini's *Decameron* is indeed the expression of how he would renew the mandate of the writer-cinematographer insofar as 'the whole cinema becomes a free indirect discourse operating in reality. The forger and his power, the film-maker and his character, or the reverse, since they only exist through this community which allows them to say "we, the creators of truth"'.[99]

Conclusion

Pasolini's *Decameron* reveals how occasionally in history a people will take back the storytelling function from those institutions that would appropriate it and monopolize it, translating it into a function of ideology. Boccaccio himself adopts the vernacular as the medium of a new hegemonic culture, with different stories to tell. His efforts are a continuation of Dante's project of establishing a literary tradition in the vernacular, adequate to the social conditions of the late Middle Ages, as Dante describes it in the *De vulgari eloquentia* – a text that Gramsci describes as 'an act of national-cultural politics (in the sense that "nations" had at that time and in Dante').[100] Pasolini's cultivation of the cinematic medium is an aspect of a similar political logic, an attempt to make cinema 'una possibile lingua di comunicazione umana in potenza, un possibile sistema o struttura linguistica, di rapporto sociale.'[101] Just as Boccaccio rejects Latin as an artificial language of storytelling, and a form of élite recreation, and thus adopts the *vulgar eloquio*, so will Pasolini in turn reject the Italian literary vernacular as an 'artificial' and 'normative' language,[102] and turn to cinema, the *schermo eloquio*, as a potential common language or *koiné*. And just as Boccaccio's vernacular prosaics was the expression of an (ever postponed) drive towards the formation of the Italian nation-state, Pasolini's is a 'transnational,' 'translinguistic' language that offers itself to an altered idea of social aggregation during a post-industrial (Pasolini called it 'neocapitalist') era witnessing the end of the nation-state.

Le strutture della lingua del cinema si presentano dunque più che come internazionali e interclassiste, come transnazionali e transclassiste: *prefigurano una possibile situazione socio-linguistica di un mondo reso tendenzialmente unitario dalla completa industrializzazione e dal conseguente livellamento implicante la scomparsa delle tradizioni particolaristiche e nazionali.*[103]

The structures of the language of cinema therefore present themselves as transnational and transclassist rather than as international or interclassist. *They prefigure a possible sociolinguistic situation of a world made tendentially unitary by complete industrialization and by the consequent leveling which implies the disappearance of particular and national traditions.*

Pasolini's film offers an image of storytelling that is emblematic of these types of issues and that forms an appropriate conclusion to our discussion of the film. In part 1 of the film, we are presented with an ancient Neapolitan storyteller giving a public reading of Boccaccio's *Decameron*. He begins to tell a story (Day 9.2), reading from Boccaccio's Tuscan original, but very quickly puts down the text, impatient with its language and rhetorical style and he exclaims: 'Signori miei, mò ve spiego alla napoletana…' ('Ladies and Gentlemen, now I'll tell it Neapolitan-style …').[104] He is seen to improvise, and thus revitalize, the story in dialect. (Pasolini also furnishes us with several close-ups of the groins of some of the listeners; this, along with Ciappelletto's invasion of their privacy as pick-pocket, lends the scene an erotic charge that may resemble that described by Zumthor, as discussed earlier.) Pasolini's *Decameron* repeats this storyteller's act. It is an adaptation *alla napoletana*, both literally and metaphorically, insofar as Pasolini populates his film with Neapolitans; replaces Boccaccio's Tuscan with the Neapolitan dialect; rejects the novel's structure and form of address; restores something of the (ch)oral or 'epic' nature of storytelling; appropriates Boccaccio's stories, belonging once to high culture and literary canons, and translates them into the language and medium of the popular audience; and finally he addresses his audience as 'southerners,' as an exploited and dominated population.

Thus, Pasolini's revitalization of Boccaccio reveals, just as Gramsci did before him, how the *questione della lingua* is an interrogation of the exercise of power. Yet the most heated debates concerning language occur during moments of social transition or crisis. As we quoted earlier, Gramsci writes that 'in one way or another, whenever the language question arises, it means that a series of other problems is imposing itself: the formation and broadening of the ruling class, the need to establish more intimate and secure relations between the ruling groups and the national-popular masses – that is, to reorganize cultural hegemony.'[105]

We have discussed how Pasolini criticizes the avant-garde for the way its transgressions function to reiterate the rule, how they work as a cultural 'Dioneo' necessary for the maintenance of hegemony, for the concealment, in Pasolini's society, of the production of the 'norm.' Pasolini's adaptation does not overturn its model (it does not carry out this form of filial, parodic, or revolutionary aggression towards authority). Rather, he translates Boccaccio into a new style, the free indirect, in order to multiply the addressees, to bring his spectators, collectively, to 'recognize the experiences from which the deduction of the norm is born,' in order to transfer to his audience, ideally, the power of the collective utterance that is cinema, the blank screen (like the blank third panel of the artist's triptych) that gains its eloquence from what the people project upon it.

Nel *Decameron* io ho girato come so e come voglio girare: più che mai nel mio stile. Ma mentre in *Porcile* e *Medea* il mio gioco era atroce, ora esso è lieto, stranamente lieto. Un'opera lieta (fatta con tanta serietà, naturalmente) mi sembra contraddire ad ogni aspettativa, è una disobbedienza completa. (Ma può darsi che io stia mentendo.)

With the *Decameron* I filmed the way I know and want to film: more in my style than ever. But while in *Porcile* and *Medea* my game was horrible, now it is cheerful, strangely cheerful. It seems to me that a cheerful work (made with great seriousness, naturally) contradicts every expectation: it is completely disobedient. (But maybe I'm lying.)[106]

5

Afterword: Homosexualities, the Sacred, and the Paying of Debts

Manifestar significar per verba non si poria,
ma per urli sì.[1]

Io non credo che l'attuale forma di tolleranza sia reale. Essa è stata decisa
'dall'alto': è la tolleranza del potere consumistico, che ha bisogno di un'assoluta
elasticità formale nelle 'esistenze' perché i singoli divengano buoni
consumatori. Una società spregiudicata, libera, in cui le coppie e le esigenze
sessuali (eterosessuali) si moltiplichino è di conseguenza avida di beni di
consumo.

I do not believe that the current form of tolerance is real. It was decided upon
'from above': it is the tolerance of consumerist power, which requires an
absolute formal elasticity in 'existences' so that individuals might become good
consumers. An unscrupulous society, free, in which couples and sexual
exigencies (heterosexual) multiply and consequently create a thirst for consumer
goods.[2]

A brief meditation is here necessary to deal with the question of Pasolini's
homosexuality and its significance for the study of his work. The fact of
an artist's homosexuality is, in recent theoretical debates, often held to be
determinant of his or her production; often this position also holds that
any discussion of a gay artist's work that does not privilege somehow
the significance of the artist's sexuality is guilty of a certain repression,
denial, or phobia regarding that sexuality. For me this must remain
an open question (vexed by issues of essentialism and determinism).
However, if the view I have described has any validity, it is not in terms
of a call to admit gay contents, homosexual motifs, visual 'signatures'

of the artist's sexual identity, but rather to approach the identity of the artist as itself a method, a construct, that exercises itself in the form of the film in the negotiations of inclusions and exclusions that take place in the elaboration of a narrative system.[3] While clearly we can speak of Pasolini in terms of a gay aesthetic, this aesthetic will be one suggested more along Barthesian lines of stylistic sensitivity as opposed to thematic inventories: a post-affirmative aesthetic of alterity and readerly ' bliss' that remains more concerned with what is excluded from a work than with the nature of its inclusions.[4]

Pasolini approached homosexuality in a non-essentialist, and ever-ambivalent, manner: as a form of aberration in a structure or system whose economy returned profits to those in competition to control it. Pasolini's 'diversity' was 'scandalous' to the extent that it spoke of forms of living and pleasure that failed to make a 'return' on society's investment – styles of unproductive, non-propagating 'expenditure.' Homosexuality was not an alternative, but an alterity that throughout his life he hesitated to describe – not simply out of some form of denial or self-loathing, as some have suggested (with only partial validity), but out of a refusal to render his diversity an object of representation or figuration. This refusal must be seen as indicative of his faith in forms of alterity, unrecognizability, mystery – what he at times referred to as forms of the 'sacred,' as I will conclude below by way of a brief analysis of *Teorema* – and in how these forms were apprehensible at the limits of representation or figuration, prowled around the shadows of the sayable. Ultimately, for Pasolini, these forms served as reminders of the mortality of representation, the *memento mori* that point towards a future when all that will survive of our world will be ruins.[5]

This refusal to make the alterity of homosexuality into an alternative led Pasolini consistently to refuse to endorse the gay movement or to identify with its programs – for the same reasons he scolded the Radical party, in one of his last written speeches, for understanding the project of democratic activism as one of guaranteeing the working classes, or other subaltern groups, an equal access to capitalist markets.[6] Freedom and happiness, here, became synonymous with consumerism; access to the global market-place became the *telos* of struggle and human fulfilment. For Pasolini, right up until his dying day, the Communist party was the only political grouping that continued to insist that the ontology of capital had a history, an ideology. Pasolini's 'pirate writings' consistently denounced the 'false' ontology of capital, and the hallucinatory nature of consumer society's liberty and tolerance.[7] Furthermore, the invisibility of the ideology of this society indicated the extent of its monopolization of the social imaginary: when there is no alternative, or better, when there is nothing else outside of this world-view – if only partially apprehended, and necessarily so – then the possibilities of change are radically diminished. In Pasolini's lexicon, alterity and diversity were code-words that indicated his scandalous pact with the forces of subversion.[8] The gay movement trades away much of its resistant potential by adopting the institutional forms of political activism, requiring 'equal participation' in a heterosexual society, requesting the rank of 'normality' with all of its secular and religious rituals and privileges. What could be more welcome to the powerful entities governing our societies – perhaps after a cynical display of moral outrage – than the spectre of political groupings, movements, campaigns, that claim to represent a constituency that wants in, a margin that wants a place near the centre? As long as happiness, health, and liberty are seen as existing, ultimately accessible (after the mythical sacrifices), within the material and spiritual boundaries established in capitalist societies, then the basic legitimacy of that society will remain beyond doubt. Pasolini's famous metaphor of his own society as the Palace ('Il Palazzo'), in which politics is likened to the courtly struggle to be seated near the King's dinner table, retains its resonancy to this day. His admonishment is not to seek representation and recognition – the desire of the courtesan – but to remain unrecognizable: 'Against all of this you must not do anything else (I believe) than simply continue to be yourselves: this means to be continually unrecognizable. Forget the great successes right away, and continue – unafraid, obstinate, eternally contrary – to insist upon and desire an identification with the different [il diverso]; to scandalize; to curse.'[9]

But let's return to our initial proposal: I do not read Pasolini's homosexuality in the motifs and themes of his films (the seductive images of young boys, close-ups of the crotches on men, secret forms of communication and identification, or the problem of Pasolini's occasional misogyny, and so on).[10] Pasolini's 'homosexual aesthetic' resides not within the images of his films. Rather, this 'aesthetic,' if it is one, is to be found 'outside' the images or, better, in how his images display their weaknesses and limits,[11] their histories and their futures, and their very nature as artifice (often bordering on camp or kitsch, to recall Sontag's important work).[12] Pasolini's style is one designed to present the spectator with images that allude indirectly to what is not there, to something that has been excluded; images that show the film itself, in its composition and completion, as the product of a set of inclusions and exclusions, bearing a narrative whose economy and pleasure depend upon the exclusion of elements that would threaten it with unmotivated detour and exhaustion.[13] That is, in the narrative film, especially those of the commercial variety, all of the elements, actors, properties, and actions it contains must derive their meaning within the film's narrative universe – they will become the synecdoche of the film's fullness, details in which is glimpsed the meaning of the whole. Elements that do not produce, or return, a meaning that contributes to the progress of the narrative are to be eliminated, excluded. In the essay 'Tetis,' Pasolini remarked upon this role of the director as one whose aesthetic task is that of deciding what to exclude and what to include – and he insisted that it was the artist who pushed at the limits of what could be included, at the boundaries of the expressible. In a film, what transgresses the limits of the representable will necessarily exist as something that will put the progress of the narrative into crisis (or 'suspend' it, as Pasolini would say) – present the spectator with elements whose meaning is nebulous, obtuse, alien. These 'foreign' elements within the dominant language of the narrative resuscitate the hermeneutic capacities of spectators and require of them an effort of interpretation: narrative pleasure is overwhelmed by the excessive, unproductive bliss of interpretation. This bliss – of Barthesian provenance (*The Pleasure of the Text*) – is heretical insofar as it does not contribute to the story's progress, does not maintain the transparency of the image, is not productive of significance or value: it relates only a 'signifying,' a process of meaning, an intensification of perceptual faculties *'contra naturam,'* to use Barthes's ironic phrase.[14] One of the lessons of the Centaur in Pasolini's *Medea* (half-man and half-beast) is that 'there is nothing natural in nature.' This view translates into Pasolini's antinaturalist cinema of 'poetry,' designed to 'demystify the innocence of technique to the last drop of blood';[15] this demystification takes the form of the 'indebted' style of pastiche, borrowing, and contamination that, as we have seen in previous chapters, threaten the naturalism of the filmic image with the opacity of obsolete codes.

According to Lyotard, it is in the work of experimental filmmakers that we find staged the processes of narrative 'disciplining' and 'normalization.' This is always simultaneously a staging of scene and society: 'Just as the libido must renounce its perverse overflow to propagate the species through a normal genital sexuality allowing the constitution of a "sexual body" having that sole end, so the film produced by an artist working in capitalist industry (and all known industry is now capitalist) springs from the effort to eliminate aberrant movements, useless expenditures, differences of pure consumption.'[16] For Lyotard, narrative stages the libidinal economy of human subjects and communities, forced to submit to the laws of efficiency and productivity, pushed to police their desires and actions to excise whatever is non-propagating, irresponsible to common survival. He suggests that

> normalization consists of the exclusion from the scene of whatever cannot be folded back upon the body of the film, and outside the scene, upon the social body. The *film*, strange formation reputed to be normal, is no more normal than the *society* or the *organism*. All of these so-called objects are the result of the imposition and hope for an accomplished totality. They are supposed to realize the reasonable goal par excellence, the subordination of all partial drives, all sterile and divergent movements to the unity of an organic body. The film is the organic body of cinematographic movements. It is the *ecclesia* of images: just as politics is that of the partial social organs ... The fundamental problem is the exclusion and forclusion of all that is judged unrepresentable because non-recurrent.[17]

For Pasolini as well, what counted was a politics of cinematic representation as an allegory of community, as a figuration of an impossible society.[18] That is, just as narrative progression and the transparency or realism of filmic images depend upon the exclusion of whatever elements would pose a threat of breakdown or opacity, so does the formation and propagation of a community depend upon mechanisms of exclusion and repression of disorderly social elements. Communities, that is, have an unconscious, what Fredric Jameson once called a 'political unconscious' – an unconscious that is usually located historically and spatially as a *ghetto*, a *lager*, a prison, a reservation, or a 'closet.'[19]

In this study of the *Trilogia della vita* we have described Pasolini's style of contamination as an ideological form of pastiche, a style that demonstrates the debts of cinematic representation. It is a style of filmmaking that includes what commercial filmmakers must exclude: images that foreground their artifice, narrative elements that exceed any definite plot-function, and experimentations in point of view that cause the spectator to ponder the historical and ideological determinants of representation and of vision itself.[20] One could be tempted to draw this style together under the umbrella-term of a gay aesthetic (and clearly Pasolini's homosexuality, his own personal experience as a *diverso*, was at the productive heart of his method). However, the alterity that Pasolini's films refer to, freely and indirectly, or allegorically, is not an essence – it is not homosexuality nor is it labour power. Rather, it is an alterity, a political unconscious, that is found repressed within all subjects and all communities, an 'otherness' repressed in the processes of subjective and political 'empowerment' (we could call it, along with Barthes, 'homosexualities' in the plural): and it is this unrecognizable alterity, this threat of disempowerment, that returns (like all repressions) to offer the possibility of equality and the reminder of mortality. In the words of Rinaldo Rinaldi:

Unrecognizability, as the only principle of paradoxical identity, is the key to Pasolini's project. It is a key that is not difficult to link to a form of homosexuality that Pasolini, in the last years of his life, used as a provocation, a polemical weapon, a distinctive signal of a global transgression – even literary. It is another way to declare his own unrecognizability, through the paradox of an apparently easy recognizability, scandalous and public: not to show oneself inside the sexual system of the Father, of the Law; refuse to identify with any significant sexual difference. Homosexuality traverses the masculine-feminine system to appear as neuter, as that Artaudian neutral non-gender: a 'void' that 'expands' between two 'breaths,' between two 'moments,' between two genders. But it is also a funereal 'massacre,' 'asphyxiated void,' blocked and destroyed respiration. It is the interval between categories, discontinuity, fissure, but it is also the apocalypse that massacres all categories.[21]

If there is a nostalgia, a desire for the *nostos*, in the *Trilogia della vita*, it is in reaction to the perception of the nearly complete derealization and reification of the present – that is, it is a nostalgia for the present. This nostalgia takes another form in one of Pasolini's greatest films, *Teorema*, released in the mythical year of 1968, which here demands mention. This film relates the story of a bourgeois family and their servant who become the hosts of a mysterious, unidentified 'Visitor' (an avid reader of Rimbaud, described as Pasolini as the bearer of 'authenticity,' who has arrived from an unnamed space of 'otherness' or divinity).[22] All of the characters fall in love with this young man, whose body is obsessively framed by Pasolini's camera, and have sex with him, become dependent upon him, indebted to him. Soon thereafter, the Visitor leaves as mysteriously as he had arrived, leaving the characters with merely the signs and memory of his passing (with the nostalgia of converts), and forcing them to carry out obsessive rituals designed to evoke and renew his presence.[23]

This encounter, the moment of conversion, proves to be the destruction of all the characters, a total subversion of the structures governing their daily lives, an implosion of subjectivity: the film is an allegory of disempowerment. The only character who is able to survive this 'enlightenment' (and the allegory of 'enlightenment' is different for all the characters: revolutionary for the father; sexual for the mother; psychological for the daughter; aesthetic for the son) is the servant, Emilia. The bourgeois characters are not able to survive the 'authenticity' that they experience, through the mediation or inter-course of the Visitor, because their only foundation, which proves unwieldy, is found in empty social rituals and solipsistic self-representations – that is, in language, or what we might call the Symbolic. And the meanings generated in this Symbolic, in this language – according to the theorists of language and culture, even the 'engaged' forms of structuralism and semiotics – are arbitrary, and the identities that are formed there are shifting, continually *sous rature*. In *Teorema*, the impact of the Visitor, the 'cruelty' of his intervention, is that of rendering the characters' identities absurd: consequently, the father relinquishes his factory to the workers (who don't want it); the mother surrenders herself to an infinite succession of unsatisfactory lovers; the daughter retreats into psychosis; the son becomes an avant-garde artist. These people are utterly defeated and alone; their 'lack' or incompleteness, their indebtedness, is experienced as meaninglessness.

The servant Emilia, however – named after Emilia-Romagna, the traditionally communist, predominantly agricultural, region of Italy – is the only character to survive. This is often explained by critics in terms of Pasolini's naïve belief in the revolutionary capacities of the sub-proletariat, or in terms of a decadent religious sentiment. Though there is partial truth in these explanations, it seems to me that Emilia's salvation is possible because her experience of powerlessness, lack, absurdity, and cruelty is not new to her. Indeed, these are the factors that have defined her entire identity, shaped her life. Furthermore, this experience is one that she shares with others of her kind – in the film she returns to her home, where people greet her by her first name, recognize her – and, indeed, this sharing of misery is the common denominator of the collectivity that is presented in the film, this powerlessness the very basis of its community. For Emilia, this experience, and the acknowledgment of her indebtedness to an otherness allegorized in the Visitor, offer the possibility of meaning, of having a meaning, and being meaningful.[24] The power of making meaning, or somehow revealing the processes of *signifying* – the power of creation *ex nihilo* – is figured through Emilia's adoption of prophetic, mystical capabilities (she begins to perform miracles) – and, clearly, for Emilia her power is an affliction (analogous to the *malessere* of poets, sibyls, and saints). What the Visitor has awakened within this character is an affliction of meaning. To recall the title and theme of Pasolini's *Trasumanar e organizzar* – a title that invokes Saint Paul by way of Dante's *Paradiso* – Emilia is an emblem of a conversion, a going 'beyond human' (*trasumanar* is Dante's untranslatable neologism) that imposes an ethical responsibility, a duty of 'organization.'[25] In the film, Emilia becomes the centre of her community, a point of attraction, an emblem of common aspirations. What has been awakened is the power to produce sense, suspend and re-make meaning, through the experience and recognition of the essentially open-ended, un-fixed, ever-shifting nature of the Symbolic, or through the collapse of the Symbolic. In *Teorema*, the nameless Visitor becomes the agent of rupture, both divine and revolutionary – an allegorical figuration of a dis-empowering force, the eruption of difference within the fabric of the family narrative. This force is at once destructive and constructive, poison and cure: for the bourgeois characters, there is retreat into irresponsible solipsism, individual defeat, and the end of the social (and this family is presented as typical of a class that has made of this condition a universal aesthetic and a philosophy – we might call it post-modern, with the son, Pietro, as its condemned practitioner); while for Emilia and those like her, the Visitor's message holds out the possibility of community and a renewal of the social, a signifying responsibility.

In a certain sense, the three films of the *Trilogia della vita* are also about Emilia's community: their nostalgia is one for pre-modern, pre-bourgeois societies – those of the playful characters in the *Decameron*; societies on the brink of destruction in *Canterbury*; or figured as 'Third World' or non-Western in *Il fiore delle mille e una notte*. These societies are all somehow 'incomplete,' since the source of their completion and perfection is found outside of them, in a 'beyond' or *aldilà*. In all three films, the societies and characters represented are all in some way negotiating with an invisible 'beyond,' a realm of divinity, in whatever guise it assumes: Christian in the *Decameron* and *Canterbury* (with the associated problems of sin and the visionary nature of artistic creation), magical in the *Arabian Nights* (with its magical forces, flying genies and mythical lions represented through special-effect techniques that might provide a definition of kitsch). These communities are in fact 'driven' by their constitutive incompleteness, as are the films that Pasolini has made about them. As Pasolini's character says at the conclusion of the *Decameron*, 'why finish a work of art when it is so beautiful simply to dream it?'

Pasolini's nostalgia is not simply for a 'return' to a past, to an ideal that clearly never existed (this criticism of Pasolini is both common and rather facile), but for a return of another sort: a return of the signifying function, of the signifying responsibility to artists, a return to engagement in the production of a critical collectivity, a community of the equally powerless, whose self-consciousness, once achieved, would reveal the absurdity of power, and the illegitimacy of the powerful.[26] This function presumes an incomplete society – *da farsi* – whose completion becomes the desire of the community, the content of a collective dream (as it is described in Pasolini's novel *A Dream of Something*).[27]

The nostalgia for community was also approached by Pasolini as the problem of the Irrational and the Sacred (thus his interest in mechanisms of periodic sacrifice, as thematized in nearly all of his works in the martyrdom of sacred victims).[28] That is, what bears the name of the sacred – and it was, and remains, heretical even to utter the word in post-Enlightenment cultures[29] – is, to adopt Wlad Godzich's suggestive terminology, 'an excluded space of otherness' towards which people carry a debt; and it is universal indebtedness that is 'the only ground on which equality, as a social fact, can be thought of.'[30] In a poem Pasolini wrote on commission for the journal *Cattolicesimo rivoluzionario* (though it never appeared on its pages, but is found in the volume *Trasumanar e organizzar*), he identifies his position as a *diverso* with the plight of the Jews, and claims the ghetto as his home (in a manner that anticipates, in certain ways, Lyotard's figuration of marginalized classes and identities as 'the jews'):[31]

I am therefore codified as Chief
of the Ghetto where is found all of Humanity,
insofar as it is completely excluded with respect to God.[32]

Clearly, this equality will not be the product of an empowerment of the powerless, a giving-voice to the voiceless, an enlightened fine-tuning of political representation. It is a 'humanity' that is the product of an 'enigma': 'here is the point: enigma.'[33] The generosity of Pasolini's work rests, rather, in its obsessive gesturing (in the excess of its style and theme)[34] towards an alterity, diversity, or perversity that disempowers, but disempowers equally: something I would not call a gay aesthetic but, once again to recall Barthes's phrase, an aesthetic of homosexualities. What is more radical, more heretical, more utterly egalitarian – and here is to be found the so-called religious, 'Pauline' content of Pasolini's work, an invocation of a 'humble Italy,' bereft of the transcendent[35] – than a call for equal disempowerment and the absolute renunciation of the privileges and obligations of capital?

> più è sacro dov'è piu' animale
> il mondo: ma senza tradire
> la poeticità, l'originaria
> forza, a noi tocca esaurire
> il suo mistero in bene e in male
> umano. Questa è l'Italia, e
> non è questa l'Italia: insieme
> la preistoria e la storia che
> in essa sono convivano, se
> la luce è frutto di un buio seme.

> the world is more sacred where it is
> more animal: but, without betraying
> the poeticity, the originary
> force, we must exhaust
> its human mystery for better or for worse.
> This is Italy, and
> this is not Italy: together
> the prehistory and the history that
> are within her co-exist, if
> light is the fruit of a dark seed.[36]

Notes

CHAPTER 1 Pasolini *regista civile*

1 'Vivo ora per ora, inquadratura per inquadratura.' Pasolini, *Lettere 1955–1975*. Ed. Nico Naldini (Turin: Einaudi, 1988), 735.
2 See Pasolini, *Lettere 1955–1975*.
3 See Franco Fortini, 'Pasolini o il rifiuto della maturità,' *Nuovi saggi italiani*. Vol. 2 (Milan: Garzanti, 1987), 213–14. With the publication of his *Attraverso Pasolini* (1993), Fortini himself has shed more light on the often conflictual relationship that existed between these two poets.
4 For a discussion of the impact of Neorealist cinema upon Pasolini, see Antonio Bertini, ed., *Teoria e tecnica del film in Pasolini* (Rome: Bulzoni, 1979), 34–5.
5 Pasolini, 'Proiezione al "Nuovo" di *Roma città aperta*,' *Le poesie* (Milan: Garzanti, 1971), 189–90; English translation from *A Future Life* (Rome: Associazione 'Fondo Pier Paolo Pasolini,' 1989), 32.
6 On the new audiovisual 'koiné,' and an institutional response to its challenge, see Harold M. Foster, *The New Literacy: The Language of Film and Television* (Urbana, IL: National Council of Teachers of English, 1979). For one of the most interesting approaches to the issue of literacy and technology, see Walter J. Ong, *Orality and Literacy* (London, New York: Methuen, 1982); see also Donis A. Dondis, *A Primer of Visual Literacy* (Cambridge, MA: MIT Press, 1973).
7 Pasolini, *Empirismo eretico* (Milan: Garzanti, 1972) [hereafter *EE*], 233; *Heretical Empiricism*, trans. L.K. Barnett and B. Lawton (Bloomington and Indianapolis: Indiana University Press, 1988) [hereafter *HE*], 225.
8 Nico Naldini, *Pasolini: Una vita* (Turin: Einaudi, 1989), 243 (translation mine).

9 My own approach to Pasolini's texts will be guided by a Goldmannian notion of structural homology as it has been elucidated by Cesare Segre in *Avviamento all'analisi del testo letterario* (Turin: Einaudi, 1986): 'History thus seems to reveal itself under two principal aspects: as historical content and as historicity of codes. An attentive analysis reveals these two aspects as more homogenous, since in the text what is important is not so much the data or the historical re-evocation, but rather the "imaginary universe," to use Goldmann's phrase; that is, an interiorized historicity that is structured as system. This "imaginary universe" has the status of model, and constitutes a schema for the functioning of codes' (132–3). For an essential discussion of homologies between the spheres of material production and linguistic forms, see Ferruccio Rossi-Landi, *Il linguaggio come lavoro e come mercato* (Milan: Bompiani, 1968); see also Rossi-Landi, *Semiotica e ideologia* (Milan: Bompiani, 1972), 59–63 and 248–58. For his important Benjaminian elaboration of these theories in terms of allegory, see Romano Luperini's 'Semantica e interpretazione,' *Allegoria* 9 (1986), 11–66; see also his excellent *L'Allegoria del moderno: saggi sull'allegorismo come forma artistica del moderno e come metodo di conoscenza* (Rome: Editori Riuniti, 1990).

10 See Lucien Goldmann, *Per una sociologia del romanzo* (Milan: Bompiani, 1964).

11 See Pasolini, *A Future Life* (Rome: Associazione 'Fondo Pier Paolo Pasolini,' 1989), 163.

12 For a very interesting discussion of Pasolini's post-national theory of cinema, see Beverly Allen, 'The Shadow of His Style,' in *Pier Paolo Pasolini: The Poetics of Heresy*, ed. B. Allen (Saratoga, CA: Anma Libri, 1982): 'The subtle and potentially subversive homology that may exist, according to Pasolini, between a written text and reality, may also fall victim to a kind of nationalism which only the universality of the cinematic sign (regardless of the film's spoken language) is capable of undermining; for Pasolini cinema became a "hyper-space" for his "apedagogical pedagogy" because its *langue* or *langage* is not limited to a specific nationality' (3).

13 See G.P. Brunetta, *Forma e parola nel cinema. Il film muto: Pasolini, Antonioni* (Padova: Liviana, 1970); and see Pasolini, *A Future Life*, 163, where Pasolini describes the 'silent' style of his *Canterbury*.

14 Pasolini, *EE*, 128–9; *HE*, 123–4 (emphasis in original).

15 *EE*, 129; *HE*, 124 (emphasis in original).

16 Pasolini, *A Future Life*, 171.

17 Pasolini, *Le poesie*, 297 (translation mine).

18 And this study will be concerned solely with the visual language of the films of the *Trilogia*, with occasional references to the significance of dialect in the dialogues (especially in the *Decameron*). However, it must be noted

that Pasolini's decision to seek the collaboration of Ennio Morricone on the musical commentary seems motivated by the fact that both artists share a citational compositional method; both produce work dominated by pastiche and self-conscious irony. Moreover, it is ironic that both Morricone and Tonino Delli Colli (as director of photography) were both working with Sergio Leone on his parodic 'spaghetti westerns' during the same period they were collaborating with Pasolini. For Morricone's often less than enthusiastic comments concerning his work with Pasolini, see his interview in Bertini, *Teoria e tecnica del film in Pasolini*, 169–75.

19 Quoted in Sandro Petraglia, *Pier Paolo Pasolini* (Florence: La Nuova Italia, 1974), 46–7 (translation mine).

20 Quoted in Nicole Gingras, 'Peter Greenaway: The Photographic Effect and the Disquieting Stability,' *Parachute* 52 (1988): 23, 25. We could mention several other filmmakers who, since the sixties, have shown themselves to be engaged in such stylistic experimentation and ethical concerns: Bertolucci, Godard, Jost, Scorsese, and Tarkovsky offer notable examples.

21 In Italian, to be estranged, lost, or bewildered is to be *spaesato*: literally, to be outside one's country.

22 Giorgio Agamben, *La comunità che viene* (Turin: Einaudi, 1990); *The Coming Community*, trans. Michael Hardt (Minneapolis: University of Minnesota Press, 1993).

23 Pasolini, *EE*, 85; *HE*, 79.

24 On Pasolini's 'Abiura' as a strategy of 'deflection,' see Roland Barthes, *Leçon* (Paris: Seuil, 1978).

25 Pasolini, 'La presenza,' in *Le poesie*, 747.

CHAPTER 2 Allegories of Contamination in *The Trilogy of Life*

1 'Il mio gusto cinematografico non è di origine cinematografica, ma figurativa. Quello che io ho in testa come visione, come campo visivo, sono gli affreschi di Masaccio, di Giotto – che sono i pittori che amo di più, assieme a certi manieristi (per esempio il Pontormo). E non riesco a concepire immagini, paesaggi, composizioni di figure al di fuori di questa mia iniziale passione pittorica.' Quoted in Adelio Ferrero, *Il cinema di Pier Paolo Pasolini* (Venice: Marsilio, 1977), 42.

2 M. McLuhan and H. Parker, *Through the Vanishing Point* (New York: Harper and Row, 1968), 1.

3 See Pasolini, 'Il cinema di poesia,' in *EE*, esp. 173.

4 See David Bordwell, *Narration in the Fiction Film* (Madison: University of Wisconsin Press, 1985), 156–204.

5 See Noël Burch, *Theory of Film Practice* (Princeton: Princeton University Press, 1981); David Bordwell, *Narration in the Fiction Film*, 4–7; on film as a 'complement of theatre,' see André Bazin, ' Theater and Cinema – Parts 1–2,' in *What is Cinema?* (Berkeley: University of California Press, 1967), 1: 76–124; Stephen Heath, 'Narrative Space,' in *Questions of Cinema* (Bloomington: Indiana University Press, 1981), 19–75; Kristin Thompson, *Breaking the Glass Armor* (Princeton: Princeton University Press, 1988).

6 Bordwell, *Narration in the Fiction Film*, 4–7.

7 V. Pudovkin, *Film Technique* (New York: Grove, 1970), 38–47.

8 See the 'Manifesto della cinematografia futurista' in Mario Verdone, *Cinema e letteratura futurista* (Rome: Bianco e nero, 1967).

9 Pasolini, *EE*, 279; *HE*, 274.

10 Stan Brakhage, *Brakhage Scrapbook* (New Paltz, NY: Documentext, 1982), esp. 205.

11 See *EE*, 281–8 and 293–301.

12 *EE*, 282; *HE*, 277.

13 Marco Vallora, 'Pier Paolo Pasolini tra manierismo e metaletteratura,' in *Per conoscere Pasolini* (Rome: Bulzoni and Teatro Tenda, 1978), 120 (translation mine).

14 In this regard, see Jaqueline Rose, 'Sexuality and Vision: Some Questions,' in Hal Foster, ed., *Vision and Visuality* (Seattle: Bay Press, 1988), 115–27.

15 *Le poesie*, 329.

16 *A Future Life*, 171.

17 Quoted in Stanley Reed, 'The Filmmaker and the Audience,' in Jean Creedy, ed., *The Social Context of Art* (London: Tavistock, 1970), 136.

18 See Louis Althusser, 'Ideology and Ideological State Apparatuses,' in *Lenin and Philosophy* (London: New Left Books, 1971), 127–88, and 'Freud and Lacan,' in ibid., 189–220; Teresa de Lauretis, *Alice Doesn't* (Bloomington: Indiana University Press, 1984), and *Technologies of Gender* (Bloomington: Indiana University Press, 1987); and Stephen Heath, *Questions of Cinema*.

19 'Ideology and Ideological State Apparatuses,' 155–9.

20 Catherine Belsey, *Critical Practice* (London: Methuen, 1980), 57.

21 'Ideology and Ideological State Apparatuses,' 121–73.

22 Ibid., 171.

23 Ibid., 174.

24 De Lauretis, *Technologies of Gender*, 12.

25 'Freud and Lacan,' 206 (emphasis his).

26 See Kaja Silverman, *The Subject of Semiotics* (New York: Oxford University Press, 1983), 155.

27 Silverman, *The Subject of Semiotics*, 166.

28 See de Lauretis, *Technologies of Gender*; Colin MacCabe, 'Theory and Film: Principles of Realism and Pleasure,' *Screen* 17, no. 3 (1976); and Mary Anne Doane, Patricia Mellencamp, and Linda Williams, eds, *Re-Vision: Essays in Feminist Film Criticism* (Frederick, MD: University Publications of America and The American Film Institute, 1984).

29 See Colin MacCabe, 'Realism and the Cinema: Notes on Some Brechtian Theses,' *Screen* 15, no. 2 (1974).

30 *Godard: Images, Sounds, Politics* (Bloomington: Indiana University Press, 1980), 38.

31 Ibid., 34.

32 See Laura Mulvey, 'Visual Pleasure and Narrative Cinema,' *Screen* 16, no. 3 (1975), 6–18; Ellie Ragland-Sullivan, *Jacques Lacan and the Philosophy of Psychoanalysis* (Urbana: Illinois University Press, 1986), esp. 267–308; Rosalind Coward, 'Lacan and Signification,' *Edinburgh Magazine*, no. 1 (1984), 6–21; and Annette Kuhn, *Women's Pictures: Feminism and Cinema* (London: Routledge and Kegan Paul, 1982).

33 See Jacques Alain-Miller, 'Suture,' *Screen* 18, no. 4 (1977–8), 24–34; Jean Pierre Oudart, 'Cinema and Suture,' *Screen* 18, no. 4 (1977–8), 35–47; Stephen Heath, 'On Suture,' *Questions of Cinema*, 76–112. For recent arguments against suture theory, See Noël Carroll, *Mystifying Movies* (New York: Columbia University Press, 1988), 183–99; and David Bordwell, *Making Meaning* (Cambridge, MA: Harvard University Press, 1989), 83–104.

34 Giuseppe Zigaina, 'Total Contamination in Pasolini,' *Stanford Italian Review* 4, no. 2 (1984), 267–85; and Marco Vallora, 'Alì dagli occhi impuri,' *Bianco e nero*, January–April 1976, 156–204.

35 Althusser, 'Il piccolo teatro,' in *For Marx* (London: Verso, 1979), 145.

36 'L'ambiguità,' in Antonio Bertini, ed., *Teoria e tecnica del film in Pasolini*, 112 (translation mine).

37 Jean Duflot, *Il sogno del centauro* (Rome: Editori Riuniti, 1983), 58 (translation mine).

38 Quoted in J. Snyder, 'Benjamin on Reproducibility and Aura,' in Gary Smith, ed., *Walter Benjamin: Philosophy, Aesthetics, History* (Chicago and London: University of Chicago Press, 1989), 163.

39 See Enzo Golino, *Pier Paolo Pasolini: Il sogno di una cosa* (Bologna: Il Mulino, 1985).

40 The phrase is Jean-Francois Lyotard's: See 'Interview,' *Diacritics* 14, no. 3 (Fall 1984), 18.

41 I gain this understanding of 'mannerism' and its relation to any rigidified 'classical' style in art from Arnold Hauser, though I have abstracted the category from the actual historical period, following the Renaissance,

commonly referred to as 'mannerist' (during which we find the works of such artists as Caravaggio, Pontormo, and Rosso Fiorentino). However, the analogies between Pasolini's style and that of the historical mannerists, both as a reaction to classicism and a stress on derivation and citation, not to mention possible analogies with the artists of the baroque in general, provide crucial insights into his 'neo-mannerist' or 'neo-baroque' works. See Arnold Hauser, *Mannerism: The Crisis of the Renaissance and the Origin of Modern Art* (London: Routledge and Kegan Paul, 1965).

42 See *EE*, 108–18, and 120, where he writes that the questions of plurilinguism and monolinguism 'implicano tutta la mia ideologia di scrittore.'

43 Marco Vallora, 'Alì dagli occhi impuri,' 173 (translation mine).

44 H.R. Jauss, *Toward an Aesthetic of Reception* (Minneapolis: University of Minnesota Press, 1982), 3–45 and 139–85.

45 See Pasolini, 'Il cinema di poesia,' in *EE*, 171–91.

46 Antonio Costa, 'Effetto dipinto,' *Cinema e cinema* 54–5 (January–August 1989), 37–48. See also André Bazin, 'Painting and Cinema', in *What Is Cinema?* Berkeley: University of California Press, 1967, 1:164–9; Bazin distinguishes the 'centripetal' frame of paintings from the 'centrifugal' screen of the cinema, and concludes with the suggestion that cinema will not destroy painting but will 'save' it by bringing it to general attention.

47 Ibid., 48.

48 Ibid., 42 (translation mine).

49 Alberto Moravia, *Al cinema* (Milan: Bompiani, 1975), 210.

50 Pasolini, 'Confessioni tecniche,' *Paese Sera*, 27 September 1964, 11.

51 Bertini, ed., *Teoria e tecnica del film*, 23–4.

52 Pasolini, 'La ricotta,' in *Alì dagli occhi azzurri* (Milan: Garzanti, 1989 [1965]), 480.

53 Ibid., 482–3 (translation mine); *ciachista* is the Italian term for 'clap-board person.'

54 Hauser, *Mannerism*, 192.

55 G. Grignaffini, 'Rosso sangue,' *Cinema e cinema* 54–5 (January–August 1989): 25. I would add the name of Peter Greenaway to the list of filmmakers interested in the intersection of painterly and cinematic models. As Greenaway remarks, concerning his own films, 'I have always been fascinated by the viewer's relationship with paintings, one which is completely different from the 'empathy' with which we often react to film, or literature, almost always to the theatre and of course opera. I want to introduce this viewer-painting relationship, this distance, into my cinematography.' Quoted in Nicole Gingras, 'Peter Greenaway: The Photographic Effect and The Disquieting Stability,' *Parachute* 52 (1988): 23.

56 Hauser, *Mannerism*, 85.

57 Ibid., 111.

58 A.C. Quintavalle, *Prospettiva e ideologia* (Parma: Editrice Studium Parmense, 1967), 18. See also Jean-François Lyotard, 'Representation, Presentation, Unpresentable,' in *The Inhuman* (Stanford: Stanford University Press, 1991): 'Painting obtained its letters of nobility, was placed among the fine arts, was given almost princely rights, during the Quattrocento. Since then, and for centuries, it made its contribution to the fulfilment of the metaphysical and political programme for the organization of the visual and the social. Optical geometry, the ordering of values and colors in line with a Neoplatonically inspired hierarchism, the rules for fixing the high points of religious or historical legend, helped to encourage the identification of new political communities: the city, the State, the nation, by giving them the destiny of seeing everything and of making the world transparent (clear and distinct) to monocular vision. Once placed on the perspectivist stage, the various components of the communities – narrative, urbanistic, architectural, religious, ethical – were put in order under the eye of the painter, thanks to the *costruzione legittima*' (119–20).

59 A.C. Quintavalle, *Prospettiva e ideologia*, 19.

60 Linda Hutcheon, *A Theory of Parody* (New York and London: Methuen, 1985), 7.

61 *EE*, 69 (his emphasis).

62 Michel Foucault, 'Las Meninas,' in *The Order of Things* (New York: Vintage, 1970), 3–16.

63 Ibid., 6.

64 Ibid., 16.

65 Pasolini's interest in representations of Carnival and Lent began as early as 1943, according to Stefano Casi in his study of Pasolini and the theatre. Casi recounts how, on the last day of Carnival of that year, Pasolini and his friend Cesare Bartotto improvised a theatrical sketch of Carnival and Lent in Friulian dialect, based on Ermes di Colloredo's *Contrast fra Carneval e Cresime*. See Casi, *Pasolini: un'idea de teatro* (Udine: Campanotto Editore, 1990), 40.

66 See Pasolini, 'L'ambiguità,' in Bertini, ed., *Teoria e tecnica del film in Pasolini*, 109–13.

67 Pasolini, 'C'est le *Decameron* qui m'a choisi,' *La Galerie*, December 1971: 89.

68 Quoted in G. Gambetti, 'Pasolini da Boccaccio a Chaucer: Per una "*Trilogia popolare, libera, erotica*,"' *Cineforum*, March 1974: 222 (translation mine).

69 See Ben Lawton, 'The Storyteller's Art: Pasolini's *Decameron*,' in Horton and Magretta, eds, *Modern European Filmmakers* (New York: Ungar, 1981), 210–11.

Lawton here identifies these paintings and provides a similar discussion of their thematic import.

70 M. Bakhtin, *Rabelais and His World* (Boston: MIT Press, 1964).

71 'The Storyteller's Art,' 121.

72 Pasolini, 'Tetis,' in V. Boarini, ed., *Erotismo, eversione, merce* (Bologna: Cappelli Editore, 1974), 100. An English translation of this essay is found in *Pasolini: Contemporary Perspectives*, P. Rumble and B. Testa, eds (Toronto: University of Toronto Press, 1994).

73 Pasolini quoted in Bertini, *Teoria e tecnica del film* ,112–13.

74 See Lawton, 'The Storyteller's Art,' for an Oedipal reading of this sequence.

75 G. Brunetta, 'Itinerario di Pier Paolo Pasolini verso il mito di Edipo,' *Rivista di Studi Italiani* 2 (1984), 97. While providing an autobiographical reading of *Edipo Re*, Brunetta is careful to note that 'l'orizzonte autobiografico si è molto dilatato fino a coinvolgere il senso del destino umano.'

76 See William Van Watson's reading of the Oedipus and Laius figures in Pasolini's theatrical works, in *Pier Paolo Pasolini and the Theatre of the Word* (Ann Arbor and London: UMI Research Press, 1989).

77 Michael Gibson, *Bruegel* (Seacaucus, NJ: Wellfleet Press, 1989), 8.

78 Ibid.

79 Concerning Pasolini's novels, Franco Fortini writes: 'The inspiration and prime mover of everything Pasolini writes is antithesis ... Antithesis can be found at all levels of his writings ... including even his preferred rhetorical figure, that sub-species of oxymoron called syneciosis in ancient rhetoric, by which one affirms two contrary attributes of the same object.' Quoted in Zigaina, 'Total Contamination in Pasolini,' 271. Pasolini calls himself a non-dialectical thinker 'perché la natura non conosce "superamenti." Ogni cosa in essa si giustappone e coesiste.' See Duflot, *Il sogno del centauro*, 53.

80 Brian Henderson understands this sort of flattening of the image as an example of 'non-bourgeois' style. See 'Towards a Non-Bourgeois Camera Style,' in Mast and Cohen, eds, *Film Theory and Criticism* (New York: Oxford University Press, 1979), esp. 839–42.

81 *EE*, 85.

82 See Erwin Panofsky, *Renaissance and Renascences in Western Art* (Stockholm: Almquist and Wiksell, 1960), 119; John White, *The Birth and Rebirth of Pictorial Space* (Cambridge, MA: Harvard University Press, 1987 [1957]), 40ff.

83 White, *The Birth and Rebirth of Pictorial Space*, 69, 140.

84 Ibid., 103.

85 See Fredric Jameson, 'Postmodernism or the Cultural Logic of Late Capital,' *New Left Review* 146 (1984), 53–92. Jameson has turned this into a book-length study, See *Postmodernism or the Cultural Logic of Late Capital* (Durham: Duke

University Press, 1990). For a critical assessment of Jameson's formulations, See Linda Hutcheon, *A Poetics of Postmodernism* (London: Routledge and Kegan Paul, 1988), esp. 22–36.

86 See Roland Barthes, *The Pleasure of the Text* (New York: Hill and Wang, 1975), 4: 'The subject gains access to bliss by the cohabitation of languages *working side by side.*'

87 See Pasolini, *EE*, 99.

88 'Dialogo 1,' *Cinema e film* 1, no. 1 (1966), 8; this interview is included in *EE*, 231–40; *HE*, 231 (translation modified).

89 Ibid.

90 Roland Barthes, 'Literature Today,' *Critical Essays* (Evanston: Northwestern University Press, 1972), 154.

91 *EE*, 230; *HE* 221, trans. modified.

92 Quoted in Naldini, *Pasolini: Una vita*, 392 (translation mine).

93 Ibid.

94 For a detailed account of the court battles surrounding the *Trilogia*, see Laura Betti, ed., *Pasolini: Cronaca giudiziaria, persecuzione, morte* (Milan: Garzanti, 1977), 180–207.

95 Pasolini, 'Il cinema di poesia,' *EE*, 185–6; *HE*, 180 (trans. altered; first and second emphases mine).

96 According to Ferruccio Rossi-Landi, an author has the ability 'to *exceed* [*eccedere*], to produce something that is not foreseen in the cycle of social reproduction.' See 'L'autore fra riproduzione sociale e discontinuità: Dialogo con Ferruccio Rossi-Landi,' in *Lectures* 15 (1984); quoted in A. Biancofiore and A. Ponzio, 'Intorno ai "Criteri per lo studio ideologico di un autore" di Ferruccio Rossi-Landi,' *Allegoria* 11–12 (1987), 93. In clarifying Rossi-Landi's notion of excess, Biancofiore and Ponzio refer to Pasolini's 'Gramscian' idea of the author's 'mandate' as one of affirming the 'rights of expressivity against the purely instrumental use of language' as found in his essays in *Heretical Empiricism*.

97 Pasolini, *EE*, 187; *HE*, 182.

98 *EE*, 99; *HE*, 92.

99 See Giorgio Agamben, *The Coming Community*, trans. Michael Hardt (Minneapolis: University of Minnesota Press, 1993).

100 For an account of some of the visual sources for several of Pasolini's films, including the *Trilogia*, see the interview with Dante Ferretti, Pasolini's scenographer, in A. Bertini, ed., *Teoria e tecnica del film*, 187–94.

101 Ibid., 186–93.

102 Quoted in Naldini, *Pasolini: Una vita*, 409.

103 Petraglia, *Pier Paolo Pasolini*, 105 (translation mine).

104 Quoted in John Michalczyk, *The Italian Political Filmmakers* (London and Toronto: Associated University Presses, 1986), 99.

105 Pasolini interviewed in P. Willemen, ed., *Pier Paolo Pasolini* (London: British Film Istitute, 1977), 69–70.

106 Ibid., 71.

107 See Harold Bloom, *Anxiety of Influence* (New York: Oxford University Press, 1973).

108 Omar Calabrese, *L'età neobarocca* (Rome-Bari: Laterza, 1989), 63 (translation mine).

109 Ibid., 64.

110 For a detailed account of the 'caso Canterbury,' see Laura Betti, ed., *Pasolini: Cronaca giudiziaria, persecuzione, morte*; see esp. 186–93.

111 'Effetto-dipinto,' 48.

112 Thompson, *Breaking the Glass Armor: Neoformalist Film Analysis* (Princeton: Princeton University Press, 1988), 259; and see also 'The Concept of Cinematic Excess,' in P. Rosen, ed., *Narrative, Apparatus, Ideology: A Film Theory Reader* (New York: Columbia University Press, 1986), 130–42.

113 Quoted in Thompson, 'The Concept of Cinematic Excess,' 130–1.

114 For an extended discussion of excess, evasion, and slippage in narrative film, within the context of an analysis of Orson Welles's *Touch of Evil*, see Heath's 'Film, System, Narrative,' in *Questions of Cinema* (Bloomington: Indiana University Press, 1981), 131–44.

115 See Roland Barthes, 'The Third Meaning,' in *The Responsibility of Forms*, trans. R. Howard (Berkeley: University of California Press, 1985), 41–62: 'obtuse meaning is discontinuous, *indifferent* to the story and to the obvious meaning (as signification of the story); this dissociation has a *contra naturam* or at least a distancing effect with regard to the referent (55).' See also Gregory Ulmer, *Applied Grammatology* (Baltimore: Johns Hopkins University Press, 1985), 306–7, for a post-structuralist account of the 'third sense of the image' (Ulmer focuses on the films of Sergei Eisenstein in particular).

116 Thompson, *Breaking The Glass Armor*, 251.

117 For a discussion of Pasolini's debt to the Russian Formalists, See Naomi Greene, *Pier Paolo Pasolini: Cinema as Heresy* (Princeton: Princeton University Press, 1990), 110.

118 Quoted in Thompson, *Breaking The Glass Armor*, 10.

119 Ibid.

120 Deleuze, *Cinema 2* (Minneapolis: University of Minnesota Press, 1989), 223.

121 'Cinema di poesia,' 185.

122 Quoted in Naldini, *Pasolini: Una vita*, 360. Pasolini's short film *Le mura di San'A* (1974), was made as an appeal to UNESCO to help save these ancient

walls from demolition. He became aware of this issue during the filming of *Il fiore delle mille e una notte* on location in Yemen.

123 *Bruegel*, 44.

124 'Cinema di poesia,' 185.

125 See Thompson, 'The Concept of Cinematic Excess,' 130–1.

126 I find this notion of structure in Pasolini's explanation of his own *Appunti per un film sull'India* and *Appunti per un'Orestiade africana*, both to be considered as 'sketches' of a possible film (each of which, moreover, are about a society *da farsi*) whose completion is left to the imagination of the spectator. See Naldini, *Pasolini: Una vita*, 326 and 341. Interesting also in this regard is his attitude towards the structure of the scenario, what he calls 'una struttura che vuol essere altra struttura': See *EE*, 192–201. See also Antonio Bertini, 'La metafora della sceneggiatura,' in *Teoria e tecnica del film*, 71–83; Vallora, 'Alì dagli occhi impuri,' 177; and Naldini, ed., *Pasolini: Lettere 1955–1975*, 600–1, for Pasolini's letters to Fortini, where this notion of a structure *da farsi* is carried over to other forms of organization, insofar as Pasolini urges Fortini to join the existing editorial committee of *Nuovi argomenti*, a journal that, in Pasolini's mind, will always remain 'una rivista futura possibile.'

127 G. Brunetta, *Storia del cinema italiano* (Rome: Editori Riuniti, 1979), 662.

128 For a discussion of the issue of voyeurism in the film, and its problematization of bourgeois morality and sexuality, see Martin Green, 'The Dialectic of Adaptation: The Canterbury Tales of Pier Paolo Pasolini,' *Literature/Film Quarterly* 4 (1976), 50.

129 Michel Foucault, *Discipline and Punish* (New York: Vintage, 1979), esp. 3–72.

130 See Cesare Palumbo, *Assassiniamo il poeta: Pier Paolo Pasolini* (Cosenza: Edizioni Pellegrini, 1978); and also Maria-Antonietta Macciocchi, 'Pasolini: Assassinat d'un dissedent,' *Tel Quel* 76 (Summer 1978).

131 See Sam Weber, *Institution and Interpretation* (Minneapolis: University of Minnesota Press, 1987), 132–57.

132 See Brunetta, *Storia*, 662; and for a discussion of Bosch in *Canterbury*, see Green, 'The Dialectic of Adaptation,' 51.

133 Frederic Jameson, *The Political Unconscious* (Ithaca: Cornell University Press, 1981).

134 *EE*, 257.

135 *EE*, 199; *HE*, 193–4.

136 'li ho fatti per oppore al presente consumistico un passato recentissimo dove il corpo umano e i rapporti umani erano ancora reali, benché arcaici, benché preistorici, benché rozzi, però tuttavia erano reali, e opponevano questa realtà all'irrealtà della civiltà consumistica' (Naldini, *Pasolini: Una vita*, 348, translation mine).

137 'Le mille e una notte sono un modello narrativo ... Il narrare illimitato. Una cosa dopo l'altra, e una dentro l'altra, all'infinito' (Pasolini in Naldini, 380; translation mine).

138 In Lawton, 'The Storyteller's Art,' 204.

139 Pasolini, A Future Life, 171.

140 EE, 85.

141 See Greene, Pier Paolo Pasolini: Cinema as Heresy, 191–2.

142 For a discussion of Pasolini's representation of homosexuality, in particular in the Trilogia, see Richard Dyer, 'Pasolini and Homosexuality,' in P. Willemen, ed., Pier Paolo Pasolini, 57–63. See also Ben Lawton, 'The Evolving Rejection of Homosexuality, the Sub-Proletariat and the Third World in The Films of Pier Paolo Pasolini,' Italian Quarterly, 21 (1980), 167–73.

143 Greene, 189.

144 See Pasolini, 'A quattr'occhi con Pasolini,' 159.

145 John Barth has been an important figure in Italian cultural debates concerning post-modern literature, in particular (see Carravetta and Spedicato). Recent approaches towards a 'post-modern' Pasolini might find a theoretical comparison of these two authors productive.

146 Barth, Chimera (Greenwich, CT: Fawcett, 1972), 32 (emphasis mine); for a theoretical discussion of embedded tales, see Barth, 'Muse Spare Me,' in Quinn, ed., The Sense of the Sixties (New York: Free Press, 1968). See also Barth, 'Tales within Tales within Tales,' in The Friday Book (New York: Putnam, 1984), 218–38; and The Tidewater Tales, 639–51.

147 'Tales within Tales,' 221.

148 Ibid., 235.

149 Ibid., 219.

150 Barthes, Image, Music, Text, trans. Stephen Heath (London: Fontana, 1977), 147.

151 Jean-Francois Lyotard, 'Acinema,' Wide Angle 2, no. 3 (1978), 55.

152 EE, 126–47.

153 Pasolini's clearest visual sources in the Decameron and I racconti di Canterbury include Giotto, Masaccio, Bruegel, and Bosch.

154 See Bertini, ed., Teoria e tecnica del film, 191.

155 See Brunetta, Storia del cinema italiano, 662.

156 White, The Birth and Rebirth of Pictorial Space, 68.

157 See Jonathan Crary, Techniques of the Observer (Boston: MIT Press, 1992).

158 See de Lauretis, Technologies of Gender.

159 See Jean Louis Comolli, 'Technique and Ideology,' Film Reader 2 (1977); and Lucia Corrain, 'La grammatica della duplicazione,' Carte semiotiche 1 (1985).

160 'La mia polemica era contro la cultura della classe dominante eurocentrica' (in F. Faldini and G. Fofi, eds, *Il cinema italiano d'oggi* (Milan: Mondadori, 1984), 9; translation mine).

161 Naldini, *Pasolini: Una vita*, 250.

162 Though I do not agree entirely with all his conclusions, see Chris Bongie's recent critique of Pasolini's 'exoticist' *tiersmondisme* in 'A Post-Script to Transgression: The Exotic Legacy of Pier Paolo Pasolini,' in *Exotic Memories: Literature, Colonialism, and the Fin de Siècle* (Stanford, CA: Stanford University Press, 1991), 188–228.

163 'Oggi il dialetto è un mezzo per opporsi all'acculturazione. Sarà, come sempre, una battaglia perduta' (in Naldini, *Pasolini: Una vita*, 388; translation mine).

164 For a collection of Pasolini's writings on the Friulian dialect and his early involvement in the Friulian autonomy movement, see Pasolini, *Un paese di temporali e di primule*, ed. Nico Naldini (Parma: Guanda, 1993).

165 Pasolini, *Il portico della morte*, ed. Cesare Segre (Rome: Associazione 'Fondo Pier Paolo Pasolini,' 1988), 63; translation mine.

166 'è sempre prodotto di un ibrido morale – qui verrebbe voglia di dire storico' (*Il portico della morte*, 105: translation mine).

167 Pasolini reports that he was ostracized at the University of Bologna for this (See Naldini, *Pasolini: Una vita*, 388, and 99–109).

168 *Lettere luterane* (Turin: Einaudi, 1976), 24.

169 'La natura, insomma, è già artificio, cultura, spettacolo; non esiste più nulla di elementare, primario; ogni cosa rimanda ad un codice preesistente, l'arte scende nella vita … La realtà si atteggia ad arte, meglio è già arte, i riferimenti colti sono "naturali," non già imposti dalla cultura del poeta' (Vallora, 'Pier Paolo Pasolini tra manierismo e metaletteratura,' 120; translation mine).

170 *EE*, 282–3.

171 Ibid., 283; for Eco's critique of Pasolini's 'naïve notion of reality in his description of the language of cinema, see *La struttura assente* (Milan: Bompiani, 1989 [1968]), 149–63.

172 Ibid.

173 'tutte le mie caotiche pagine su questo argomento … tendono a portare la Semiologia alla definitiva culturizzazione della natura (ho ripetuto sette otto volte che una Semiologia Generale della realtà sarebbe una filosofia che interpreta la realtà come linguaggio)' (*EE*, 283; emphasis his, translation mine).

174 Ibid.; emphasis mine.

175 'facendo dell'intero vivere un parlare' (*EE*, 288).

176 Pasolini, *A Future Life*, 153.

177 See T. de Lauretis, 'Re-reading Pasolini's Essays on Cinema,' *Italian Quarterly* 82–83 (1980); A. Costa, 'Pasolini's Semiological Heresy,' in P. Willemen, ed., *Pier Paolo Pasolini* (London: British Film Institute, 1977); C. Wagstaff, 'Reality into Poetry,' *The Italianist* 5 (1985).

178 Rose, 'Sexuality and Vision,' 125.

179 Ibid.

180 Quoted in Heath, *Questions of Cinema*, 29.

181 'non produce solo merce, produce insieme rapporti sociali, umanità' (Pasolini, *Lettere luterane*, 183; translation mine).

182 See Naldini, *Pasolini: Una vita*, 392.

183 Ibid.; translation mine.

184 Ibid.

185 On *Canterbury* as an anticipation of *Salò*, See L. Miccichè, 'Pasolini: La morte e la storia,' *Cinema sessanta* 121 (May–June 1978).

186 Quoted in Adelio Ferrero, *Il cinema di Pier Paolo Pasolini*, 42.

187 Fortini, 'Pasolini e il rifiuto della maturità,' in *Nuovi saggi italiani* (Milan: Garzanti, 1987), 2:213–14. This essay, along with others concerning Pasolini's work, as well as selected correspondence between Fortini and Pasolini, is also found in Fortini's fascinating documentation of his difficult relationship with Pasolini, *Attraverso Pasolini* (Turin: Einaudi, 1993).

188 T. Adorno and H. Eisler, *Komposition für den Film* (Münich: Roger and Berhard, 1969), 41; quoted in G. Koch, 'The Body's Shadow Realm,' in *October* 50 (Fall 1989), 13.

189 *EE*, 273–80.

190 *Le poesie*, 522.

191 *Brakhage Scrapbook*, 205. Brakhage is one of the only American filmmakers, along with Warhol, that Pasolini mentions in *Empirismo eretico* (258), though his name is mis-typed as Burkage.

192 *EE*, 173.

193 See *EE*, 176–7.

194 'dobbiamo batterci, dunque, per demistificare l' "innocenza della tecnica," fino all'ultimo sangue' (*EE*, 230; translation mine).

195 'una vecchia figuratività nel fianco della giovane leva' (*Le poesie*, 521). Although the actual work he is describing is his *Divina mimesis*, his descriptions found in this poem are entirely relevant to the *Trilogia* along with many of his other films.

196 Here the reader is referred to Marcuse's resonant formulations on the autonomous or utopian character of 'unfree art,' found in a brief treatise containing his meditations on the aesthetics of Adorno, Benjamin, Goldmann, Horkheimer, Lukacs, and Sartre. See *The Aesthetic Dimension: Towards a Critique of Marxist Aesthetics* (Boston: Beacon Press, 1978): 'The

utopia in great art is never the simple negation of the reality principle but its transcending preservation in which past and present cast their shadow on fulfillment. The authentic utopia is grounded in recollection. "All reification is forgetting" (Adorno). Art fights reification by making the petrified world speak, sing, perhaps dance. Forgetting past suffering and past joy alleviates life under a repressive reality principle. In contrast, remembrance spurs the drive for the conquest of suffering and the permanence of joy. But the force of remembrance is frustrated: joy itself is overshadowed by pain. Inexorably so? The horizon of history is still open. If the remembrance of things past would become a motive power in the struggle for changing the world, the struggle would be waged for a revolution hitherto suppressed in the previous historical revolutions' (73).

197 *Le poesie*, 670.

198 Ibid., 670–1.

199 'con un amore così violento per il "tempo perduto," da essere una denuncia non di qualche particolare condizione umana ma di tutto il presente (permissivo per forza). Ora siamo dentro quel presente in modo ormai irreversibile: ci siamo adattati. La nostra memoria è sempre più cattiva. Viviamo dunque ciò che succede oggi, la repressione del potere tollerante, che, di tutte le repressioni, è la più atroce' (in Naldini, *Pasolini: Una vita*, 392; translation mine).

200 Crary, 'Spectacle, Attention, Counter-Memory,' 103; and on the 'organization of human sense perception,' see W. Benjamin, *Illuminations*, trans. Harry Zohn (New York: Schocken, 1969), esp. 222–3, 253–64: 'To articulate the past historically does not mean to recognize it "the way it really was" (Ranke). It means to seize hold of memory as it flashes up at a moment of danger. Historical materialism wishes to retain the image of the past which unexpectedly appears to man singled out by history at a moment of danger. The danger affects both the content of the tradition and its receivers. The same threat hangs over both: that of becoming a tool of the ruling classes. In every era the attempt must be made anew to wrest tradition away from a conformism that is about to overpower it' (255).

201 *Lettere luterane*, 177.

202 'Progetto per opere future,' in *Le poesie*, 520.

CHAPTER 3 Pasolini's Ironic Recantation

1 Pasolini, 'Abiura dalla *Trilogia della vita*,' in *Lettere luterane*, 71–6; in the Preface to the screenplays, *Trilogia della vita* (Milan: Mondadori, 1987), 7–11; and in Naldini, *Pasolini: Una vita*, 396–9.

2 'Abiura,' 71.

3 Ibid.

4 See M. Foucault, 'The Grey Mornings of Tolerance,' in Beverly Allen, ed., *Pier Paolo Pasolini: The Poetics of Heresy* (Saratoga, CA: Anma Libri, 1982).

5 See Foucault, *The History of Sexuality*, vol. 1 (New York: Vintage, 1980), 15–50.

6 'Abiura,' 72.

7 Ibid.

8 Ibid., 74.

9 Ibid.

10 Ibid., 75.

11 Ibid, 75–6.

12 Franco Fortini, quoted in Giuseppe Zigaina, 'Total Contamination in Pasolini,' *Stanford Italian Studies*, 4, no. 2 (Fall 1984), 267–85.

13 Most critics see it simply as an introduction to *Salò* rather than a conclusion to the *Trilogia*, and few see its irony. See Guido Santato, *Pier Paolo Pasolini: L'opera* (Vicenza: Neri Pozza Editore, 1980), 263; Stefano Casi, 'Il teatro di *Salò* per una tragedia personale,' *Le giovani generazioni e il cinema di Pier Paolo Pasolini* (Rome: Fondo Pier Paolo Pasolini, 1989), 140; Nico Naldini, *Pasolini: Una vita*, 396–9; and Naomi Greene, *Pier Paolo Pasolini: Cinema as Heresy*, 196–7. Of these four in particular, only Greene notes its 'theatrical' qualities (196), yet she fails to fully clarify this insight. Significantly, Roland Barthes describes Pasolini's 'Abiura' as a playful and indeed theatrical example of ironic abjuration designed to transfer oneself where one is least expected ('spostarsi'); see his *Lezione* (Turin: Einaudi, 1981), 19–20. Thanks go to Professor David Ward for bringing this passage to my attention.

14 This sort of contamination of registers is found for example in the title of one of his last books of poetry, *Trasumanar e organizzar* (Milan: Garzanti, 1971).

15 See Pasolini, *Scritti corsari* (Milan: Garzanti, 1975), 5.

16 On irony as a defensive strategy, see C. Perelman and L. Olbrechts-Tyteca, *Trattato dell'argomentazione: La nuova retorica*, vol. 2 (Turin: Einaudi, 1982 [1966]), 219.

17 Boccaccio, *Decameron*, 673.

18 Ibid.

19 Lucia Marino provides a very interesting reading of how, in the 'Proemio,' the Introduction to Day 4, and the 'Conclusione,' Boccaccio very ironically both claims and disclaims authorship of the *novelle* that make up the *Decameron*. See *The Decameron's 'Cornice': Allusion, Allegory, and Iconology* (Ravenna: Longo, 1979), 130–2.

20 Boccaccio, *Decameron*, 255.

21 Ibid., 254.

22 Ibid., 255.

23 Ibid., 676.

24 See Vanna L. Bigazzi, ed., *I volgarizzamenti trecenteschi dell'Ars amandi e dei Remedia amoris* (Florence: Accademia della Crusca, 1987).

25 See Aldo Scaglione, *Nature and Love in the Late Middle Ages* (Berkeley: University of California Press, 1963), esp. 97–8; Mirko Bevilacqua, *L'ideologia letteraria del 'Decameron'* (Rome: Bulzoni, 1978), 32–4; Francesco Bruni, *Boccaccio: L'invenzione della letteratura mezzana* (Bologna: Il Mulino, 1990), 128–32; Azzura B. Givens, *La dottrina d'amore nel Boccaccio* (Messina, Florence: G. D'Anna, 1968), esp. 200–13.

26 See Andreas Capellanus, *The Art of Courtly Love*, intro. John J. Parry (New York: Frederick Ungar, 1959 [1941]). As John Parry suggests, regarding Book 3 of Capellanus's *De amore* entitled 'E quibus rationibus amor reprobetur,' 'such a retraction was called for by the scheme of Ovid, which in a general way Andreas was following ... Doubtless he was trying to appease his ecclesiastical superiors, who may well have been offended by the tone of the first two books' (18–19).

27 See John T. McNeil and Helena M. Gamer, eds, *Medieval Handbooks of Penance'* (New York: Columbia University Press, 1990 [1938]); and also J.A. Jungmann, *Missarum Sollemnia* (Westminster, MD: Christian Classics, 1986), 386–402.

28 See Olive Sayce, 'Chaucer's "Retractions,"' *Medium Aevum* 40 (1971), 241.

29 *The Decameron's* 'Cornice,' 12.

30 Boccaccio, *De Genealogia Deorum*, ed. V. Romano, (Bari: 1951).

31 See A. Capellanus, *De amore* (Havnia: Libraria Gaddiana, 1892), 358.

32 Geoffrey Chaucer, *The Canterbury Tales* (London: J.M. Dent and Sons, 1939), 518–9.

33 See William W. Lawrence, *Chaucer and the 'Canterbury Tales'* (New York: Columbia University Press, 1950), 146, 156.

34 *The Poetry of Chaucer* (Carbondale: Southern Illinois University Press, 1977), 336.

35 Lawrence, *Chaucer and the 'Canterbury Tales,'* 166–7.

36 Elbow, *Oppositions in Chaucer* (Middletown, CT: Wesleyan University Press, 1975), 142.

37 Pinsent, 'Chaucer's Critique of the Church in the General Prologue,' in L. Cookson and B. Loughrey, eds, *Critical Essays on the General Prologue to the 'Canterbury Tales'* (Essex, England: Longman House, 1989), 39–40.

38 Brewer, 'Gothic Chaucer,' in D. Brewer, ed., *Geoffrey Chaucer* (Cambridge: D.S. Brewer, 1990), 30.

39 Coghill, *The Poet Chaucer* (London: Oxford University Press, 1968 [1949]), 64–5.

40 Malone, *Chapters on Chaucer* (Baltimore: Johns Hopkins University Press, 1951), 139–40.

41 See Sayce, 'Chaucer's "Retractions,"' 230–1.

42 See Kendrick, *Chaucerian Play: Comedy and Control in the 'Canterbury Tales'* (Berkeley: University of California Press, 1988), esp. 131.

43 Sayce, 'Chaucer's "Retractions,"' 244.

44 Ibid., 245.

45 Ibid., 244.

46 Ibid.

47 And here there is an allusion, not picked up by Sayce, to Capellanus's recantation, where he writes: 'Sumas ergo, Gualtieri, salubrem tibi a nobis propinatum doctrinam et mundi penitus vanitates omittas.' *De amore*, bk. 3, 360.

48 'Chaucer's "Retractions,"' 245–6.

49 Deleuze, *Cinema 2*, 150.

50 Pasolini, *EE*, 85; *HE*, 79.

51 Deleuze, *Cinema 2*, 223.

52 *EE*, 191; *HE*, 185.

53 'It's true, *Salò* will be a 'cruel' film, so cruel that (I suppose) I will necessarily have to distance myself from it, pretend to not believe in it and play in a sort of cold manner.' Quoted in Naldini, *Pasolini: Una vita*, 391.

54 'Poeta delle ceneri,' *Nuovi argomenti* 67–68 (July–December 1980), 12.

55 Quoted in Naldini, *Pasolini: Una vita*, 306.

56 Ibid., 243. Here, as so often, Pasolini quotes himself, though without providing the reference.

57 But whereas Dante is '"made Italian" by exile,' as Mengaldo asserts, Pasolini is 'made transnational by exile.' See P.V. Mengaldo, s.v. 'De vulgari eloquentia,' *Enciclopedia Dantesca*, vol. 2 (Rome: Istituto della Enciclopedia Dantesca, 1970), 414.

58 See Maria Corti, 'Pasolini aveva ragione,' in A. Todisco, ed., *Ma che lingua parliamo?* (Milan: Longanesi, 1984): 'Unfortunately, Pasolini was right about the homogenization of language as a result of industrial technological development' (42).

59 Pasolini, 'Poeta delle ceneri,' 12.

60 'thanks to which, in some way, art is able to negate that which negates it.' Quoted in Lino Miccichè, 'Contestazione e controcontestazione,' in *Per conoscere Pasolini* (Rome: Bulzoni and Teatro Tenda, 1978), 52.

CHAPTER 4 Framing Boccaccio

1 See Marc Gervais, *Pier Paolo Pasolini* (Paris: Seghers, 1973), 15: Gervais suggests that with *Accattone* Pasolini offers a 'cinema dominated by an

abrupt tonality, where faces look at us and speak to us directly ... *Accattone* marks the beginning of a style of confrontation, even of assault.'

2 See Zygmunt Barański, 'Pasolini's Theorems' (forthcoming).

3 *EE*, 274; *HE*, 268.

4 See *Pasolini: Cronaca giudiziaria, persecuzione, morte* (Milan: Garzanti, 1977).

5 Quoted in Lawton, 'The Storyteller's Art.'

6 See especially Lawton; and Millicent Marcus, 'The *Decameron*: Pasolini as a Reader of Boccaccio,' *Italian Quarterly* 82–3 (Fall/Winter 1980–1), 175–80.

7 J. Potter, *Five Frames for the 'Decameron': Communication and Social Systems in the 'Cornice'* (Princeton: Princeton University Press, 1982). M. Cottino-Jones also provides an excellent discussion of Boccaccio's ethical response to the crisis figured by the plague, in her *Order from Chaos: Social and Aesthetic Harmonies in Boccaccio's 'Decameron'* (Washington: University Press of America, 1982).

8 On medieval medical treatises concerning melancholy or *aegritudo amoris*, and therepeutic regimes, see Massimo Ciavolella, *La 'malattia d'amore' dall'antichità al medioevo* (Rome: Bulzoni, 1976); regarding the importance of medical treatises and 'plague tracts,' see G. Olson, *Literature as Recreation in the Later Middle Ages* (Ithaca: Cornell University Press, 1982).

9 Pasolini, 'Cinema and Literature,' *Antaeus* (Winter 1976), 133.

10 For Pasolini's notes concerning Dante, see especially 'La volontà di Dante a essere poeta,' *EE*, 108–18.

11 Ibid.

12 See M. Bakhtin, 'Epic and Novel,' in *The Dialogic Imagination* (Austin: University of Texas Press, 1981); Vittore Branca, *Boccaccio medievale* (Florence: Sansoni, 1964); G. Lukács, 'Il romanzo come epopea borghese,' in *Problemi di teoria del romanzo* (Turin: Einaudi, 1976), 133–78.

13 Antonio Gramsci, *Quaderni del carcere* (Turin: Einaudi, 1975), 2346.

14 For an approach to such precursor anxieties in terms of issues of 'influence,' see Harold Bloom, *Anxieties of Influence*; and for discussion of the figure of the father in Pasolini's writing, see Gian Carlo Ferretti, 'Mio padre, quando sono nato,' *Nuovi argomenti*, no. 8 (October–December 1983), 123–34.

15 See G.P. Brunetta, 'La conquista dell'impero dei sogni: D'Annunzio e Pirandello,' *Annali d'Italianistica* 6 (1988), 18–37; Jennifer Stone, 'Cineastes' Texts,' *Yearbook of the British Pirandello Society* 3 (1983), 45–66.

16 See M. Verdone, 'Futurismo: Film e letteratura,' *Annali d'Italianistica* 6 (1988), 69–79; and M. Landy, 'Neorealism, Politics, and Language in the Films of the Tavianis,' *Annali d'Italianistica* 6 (1988), 236–51.

17 See G. Bluestone, *Novels into Film* (Baltimore: Johns Hopkins University Press, 1957); Pio Baldelli, *Film e opera letteraria* (Padova: Marsilio, 1964);

John Harrington, *Film and/as Literature* (Englewood Cliffs, NJ: Prentice Hall, 1977); W. Aycock and M. Schoenecke, *Film and Literature: A Comparative Approach to Adaptation* (Lubbock: Texas Tech University Press, 1988); J.G. Boyum, *Double Exposure: Fiction into Film* (New York: New American Library, 1985); G.P. Brunetta, ed., *Letteratura e cinema* (Bologna: Zanichelli, 1976); C. Eidsvik, 'Towards a "Politique des adaptations,"' *Literature/Film Quarterly* 3 (1975), 255–63; A. Horton and J. Magretta, eds, *Modern European Filmmakers and the Art of Adaptation* (New York: Ungar, 1981); J. Mayne, *Private Novels Public Films* (Athens, GA: University of Georgia Press, 1988); B. Morisette, *Novel and Film: Essays in Two Genres* (Chicago and London: University of Chicago Press, 1985); C. Orr, 'The Discourse on Adaptation,' *Wide Angle* 2 (1984), 72–6; R. Richardson, *Literature and Film* (Bloomington: Indiana University Press, 1969); M.C. Ropars-Wuilleumier, *De la litterature au cinéma: genese d'une écriture* (Paris: Colin, 1970).

18 See S. Eisenstein, 'Dickens, Griffith and the Film Today,' in Jay Leyda, ed., *Film Form* (New York: Harcourt, Brace and Jovanovich, 1949).

19 See G. Ulmer, 'Film: Sergei Eisenstein,' in *Applied Grammatology* (Baltimore: Johns Hopkins University Press, 1985), 265–315.

20 For an example of the academic response to Pasolini's *Decameron*, see Giovanni Grazzini, 'Boccaccio sullo schermo,' *Studi sul Boccaccio* 7 (1973), 369–73.

21 Indeed, it is interesting to note how Pasolini will be held responsible for the many pornographic remakes, by other directors, of the *Decameron* that followed the release of his own. See Giovanni Grazzini, 'Al cinema col Boccaccio,' in *Boccaccio e d'intorni* (Florence: Olschki, 1983), 323–6.

22 A positive evaluation is offered, however, by A.A. Iannucci, 'Dante, Television and Education,' *Quaderni d'italianistica* 10, nos. 1–2 (Spring/Fall 1989), 1–34; for an ambivalent 'official' response to Pasolini's adaptation, see Giovanni Grazzini, 'Boccaccio sullo schermo,' 369–73; and by the same author, 'Al cinema col Boccaccio.'

23 *EE*, 279.

24 Ibid., 280.

25 See ibid., 3–22.

26 On the *cornice* as protective screen, though not in precisely this sense, see G. Almansi, *The Writer as Liar: Narrative Techniques in the 'Decameron'* (London and Boston: Routledge and Kegan Paul, 1975), 14.

27 'Cinema and Literature,' 133.

28 See Grazzini, 'Boccaccio sullo schermo.'

29 'Cinema e litteratura,' 133.

30 See 'The *Decameron*: Pasolini as Reader of Boccaccio,' as well as her recent expanded study of Pasolini's *Decameron* and *Il Vangelo secondo Matteo*, within

the context of a theoretical discussion of literary adaptation, in *Filmmaking by the Book* (Baltimore: Johns Hopkins University Press, 1993).

31 See V. Branca, *Boccaccio medievale*, 301–7; G. Barberi-Squarotti, *Il potere della parola* (Naples: Federico and Ardia, 1983), 5–63; and J. Potter, *Five Frames for the Decameron* (Princeton: Princeton University Press, 1982).

32 See Boccaccio, *Il Decameron*, Introduction to Day One, 43.

33 For its description, see the Introduction to Day Three, 180.

34 See Potter, *Five Frames for the Decameron*, 11–40; Barberi-Squarotti, *Il potere della parola*, 44.

35 See G. Petronio, 'La posizione del *Decameron*,' in *L'Autore e il pubblico* (Padova: Studio Tesi, 1981), 36; for an excellent overview of the controversial matter of Boccaccio's moral or didactic intent in the *Decameron*, though not for his conclusions regarding the 'natural' and 'healthy' moralism of Boccaccio, see R. Hastings, 'To Teach or Not to Teach: The Moral Dimension of the *Decameron* Reconsidered,' *Italian Studies* 44 (1989), 19–40.

36 See Barberi-Squarotti, *Il potere della parola*, 8.

37 Ibid., 33.

38 'A Preface to Transgression,' in *Language, Counter-Memory, Practice* (Ithaca: Cornell University Press, 1977), 34.

39 Barberi-Squarotti, *Il potere della parola*, 34 (translation mine).

40 On the notion of the carnivalesque in the novel, see M. Bakhtin, *Rabelais and His World* (Cambridge, MA: MIT Press, 1968).

41 See U. Eco, 'The Comic and the Rule,' in *Faith in Fakes* (London: Secker and Warburg, 1986).

42 T. de Lauretis, *Technologies of Gender* (Bloomington: Indiana University Press, 1987).

43 See Petronio, 'La posizione del *Decameron*,' 19–47.

44 L. Mumford, *The City in History* (New York: Harcourt, Brace and World, 1961), 316; and see M. Foucault, *Discipline and Punish* (New York: Vintage, 1979), and N. Elias, *The History of Manners* (New York: Pantheon, 1978).

45 L. Costa-Lima, *Control of the Imaginary: Reason and Imagination in Modern Times* (Minneapolis: University of Minnesota Press, 1988), 3–34.

46 For Pasolini's account of the film's structure, see Pasolini, 'La tentazione di parlare,' *Rivista del cinematografo* 5 (May 1971), 207. And on Pasolini's early intention to adapt the text into a three-part film, drawing from fifteen of Boccaccio's *novelle*, see Pasolini's letter to producer Franco Rossellini (Rome, Spring 1970), in Naldini, ed., *Lettere: 1955–1975*, 670.

47 'The Storyteller's Art,' 206.

48 For an account of the numerology of Boccaccio's text, see Potter, *Five Frames for the Decameron*, 75–7.

49 *Cinema 2*, 126–55.

50 Branca, *Boccaccio medievale*, 157–62.

51 For an interesting discussion of money and literature, and verbal 'usury' in Jewish, Islamic, and Christian traditions, see Marc Shell, *Money, Language, and Thought: Literary and Philosophic Economies from the Medieval to the Modern Era* (Berkeley: University of California Press, 1982), esp. 49–50.

52 K. Marx, *Capital*, vol. 1 (New York: Vintage, 1977), 125–244.

53 See J. Le Goff, *Your Money or Your Life* (New York: Zone Books, 1988).

54 The tenth story of Day Eight (that of Salabaetto and Madonna Jancofiore, recounted by Dioneo) is similarly concerned with the dangers of loans and the money-form in general, identified as the untraceable and untrustworthy currency of merchants.

55 *EE*, 261.

56 'La tentazione di parlare,' 207.

57 'The Storyteller's Art,' 216.

58 On the issue of the 'proper name,' see J. Derrida, 'The Battle of Proper Names,' in *Of Grammatology* (Baltimore and London: Johns Hopkins University Press, 1976), 107–17.

59 G. Deleuze, *Cinema 2*, 132.

60 Ibid., 133.

61 Ibid.

62 Ibid., 133–4.

63 Ibid., 135.

64 *EE*, 203; and for a discussion of these ideas and the sometimes extreme responses of such theorists as Eco, Heath, and Metz, to Pasolini's seemingly naïve formulations, see T. de Lauretis, 'Re-reading Pasolini's Essays on Cinema,' *Italian Quarterly* 62–3 (1981), 159–66.

65 Here my argument is clearly beholden to the Heideggerian notion of enframing in his essays on technology and modernity as the 'age of the world picture.' See especially 'The Age of the World Picture,' in *The Question Concerning Technology and Other Essays* (New York: Harper, 1977), 115–54. Here Heidegger describes an understanding of the world as approachable only by mechanisms of representation, which is carried out, Heidegger suggests, by conceiving of the world as a collection of objects on display – as a 'world picture.' Such a representation is constituted through exclusionary operations of enframing, and is a process that presupposes a framing subject. As Heidegger writes, 'The world picture, when understood essentially, does not mean a picture of the world but the world conceived and grasped as a picture. What is, in its entirety, is now taken in such a way that it first is in being and only as in being to the extent that it is set up by man,

who represents and sets forth' (129–30). What this presupposes, suggests Heidegger, is a possibility of gaining a comprehensive representation of the world that can be ordered according to codifiable rules. What is essential to remember, for both Heidegger and Pasolini, is that this understanding of the world *as representation* cannot but presume a controlling or regulating subject: 'That the world becomes picture is one and the same event with the event of man's becoming subiectum in the midst of that which is' (130). What Pasolini, certainly, is concerned with is the extent to which a will to power is involved in the representation of the world, which is itself a fundamentally aesthetic project. The ability to subvert fantasies of power is *also* conceived of as an aesthetic project. Indeed, Pasolini's approach to the *cornice* in the *Decameron* is involved in precisely this research into the poisonous but also redemptive powers of representation or narration.

For a Derridean approach to framing, see Peter Brunette and David Willis, 'The Frame of the Frame,' in *Screen/Play: Derrida and Film Theory* (Princeton: Princeton University Press, 1989), 99–138.

66 *A Future Life*, 158.

67 'The Storyteller's Art,' 220.

68 Ibid.

69 Ibid., 221; and M. Marcus, 'The *Decameron*: Pasolini as a Reader of Boccaccio,' 179.

70 *Trilogia della vita*, 67–68.

71 Quoted in O. Stack, *Pasolini on Pasolini* (Bloomington: Indiana University Press, 1970), 28.

72 See Barthes, *S/Z* (New York: Hill and Wang, 1974); and Eco, *L'opera aperta* (Milan: Bompiani, 1962).

73 See J. Cannon, *Postmodern Italian Fiction* (Rutherford, NJ: Fairleigh Dickinson University Press, 1989); and, on the 'école du regard,' see Morisette, *Novels and Film*.

74 See U. Eco, *Lector in fabula* (Milan: Bompiani, 1979).

75 Barthes, 'The Death of the Author,' in *Image-Music-Text* (London: Fontana, 1977), 146–7.

76 Linda Hutcheon would perhaps read Pasolini's film as a characteristically post-modern form of intertextual parody (ambivalently antagonistic towards the original): 'Intertextual parody of canonical American and European classics is one mode of appropriating and reformulating – with significant change – the dominant white, male, middle-class, heterosexual, Euro-centric culture. It does not reject it, for it cannot. Postmodernism signals its dependence by its *use* of the canon, but reveals its rebellion through its

ironic *abuse* of it.' See *A Poetics of Postmodernism* (London: Routledge and Kegan Paul, 1988), 130.

77 See L. Althusser, 'Ideology and Ideological State Apparatuses,' *Lenin and Philosophy*, 127–93.

78 'Narrative Space,' in *Questions of Cinema*, 76–112.

79 'Ma ci sono dei casi, ripeto, in cui lo scrittore rinuncia fin da principio a essere scrittore-narrante.' ('But there are cases, I repeat, in which the writer renounces being writer-narrator from the very beginning.') *EE*, 87; *HE*, 80.

80 Ibid., 98.

81 Ibid., 178–9.

82 Ibid., 183.

83 Ibid., 173 (emphasis his).

84 See ibid., 202–30.

85 Ibid., 85–6.

86 Ibid., 86.

87 From an interview with Dario Bellezza, 'Io e Boccaccio,' *L'Espresso* 22 (November 1970), 22.

88 See W. Ong, *Orality and Literacy* (London, New York: Methuen, 1982).

89 *Speaking of the Middle Ages* (Lincoln, NB, and London: University of Nebraska Press, 1986), 22.

90 Ibid.

91 *Questions of Cinema*, 129.

92 *Cinema 2*, 146.

93 Ibid., see 148–9.

94 Ibid., 150.

95 Quoted in Lawton, 'The Storyteller's Art,' 204.

96 Deleuze, *Cinema 2*, 222.

97 Ibid., 223.

98 *EE*, 85.

99 Deleuze, *Cinema*, 155.

100 A. Gramsci, 'The So-Called Question of the Language,' in *Selections from Cultural Writings* (Cambridge, MA: Harvard University Press, 1985), 187.

101 *EE*, 75.

102 See esp. ibid., 9–10.

103 Ibid., 129 (emphasis his).

104 *Trilogia della vita*, 26.

105 *Quaderni del carcere*, 2346. On the *questione della lingua*, see Maurizio Vitale, *La questione della lingua* (Palermo: Palumbo, 1984).

106 From interview. Bellezza, 'Io e Boccaccio,' 22.

CHAPTER 5 Afterword

1 Pasolini, 'Manifestar (appunti),' in *Trasumanar e organizzar* (Milan: Garzanti, 1971): 'to signify political struggle through words is not possible, but by yelling, yes.' Pasolini's verse is a revision of verse 70 of the first Canto of the *Paradise* in which Dante insists on the eneffability of his mystical experience: 'Trasumanar significar per verba non si poria.' The translation of Pasolini's verse is nearly as difficult as that of Dante's original: 'How speak trans-human change to human sense? Let the example speak until God's grace grants the pure spirit the experience.' *The Paradiso*, trans. John Ciardi (New York: New American Library, 1970), I, vv. 70–2.

2 Pasolini, *Scritti corsari* (Milan: Garzanti, 1975), 259.

3 Pasolini, 'Tetis,' in Vittorio Boarini, *Erotismo, eversione, merce* (Bologna: Cappelli, 1974); and in Rumble and Testa, eds, *Pasolini: Contemporary Perspectives*.

4 See Barthes, *Roland Barthes by Roland Barthes*, trans. Richard Howard (New York: Hill and Wang, 1977), esp. p. 69: 'The opposition of the sexes must not be a law of Nature: therefore, the confrontations and paradigms must be dissolved, both the meanings and the sexes be pluralized: meaning will tend toward its multiplication, its dispersion (in the theory of the Text), and sex will be taken into no typology (there will be, for example, only *homosexualities*, whose plural will baffle any constituted, centred discourse).' See also Barthes, *The Pleasure of the Text*, trans. Richard Miller (New York: Hill and Wang, 1975); and *A Lover's Discourse*, trans. Richard Howard (New York: Hill and Wang, 1978). See also Mario Mieli's theorization of homosexuality/transsexuality in *Elementi di critica omosessuale* (Turin: Einaudi, 1977); for Mieli's account of reactions to Pasolini's murder, see pp. 150–4. When judged solely on the basis of their gay 'inclusions' or contents, Pasolini's films often draw ambivalent or antagonistic responses on the part of critics; see, for eaxmple, Richard Dyer's condemnation of *Il fiore delle mille e una notte*, in Paul Willemen, ed., *Pier Paolo Pasolini* (London: British Film Institute, 1977). See also Maurizio Viano's critique of Pasolini's 'irresponsible' *Trilogy of Life* in *A Certain Realism: Making Use of Pasolini's Film Theory and Practice* (Berkeley: University of California Press, 1993), 263–93.

5 For an excellent and insightful account of Pasolini's 'coming of age' in Friuli, and of his removal from that region in 1949, see Nico Naldini, 'Pier Paolo Pasolini, my cousin,' in Rumble and Testa, eds, *Pasolini: Contemporary Perspectives*, 14–21; on *memento mori* and melancholy, see Walter Benjamin, *The Origin of German Tragic Drama* (London: New Left Books, 1977), esp. 159–235.

6 On Pasolini's position within the Italian gay movement, a survey of writings on Pasolini's homosexuality, and a good bibliography, see Stefano Casi,

ed., *Desiderio di Pasolini* (Turin: La Sonda, 1990). See especially Giovanni Dall'Orto's critique of Pasolini's lack of gay pride in his essay 'Contro Pasolini' (149–82), and Walter Siti's pluralization of the category of 'gay culture' in his 'Postfazione in forma di lettera' (183–7).

7 In *Scritti corsari*, Pasolini recalls 'the suicide of the gay protagonist of Cocteau's *Libro bianco*, who took his own life because he had understood that, for a man, it was intolerable to be tolerated' (262).

8 See Pasolini, *Lettere luterane*, 190: 'while the extremists fight for civil rights, made pragmatically marxist, in the name of a final *identification* of the exploited with the exploiters, the communists, instead, fight for civil rights in the name of an *alterity*. An alterity (not simply an alternative) that, according to its very nature, excludes any possible assimilation of the exploited with the exploiters.'

9 Pasolini, 'Intervento al congresso del Partito Radicale,' in *Lettere luterane*, 195. This essay offered Rinaldo Rinaldi the title to his excellent study of Pasolini, *L'irriconoscibile Pasolini* (Rovito: Marra Editore, 1990).

10 For extended discussions of these features of Pasolini's work, see Naomi Greene, *Pier Paolo Pasolini: Cinema as Heresy*; and Maurizio Viano, *A Certain Realism: Making Use of Pasolini's Film Theory and Practice* (Berkeley: University of California Press, 1993). On homosexuality in Hollywood filmmaking, the reader is referred to the late Vito Russo's by now canonical *The Celluloid Closet* (New York: Harper, 1981). Other thematically oriented studies of gay cinema are found in Richard Dyer, *Now You See It: Studies on Lesbian and Gay Film* (New York and London: Routledge, 1990), and *The Matter of Images: Essays on Representations* (New York and London: Routledge, 1993).

11 And we should call to the reader's attention one of the few films that explicitly engaged in examining homosexuality in Italy, the delightfully ironic meta-documentary *Comizi d'amore* (*Love Meetings*). In this film Pasolini travels throughout the Italian peninsula interviewing Italians about their attitudes towards sex and taboos. And it is precisely when his 'informants' begin to engage in explicit discussions – especially about homosexuality – that the soundtrack goes silent, and the frame fills with the title 'auto-censura' ('self censorship'): that is, even in a documentary, a genre of communication and information, the silences and exclusions provide more insight than what is actually said.

12 See Susan Sontag, 'Notes on Camp,' in *Against Interpretation* (New York: Delta, 1967). See also Jack Babuscio, 'Camp and the Gay Sensibility,' in Richard Dyer, ed., *Gays and Film* (New York: New York Zoetrope, 1984), 40–57.

13 See John Di Stefano, 'My Affair with Pasolini,' in M. Gever, J. Greyson, and P. Parmer, eds, *Queer Looks: Perspectives on Lesbian and Gay Film and Video* (New York and London: Routledge, 1993), 292–300. Here Di Stefano launches a frontal attack on Pasolini for his 'self-loathing' and 'hypocritical' attachment to the boys of the ghettoes, which, according to my perspective, is largely beside the point. As Di Stefano writes: 'As visible as he was, in the public sphere as a gay man, he was not as radical as perhaps he wanted to be. For what he expressed, there was an equal amount left unvoiced. Pasolini was torn, his conviction diluted. He was still invisible' (300). Here, Di Stefano's ethic is one of representation, thematization, voice, identity, and empowerment, and thus Pasolini can only be found 'guilty' of not representing homosexual relationships openly and freely (ibid.). In response, I would align my own discussion with an approach suggested by Thomas Waugh, who has written in a very interesting manner on 'post-affirmative' gay filmmaking: films that narrate what he calls the 'third body' (and he refers to Pasolini's *Trilogy of Life* and *Teorema* as examples, among others). According to Waugh, post-affirmative films are those that 'manage to deconstruct without auto-destructing, that leave behind without anguish the fixed identifiers affirmed by earlier films, that seem to enjoy the struggle with definitions of identity as an ongoing process.' See Thomas Waugh, 'The Third Body: Patterns in the Construction of the Subject in Gay Male Narrative Film,' in in M. Gever, J. Greyson, and P. Parmer, eds, *Queer Looks*, 284.

14 Barthes, 'The Third Meaning,' in *Responsibility of Forms*, trans. Richard Howard (Berkeley: University of California Press, 1985), 55.

15 *HE*, 222; *EE*, 230.

16 'Acinema,' 55.

17 Ibid., 57.

18 See Ernesto Laclau, 'The Impossibility of Society,' *Canadian Journal of Political and Social Theory* 7, nos. 1–2 (Winter/Spring 1983). See also Laclau and Chantal Mouffe, 'Beyond the Positivity of the Social: Antagonisms and Hegemony,' in *Hegemony and Socialist Strategy*, 93–148.

19 On the extermination of homosexuals in the lager camps, and Pasolini's statements concerning continued victimization, see 'M. Daniel – A. Baudry: "Gli omosessuali,"' in *Scritti Corsari*, 255.

20 As Paolo Fabbri recently wrote, 'The crucial idea of the semiosis of the unspeakable sentence, of out-of-sight segments, and the project of freely creating, inside the discourse, the effect of a future addressee, is an aesthetic project that is not concluded or closed. It remains open for us.' See Fabbri, 'Free, Indirect, Discourse,' in Rumble and Testa, eds, *Pier Paolo Pasolini: Contemporary Perspectives*, 86.

21 Rinaldi, *L'irriconoscibile Pasolini*, 38. For a feminist discussion of the 'neuter' as the excluded 'third gender,' see Wanda Tommasi, 'La tentazione del neutro,' in *Diotima: Il pensiero della differenza sessuale* (Milan: La Tartaruga, 1990), 81–104.

22 Rimbaud's 'most revolutionary ambition for poetry,' according to Leo Bersani's excellent reading, 'was to make it mean as little as possible.' See Bersani, 'Rimbaud's Simplicity,' in *A Future for Astyanax: Character and Desire in Literature* (New York: Columbia University Press, 1984), 230.

23 For Pasolini's account of *Teorema*, see 'Incontro con Pasolini,' *Inquadrature* 15–16 (Fall 1968), 33–7. 'We have the arrival of a divine visitor in a bourgeois family. This visitation destroys everything the bourgeois characters thought about themselves: that visitor came to destroy. Authenticity, to use an old term, destroys inauthenticity. However, when he leaves, they all find themselves with a consciousness of their own inauthenticity and, what's more, an incapacity of being authentic – given the classist and historical impossibility of being so. Thus, each member of the family has a crisis, and the film ends, more or less, with the following moral: that whatever a bourgeois does is an error' (33). For an enthusiastic reading of 'ambisexed Eros' or 'Homeros' in *Teorema*, see Parker Tyler, *Screening the Sexes: Homosexuality in the Movies* (New York: Da Capo, 1993 [1972]), 122–4.

24 See Jean-François Lyotard, *The Inhuman*, trans. G. Bennington and R. Bowlby (Stanford: Stanford University Press, 1991): 'And what else is left to resist with but the debt which each soul has contracted with the miserable and admirable indetermination from which it was born and does not cease to be born?' (7).

25 Pasolini, *Trasumanar e organizzar*: in the title poem, the poet writes 'It is not by chance that I have the sacred and unctuous hand of Saint Paul / who pushes me to take this step. / Is not organizing contemporaneous with transhumanizing?'

26 And for Pasolini, film offered a 'possible language of potential human communication ... a language of social relationship.' See *HE*, 69.

27 Pasolini, *Il sogno di una cosa*.

28 Pasolini's approach to such topics appears to be most influenced by Freud's *Totem and Taboo*, in which the community of sons exorcises its 'debt' to the murdered father through sacrifice: a sacrifice that alludes to, but by the same gesture covers up, the original crime. See also Rene Girard, *Violence and the Sacred* (Baltimore: Johns Hopkins University Press, 1977).

29 'Laicism, yes sirs, is the fruit of bad religion. (In fact I say that it has become, itself, religion.)' Pasolini, 'L'Enigma di Pio XII,' *Trasumanar e organizzar*.

30 Wlad Godzich, 'Afterword: Religion, the State, and Post(al) Modernism,' in Sam Weber, *Institution and Interpretation* (Minneapolis: University of Minnesota Press, 1987), 162.

31 Lyotard, *Heidegger and 'the jews'*; see esp. 22. It should also be recalled that Pasolini often used the lager as a metaphor for the ghettoes of Western cities – for example, the *borgate* or slums of Rome in his novels or in the films *Accattone* or *Mamma Roma*. The ghetto contains the unproductive, homeless, and miserable elements of a society: to use narratological terminology, they are elements without a function – excessive – and therefore threaten the operativity of the system, destabilize the narrative economy.

32 Pasolini, 'L'Enigma di Pio XII,' *Trasumanar e organizzar*, 17 (emphasis in original). On the figure of the ghetto as the 'rear' of the megalopolis, the modern cityscape, see Lyotard, *The Inhuman*, 200, 202: 'To inhabit the uninhabitable is the condition of the ghetto' (200).

33 Ibid.

34 At this juncture the reader is referred to Lyotard's outstanding work on the logic of repression and denegation, and related issues of representation and recollection, which he approaches as a problem of 'the jews' as paradigmatic 'others': 'In defiance of etymology, one needs to understand "exceed" here in terms of the following three Latin verbs taken together: *ex-cedere*, to pass beyond, to go out; *ex-cidere* (from *cadere*), to fall outside of, to be dispossessed from; *ex-cidere* (from *caedere*), to detach by cutting, to excise. The soul is exceeded: dispossessed, passed beyond, excised through and by this something. This is the constitutive infirmity of the soul, its infancy and its misery.' Lyotard, *Heidegger and 'the jews,'* 17.

35 Pasolini's interest in the figure of Saint Paul, whose homosexuality he took for granted, is found clearest in one of his last screenplays for the unproduced film *San Paolo*. In this text Pasolini transports his character into modern Italy and the United States where he undergoes his martyrdom for his evangelical anti-racism. As Pasolini writes, the central theme of the film is 'the countering of "reality" with "sanctity": the world of the past – which, in its excess of presence and urgency, tends to escape into mystery, abstraction, into pure questioning – and the world of the divine which, in its religious abstraction, on the contrary, descends among men, making itself concrete and operative.' *San Paolo* (Turin: Einaudi, 1977), 7.

36 Pasolini, 'L'Umile Italia,' in *Le poesie*, 48.

Appendix: Film Credits and Synopses

Decameron

Shooting period: September–November, 1970
Locations: Ravello, Naples, Caserta, Casola, Amalfi, Vesuvius, Meta di
  Sorrento, Nepi, Viterbo, Bolzano, Yemen
Released 25 August 1971 (Trento)
Running time: 110 minutes
Silver Bear Award, Berlin Festival (1971)

Director of Photography: Tonino Delli Colli. Camera Operator: Giovanni Ciarlo. Camera Assistants: Carlo Tafani, Alessio Gelsini, Giuseppe Fornari. Art Director: Dante Ferretti. Assistant Art Director: Carlo Agate. Set Decorator: Andrea Fantacci. Music: Ennio Morricone and Pier Paolo Pasolini. Sound: Pietro Spadoni. Costume Designer: Danilo Donati. Assistant Costume Designer: Pietro Cicoletti. Costumes: Farani. Make-up: Alessandro Jacoponi. Hairdressing: Jole Cecchini. Stills Photographer: Mario Tursi. Post Production: Enzo Ocone. Continuity: Beatrice Banfi. Editors: Nino Baragli, Tatiana Casini Morigi. Assistant Editor: Anita Cacciolati. First Assistant Directors: Sergio Citti, Umberto Angelucci. Second Assistant Director: Paolo Andrea Mettel. Cast: Franco Citti (Ciappelletto), Ninetto Davoli (Andreuccio da Perugia), Jovan Jovanic (Rustico), Vincenzo Amato (Masetto), Angela Luce (Peronella), Pier Paolo Pasolini (Giotto's Pupil), Elisabetta Genovese (Caterina), Silvana Mangano (the Madonna), Guido Alberti, Gianni Rizzo, Giuseppe Zigaina, Giorgio Iovine, Salvatore Bilardo, Vincenzo Ferrigno, Luigi Seraponte, Antonio Diddio, Mirella Catanesi, Vincenzo De Luca, Erminio Nazzaro, Giovanni Filadoro, Lino Crispo, Alfredo Sivoli, E. Jannotta Carrino, Vittorio Vittori,

Monique Van Voren, Enzo Spitaleri, Luciano Telli, Anne Marguerite La-
troye, Gerard Exel, Wolfgang Hillinger, Franco Marlotta, Giacomo Rizzo,
Vittorio Fanfoni, Uhle Detlef Gerd, Adriana Donnorso, E. Maria De
Juliis, Patrizia De Clara, Guido Mannari, Michele Di Matteo, Giovanni
Esposito, Giovanni Scagliola, Giovanni Davoli, Giuliano Fratello, Lucio
Amatelli, Gabriella Frankel, Vincenzo Cristo. Production Companies:
PEA (Rome) / Les Productions Artistes Associés (Paris) / Artemis Film
(Berlin). Executive Producer: Franco Rossellini. Production Manager:
Mario Di Biase. Unit Manager: Sergio Galiano. Production Secretary: Vit-
torio Bucci. Line Producer: Alberto De Stefanis. Synch Sound: Cinefonico
Palatino. Sound Mixer: Mario Morigi, Gianni D'Amico.

Synopsis: The film consists of eight stories from Boccaccio's 14th-century
Decameron.   *Andreuccio of Perugia*: After being robbed by a woman who
pretends to be his long-lost sister, Andreuccio joins two thieves in their
raid on a dead Cardinal's tomb. After helping him into the sarcophagus
to collect the dead man's ring, the thieves treacherously close the lid.
Next day, a priest raises the lid, is horrified to receive a bite on the
leg, and runs off to leave Andreuccio free with the ring.   *Masetto and
the Nuns*: Pretending to be a deaf-mute, Masetto applies for a job as a
gardener at a convent. Encouraged by his silence, the nuns take turns to
seduce him. Masetto is soon so exhausted that, when the Mother Superior
herself approaches him, he tells her he has had enough. Undaunted, she
offers thanks to the recovery of his speech, makes him a saint, and insists
that he remain at the convent.   *Peronella*: Startled by her husband's early
return home, Peronella hides her lover at the bottom of a large jar. When
her husband tells her that he has been offered a good price for the jar, she
tells him she has had a higher offer, and the buyer is examining it now.
The lover emerges and, while her husband steps inside to clean the jar,
he and Peronella return to their lovemaking.   *Ciappelletto*: Ciappelletto,
a notorious libertine, is sent on a business trip to a Northern European
town. He falls ill and summons a priest to hear his lengthy, and false,
confession. The priest is so impressed that, when Ciappelletto dies, he
honours him with a saint's funeral.   *Lisabetta and Lorenzo*: Three Sicilian
brothers kill their sister's low-born lover. The girl learns where he is
buried and, with her nurse's help, uncovers the body, chops off the head,
and buries it in a pot of basil. Then, one night, in a vision, her lover
appears out of the basil pot to tell her who his murderers are. She swears
to seek revenge.   *Caterina*: She secretly arranges to spend the night with

her lover Riccardo on the terrace of her family's house. Her parents angrily discover them in the morning, but on remembering that Riccardo is the young Duke of Mantua, they offer to forgive him provided he agrees to marry Caterina right then and there.   *Tingoccio and Meuccio*: Two young rakes are haunted by the fear of punishment in the next world. When one of them, Meuccio, dies from sexual exhaustion, he reappears in a vision to reassure his friend Tingoccio. He tells him that in hell he has not been punished for lovemaking. Tingoccio happily runs off to a favourite girlfriend.   *Don Gianni*: A priest convinces a peasant couple that he can magically turn the wife into a horse and, with their consent, asks the wife to remove her clothes. When the priest reaches the moment of adding the horse's tail, the husband is appalled to see him thrust his penis into his wife's body.

I racconti di Canterbury

Shooting period: Winter 1971
Locations: Canterbury, Cambridge, Battle, St Oxyth, Layer Marney,
    Lavenham, Warwich, Wells, Chipping Campden
Released 2 September 1972 (Benevento)
Running time: 110 minutes
Golden Bear Award, Berlin Festival (1972)

Director of Photography: Tonino Delli Colli. Camera Operator: Carlo Tafani. Camera Assistant: Maurizio Lucchini. Art Director: Dante Ferretti. Assistant Art Director: Carlo Agate. Set Decorator: Kenneth Muggleston. Music: Selected by Pier Paolo Pasolini with the assistance of Ennio Morricone and Topic Records, Caedmon Records, Philips. Sound: Primiano Muratore. Key Grip: Augusto Diamanti. Gaffer: Alberto Ridolfi. Costume Designer: Danilo Donati. Assistant Costume Designer: Vanni Castellani. Costume House: Farani. Make-up: Otello Sisi. Hairdressing: Giancarlo De Leonardis. Stills Photographer: Mimmo Cattarinich. Post Production: Enzo Ocone. Continuity: Beatrice Banfi. Editor: Nino Baragli. Assistant Editors: Anita Cacciolati, Ugo De Rossi. First Assistant Directors: Sergio Citti, Umberto Angelucci. Second Assistant Director: Peter Shepherd. Cast: Hugh Griffith (January), Laura Betti (the Wife of Bath), Ninetto Davoli (Perkin), Franco Citti (the Devil), Josephine Chaplin (May), Pier Paolo Pasolini (Chaucer), John Francis Lane, Alan Webb,

J.P. Van Dyne, Vernon Dobtcheff, Adrian Strett, Ot, Derek Deadmin, Nicholas Smith, George Datch, Dan Thomas, Michael Balfour, Jenny Runacre, Peter Cain, Daniele Buckler, Settimio Castagna, Athol Coats, Judy Stewart-Murray, Tom Baker, Oscar Fochetti, Willoughby Goddard, Peter Stephen, Giuseppe Arrigo, Elisabetta Genovese, Gordon King, Patrick Duffett, Earmann Howell, Albert King, Eileen King, Heather Johnson, Robin Asquith, Martin Whelar, John McLaren, Edward Monteith Kervin, Franca Sciutto, Vittorio Fanfoni. Production Companies: PEA S.A.S. (Rome) / Les Productions Artistes Associés S.A. (Paris). Producer: Alberto Grimaldi. Production Manager: Alessandro von Normann. Unit Manager: Ennio Onorati. Production Secretary: Franca Tasso. Coordinators for the English Production: Adriano Magistretti, Anthony Moore. Press Office: Studio Longardi. Sound Recording: Cinefonico Palatino. Sound Effects: Luciano Anzellotti. Sound Mixer: Gianni D'Amico.

Synopsis: A group of pilgrims journeying to Canterbury enjoy an array of adventures or pass the hours of travel by recounting stories to one another. In *The Merchant's Tale*, old Sir January loses his sight shortly after his marriage to young May. His bride takes advantage of his blindness to arrange a tryst with the handsome Damian; but the gods restore the old man's vision in time for him to catch the lovers out.   In *The Miller's Tale*, in order to distract a gullible husband while he makes love to his wife, a cunning student pretends that the second Flood is at hand. The tables are turned, however, when two young rivals for the wife's affections injure the student's pride, and his tender parts, with a red-hot poker.   In *The Friar's Tale*, the devil takes the soul of a Summoner who spends his time catching people in the act of sex and blackmailing them.   *The Cook* narrates the story of Perkin, a young urchin whose slapstick sense of fun gets him fired from one job after another; and *The Steward* tells how two Cambridge students gain revenge on a dishonest miller by sleeping with his wife and daughter.   In *The Pardoner's Tale*, three young rogues who set off in search of Death discover a treasure chest beneath a tree; sooner than share the treasure, they plot to eliminate each other and meet death after all.   The much-married *Wife of Bath* relates a story from her own amorous past; while *The Summoner* paints a picture of Hell in which all the wicked Friars are gorged and excreted by the Devil.   As the pilgrims live through their adventures – or possibly just recount their stories – the poet Geoffrey Chaucer (Pasolini) is seen transcribing them for posterity.

Il fiore delle mille e una notte

Shooting period: February–May 1973
Locations: Ethiopia, North Yemen, South Yemen, Iran, Nepal
Released 20 June 1974 (Rome)
Running time: 129 minutes
Grand Prix Spécial du Jury, Cannes Festival (1974)

Screenplay Collaboration: Dacia Maraini. Director of Photography: Giuseppe Ruzzolini. Camera Operator: Allesandro Ruzzolini. Camera Assistant: Marcello Mastrogirolamo. Art Director: Dante Ferretti. Music: Ennio Morricone. Sound: Luciano Welisch. Costume Designer: Danilo Donati. Costume House: Farani. Make-up: Massimo Giustini. Hairdressing: Jole Cecchini. Wigs: Rocchetti-Carboni. Footwear: Pompei. Forwarders: Cecchetti. Stills Photogapher: Angelo Pennoni. Post Production: Enzo Ocone. Continuity: Beatrice Banfi. Editing: Nino Baragli, Tatiana Casini Morigi. Assistant Editors: Ugo De Rossi, Alfredo Menchini. Assistant Directors: Umberto Angelucci, Peter Shepherd. Cast: Ninetto Davoli (Aziz), Franco Citti (Genie), Franco Merli (Nur ed Din), Tessa Bouche (Aziza), Ines Pellegrini (Zumurrud), Margereth Clementi, Luigini Rocchi, Alberto Argentini (Prince Shahzaman), Francesco Paolo Governale (Prince Tadji), Salvatore Sapienza (Prince Yunan), Zeudi Biasiolo, Barbara Grandi, Elisabetta Vito Genovese, Gioacchino Castellina, Abadut Ghidel (Princess Dunya), Christian Alegny, Salvatore Verdetti, Jocelyne Munchenbach, Luigi Antonio Guerra, Jeanne Gauffin Matthieu, Francelise Noel, Franca Sciutto, Fessazion Gherentiel, Gian Idris, Ali Abdullah, Ghener Aielew, Mohamed Fara Scebani, Hassan Ali Ahmed, Rino Hammamet, Adila Ibrahim, Emanuel Matthews, Mohamed Ali Zedi. Production Companies: PEA (Rome) / Les Productions Artistes Associés (Paris). Producer: Alberto Grimaldi. Production Manager: Mario Di Biase. Unit Managers: Giuseppe Banchelli, Alessandro Mattei. Production Secretary: Carla Crovato. Accountants: Daniele Tiberi, Maurizio Forti. Press Office: Nico Naldini. Special Optical Effects: Rank Film Labs, England. Sound Recording: NIS Film-Rome. Sound Mixer: Fausto Ancillai.

Synopsis: Brought to auction, the slave-girl Zumurrud selects the inexperienced Nur ed Din as her new owner and enjoys initiating him sexually. That night, she tells him the story of a wager between Harun e Rashid and Queen Zobeida, who paired off a boy and a girl to see which would fall in love with the other first and thus prove his or her sex the weaker. However, against the expectations of the two players, the contest ends as a tie. Next morning, the infidel Bassum drugs Nur ed Din and kidnaps Zumurrud to return her to her former owner. A friendly woman arranges for the distraught Nur ed Din to retrieve his beloved, but he falls asleep at the rendezvous and Zumurrud is carried off by one of the Forty Thieves. Exercising her charms, she overcomes the leader of the Thieves and rides off in his clothes, arriving at a great city where her appearance fulfils a prophecy. Taken for a man, she is enthroned as king and 'married' to Hiyat, daughter of the high priest. She confides her identity to Hiyat, and tries to devise a way of luring Nur ed Din to the city. Elsewhere, the huntsman Taji encounters the nomadic Aziz at an oasis and asks to hear his story. Aziz recalls how he was attracted to the mysterious Budur on the day that he should have married Aziza; how he began a long series of secret assignments with Budur following Aziza's selfless guidance; how Aziza eventually committed suicide and how he found himself pressed into marriage with Ertay; and how Budur, learning of the marriage, castrated him. Bewitched by the story, Taji demands to be taken to Budur's house, now in a derelict state. He hires two passing holy men to restore it and enquires how they came to adopt their way of life. The elder tells how a meeting with a beautiful slave and her possessive owner, a demon, led to his being changed into a monkey; how he was found by seamen, who took him to their ruler; and how the ruler's daughter restored his natural form by a spell, at the cost of her own life. Jonaan, the younger, tells how he was shipwrecked and cast ashore on a rocky island, shrine of a tyrant god; how he toppled the god's idol, causing the island to sink; how he awoke on another island, where a merchant was concealing his son to protect him from a prophecy of murder; how he befriended the boy but then killed him during the night; and how he began a life of wandering as soon as he reached the mainland. The two men resume their travels. When the man-hating Princess Dunya chances to pass the house later, she recognizes the restored mosaics as images from her dreams. Nur ed Din has meanwhile been 'captured' by three nubile girls, who bathe and pamper him, but he tires of their pleasures and runs off. In the desert he meets a lion, who leads him to the city ruled by Zumurrud. She immediately spots her lost love, and presses him into her service. After teasing and humiliating him, she reveals her true identity, and the blissfully happy couple are reunited at last. 'What a night! God has created none like it before. Its start was bitter, but how sweet the end!'

Note: Synopses are modified versions of those found in the promotional catalogue, accompanying the travelling retrospective *Pier Paolo Pasolini: A Cinema of Poetry*, edited by Laura Betti and Ludovico Gambara Thovazzi: *Pier Paolo Pasolini: A Future Life* (Rome: Associazione 'Fondo Pier Paolo Pasolini,' 1989). Credit information is taken from this same source, as well as from the published screenplays of the *Trilogia della vita* (Bologna: Cappelli, 1975); reprinted by Mondadori (Milan: 1987).

Pasolini Filmography

Screenplays

1954 *La donna del fiume* (Dir. Mario Soldati). Co-scriptwriter.
1955 *Il prigioniero della montagna* (Dir. Luis Trenker). Co-sciptwriter.
1956 *Le notti di Cabiria* (Dir. Federico Fellini). Co-scriptwriter.
1957 *Marisa la civetta* (Dir. Mauro Bolognini). Co-scriptwriter.
1958 *Giovani mariti* (Dir. Mauro Bolognini). Scriptwriter.
1959 *La notte brava* (Dir. Mauro Bolognini). Scriptwriter.
1960 *Il bell'Antonio* (Dir. Mauro Bolognini). Co-scriptwriter.
    La giornata balorda (Dir. Mauro Bolognini). Co-scriptwriter.
    La lunga notte del '43 (Dir. Florestano Vancini). Co-scriptwriter.
    Il carro armato dell'8 settembre (Dir. Gianni Puccini). Co-scriptwriter.
    La dolce vita (Dir. Federico Fellini). Co-scriptwriter.
1961 *La ragazza in vetrina* (Dir. Luciano Emmer). Co-scriptwriter.
1962 *La commare secca* (Dir. Bernardo Bertolucci). Co-scriptwriter.
    Una vita violenta (Dirs. Paolo Heusch, Brunello Rondi). Adapted
    from Pasolini's novel, *Una vita violenta*.
1970 *Ostia* (Dir. Sergio Citti). Co-scriptwriter.
1973 *Storie scellerate* (Dir. Sergio Citti). Co-scriptwriter.

Written and Directed

1961 *Accattone*
1962 *Mamma Roma*
1963 *La ricotta*
    La rabbia

1964 *Comizi d'amore*
      Sopraluoghi in Palestina
      Il Vangelo secondo Matteo
1966 *Uccellacci e uccellini*
      La terra vista dalla luna
1967 *Che cosa sono le nuvole?*
      Edipo Re
1968 *Teorema*
      La sequenza del fiore di carta
1969 *Appunti per un film sull'India*
      Appunti per una Orestiade africana
      Porcile
      Medea
1971 *Decameron*
1972 *I racconti di Canterbury*
1974 *Il fiore delle mille e una notte*
1975 *Salò o le 120 giornate di Sodoma*

Published Screenplays

La notte brava. Filmcritica 10, nos. 91–2 (November–December 1959).
Mamma Roma. Milano: Rizzoli, 1962.
Il Vangelo secondo Matteo. Milan: Garzanti, 1965.
La ricotta. In *Alì dali occhi azzurri*. Milan: Garzanti, 1989 [1965]. Also found
     in this volume are *La notte brava*, *Accattone*, and *Mamma Roma*.
La commare secca. Filmcritica 16, no. 161 (October 1965).
Uccellacci e uccellini. Milan: Garzanti, 1966.
Edipo Re. Milan: Garzanti, 1967.
Che cosa sono le nuvole? Cinema e film 3, nos. 7–8 (Winter/Spring 1969).
Medea. Milan: Garzanti, 1970.
Ostia (written with Sergio Citti). Milan: Garzanti, 1970.
Il padre selvaggio. Turin: Einaudi, 1975.
Trilogia della vita. Bologna: Cappelli, 1975; repr. Mondadori, 1987.
San Paolo. Turin: Einaudi, 1977.
Sant'Infame (Written with Sergio Citti). Cinecritica 13 (April–June 1989).
Porno-Teo-Kolossal. Cinecritica 13 (April–June 1989).

Bibliography

Abruzzese, Alberto. 'Boccaccio come il Vangelo.' *Paese Sera* 22 (September 1970).

Abruzzese, Alberto, and Achille Pisanti. 'Cinema e letteratura.' In Alberto Asor Rosa, ed., *Letteratura italiana*, vol. 2: 807–36. Turin: Einaudi, 1983.

Adorno, Theodor, and Hans Eisler. *Komposition für den Film*. Munich: Roger and Berhard, 1969.

Agamben, Giorgio. *La comunità che viene*. Turin: Einaudi, 1990. [*The Coming Community*. Translated by Michael Hardt. Minneapolis: University of Minnesota Press, 1993.]

Ahern, John. 'Pasolini: His Poems, His Body.' *Parnassus* 2, no. 2 (Fall–Winter 1983–4): 103–26.

Alain-Miller, Jacques. 'Suture.' *Screen* 18, no. 4 (Winter 1977–8), 24–34.

Alberti, Leon Battista. *On Painting*. Translated by John R. Spencer. New Haven: Yale University Press, 1956.

Allen, Beverly (ed.). *Pier Paolo Pasolini: The Poetics of Heresy*. Saratoga, CA: Anma Libri, 1982.

Almansi, Guido. *The Writer as Liar: Narrative Techniques in the 'Decameron.'* London, Boston: Routledge and Kegan Paul, 1975.

Althusser, Louis. *Lenin and Philosophy*. Translated by Ben Brewster. London: New Left Books, 1971.

– *For Marx*. Translated by Ben Brewster. London: New Left Books, 1979.

Anzoino, Tommaso. *Pasolini*. Florence: La Nuova Italia, 1974.

Arpino, Giovanni. '*Decamerone* tutto nudo.' *La Stampa*, 8 October 1971.

Assunto, Roberto. *La critica d'arte nel pensiero medioevale*. Milano: Il Saggiatore, 1961.

Aycock, W., and M. Schoenecke (eds). *Film and Literature: A Comparative Approach to Adaptation*. Lubbock: Texas Tech University Press, 1988.

Babuscio, Jack. 'Camp and the Gay Sensibility.' In Richard Dyer, ed., *Gays and Film*, 40–57. New York: New York Zoetrope, 1984.

Bachman, Gideon. 'Il passato è sovversivo.' *Il Messaggiero* 24 (August 1973).

– 'La perdita della realtà e il cinema inintegrabile.' In L. De Giusti, ed., *Pier Paolo Pasolini: Il cinema in forma di poesia*. Pordenone, 1979.

Bakhtin, Mikhail. *Rabelais and His World*. Translated by Helene Iswolsky. Cambridge, MA: MIT Press, 1964.

– *The Dialogic Imagination*. Translated by Caryl Emerson and Michael Holquist. Austin: University of Texas Press, 1981.

Baldelli, Pio. *Film e opera letteraria*. Padua: Marsilio, 1964.

Barański, Zygmunt. 'Notes towards a Reconstruction: Pasolini and Rome 1950–51,' *The Italianist* 5 (1985), 138–49.

Barberi-Squarotti, Giorgio. 'La "cornice" del *Decameron* o il mito di Robinson.' In *Il potere della parola*, 5–63. Naples: Federico and Ardia, 1983.

Barth, John. 'Muse Spare Me.' In *The Sense of the Sixties*. Edited by Edward Quinn. New York: Free Press, 1968.

– *Chimera*. Greenwich: Fawcett, 1972.

– 'Tales within Tales within Tales.' In *The Friday Book*. New York: Putnam, 1984.

– *The Tidewater Tales: A Novel*. New York: Putnam, 1987.

Barthes, Roland. 'Literature Today.' In *Critical Essays*. Evanston: Northwestern University Press, 1972.

– *S/Z*. Translated by Richard Miller. New York: Hill and Wang, 1974.

– 'The Third Meaning.' In *The Responsibility of Forms*, 41–62. Translated by Richard Howard. Berkeley: University of California Press, 1985.

– *The Pleasure of the Text*. Translated by Richard Howard. New York: Hill and Wang, 1975.

– *Image, Music, Text*. Translated by Stephen Heath. London: Fontana, 1977.

– *Roland Barthes by Roland Barthes*. Translated by Richard Howard. New York: Hill and Wang, 1977.

– *Leçon: Leçon inaugurale de la Chaire de semiologie littéraire du Collège de France*. Paris: Seuil, 1978. [*Lezione*. Turin: Einaudi, 1981.]

– *A Lover's Discourse: Fragments*. Translated by Richard Howard. New York: Hill and Wang, 1978.

Bazin, André. *What Is Cinema?* 2 vols. Berkeley: University of California Press, 1967.

Bellezza, Dario. 'Io e Boccaccio.' *L'Espresso*, 22 November 1970.

– *Morte di Pasolini*. Milan: Mondadori, 1981.

Belsey, Catherine. *Critical Practice*. London: Methuen, 1980.

Benincasa, Carmine. *Sul manierismo come dentro a uno specchio*. Rome: Officina Edizioni, 1979.

Benjamin, Walter. *Illuminations*. Translated by Harry Zohn. New York: Schocken, 1969.
– *The Origin of German Tragic Drama*. London: New Left Books, 1977.
Benveniste, Émile. *Problems in General Linguistics*. Miami: University of Miami Press, 1971.
Berenice, A. 'Napoletano e popolaresco il "Boccaccio" di Pasolini.' *Paese Sera*, 19 June 1970.
Berger, John. *Ways of Seeing*. Harmondsworth: Penguin, 1972.
Bersani, Leo. *A Future for Astyanax: Character and Desire in Literature*. New York: Columbia University Press, 1984.
Bertini, Antonio (ed.). *Teoria e tecnica del film in Pasolini*. Rome: Bulzoni, 1979.
Betti, Laura (ed.). *Pasolini: Cronaca giudiziaria, persecuzione, morte*. Milan: Garzanti, 1977.
Bevan, David. 'Pasolini and Boccaccio,' *Literature/Film Quarterly* 5 (1977), 23–9.
Bevilacqua, Mirko. *L'ideologia letteraria del 'Decameron.'* Rome: Bulzoni, 1978.
Bianchi, Pietro. 'Dalla poesia al *Decamerone.' Il Giorno*, 4 June 1971.
Biancofiore, Angela, and Augusto Ponzio. 'Intorno ai "Criteri per lo studio ideologico di un autore" di Ferruccio Rossi-Landi.' *Allegoria* 11–12 (1987), 89–99.
Bigazzi, Vanna Lippi (ed.). *I volgarizzamenti trecenteschi dell'Ars amandi e dei Remedia amoris*. Florence: Accademia della Crusca, 1987.
Bloom, Harold. *The Anxiety of Influence*. New York: Oxford University Press, 1975.
Bluestone, George. *Novels into Films*. Baltimore: Johns Hopkins University Press, 1957.
Boarini, Vittorio (ed.). *Erotismo, eversione, merce*. Bologna: Cappelli, Editore, 1974.
Boccaccio, Giovanni. *De Genealogia Deorum*. Edited by V. Romano. Bari: 1951.
– *Decameron*. Edited by Cesare Segre. Milan: Mursia, 1987. [English translation by G.H. McWilliam. Harmondsworth: Penguin, 1972.]
Bongie, Chris. 'A Post-Script to Transgression: The Exotic Legacy of Pier Paolo Pasolini.' In *Exotic Memories: Literature, Colonialism, and the Fin de Siècle*, 188–228. Stanford, CA: Stanford University Press, 1991.
Bordwell, David. *Narration in the Fiction Film*. Madison: University of Wisconsin Press, 1985.
– *Making Meaning: Inference and Rhetoric in the Interpretation of Cinema*. Cambridge, MA: Harvard University Press, 1989.
Boyum, Joy Gould. *Double Exposure: Fiction into Film*. New York: New American Library, 1985.
Brakhage, Stan. *Brakhage Scrapbook: Collected Writings 1964–1980*. Edited by Robert A. Haller. New Paltz, NY: Documentext, 1982.

Branca, Vittore. 'Boccaccio moderno.' *Corriere della Sera*, 20 March 1975, 3.
– *Boccacio medievale*. Florence: Sansoni, 1981
Branigan, Edward R. *Point of View in the Cinema: A Theory of Narration and Subjectivity in Classical Cinema*. Berlin, New York, and Amsterdam: Mouton, 1984.
Braudy, Leo. *The World in the Frame: What We See in Films*. Chicago: University of Chicago Press, 1976.
Brewer, Derek. 'Gothic Chaucer.' In D. Brewer, ed., *Geoffrey Chaucer*. Cambridge, MA: D.S. Brewer, 1990.
Browne, Nick. 'The Spectator in the Text: The Rhetoric of *Stagecoach*.' *Film Quarterly* 29, no. 2 (Winter 1975–6).
Brunetta, Gian Piero. *Forma e parola nel cinema. Il film muto: Pasolini, Antonioni*. Padova: Liviana, 1970.
– *Storia del cinema italiano*. 2 vols. Rome: Editori Riuniti, 1979.
– 'La migrazione dei generi dalla biblioteca alla filmoteca.' *Italian Quarterly* 81 (1980), 83–90.
– 'Itinerario di Pier Paolo Pasolini verso il mito di Edipo.' *Rivista di Studi Italiani* 2, no. 2 (December 1984).
– 'La conquista dei sogni: D'Annunzio e Pirandello.' *Annali d'Italianistica* 6 (1988), 18–37.
– (ed.). *Letteratura e cinema*. Bologna: Zanichelli, 1976.
Brunette, Peter, and David Willis. *Screen/Play: Derrida and Film Theory*. Princeton: Princeton University Press, 1989.
Bruni, Francesco. *Boccaccio: L'invenzione della letteratura mezzana*. Bologna: Il Mulino, 1990.
Bruno, Edoardo. 'La sacralità erotica del *Decameron* di Pasolini.' *Filmcritica* 11 (August 1971), 217.
– *Il film e l'oggetto*. Rome: Bulzoni, 1984.
Burch, Noël. *Theory of Film Practice*. Princeton: Princeton University Press, 1981.
Calabrese, Omar. *L'età neobarocca*. Rome, Bari: Laterza, 1989.
Cannon, JoAnn. *Postmodern Italian Fiction: The Crisis of Reason in Calvino, Eco, Sciascia, Malerba*. Rutherford, NJ: Fairleigh Dickinson University Press, 1989.
Capellanus, Andreas. *De amore*. Havnia: Libraria Gaddiana, 1892. [*The Art of Courtly Love*. Translated, with an Introduction, by John J. Parry. New York: Frederick Ungar, 1959.]
Carravetta, Peter, and Paolo Spedicato (eds). *Postmoderno e letteratura: Percorsi e visioni della critica in America*. Milan: Bompiani, 1984.
Carroll, Noël. *Mystifying Movies: Fads and Fallacies in Contemporary Film Theory*. New York: Columbia University Press, 1988.

Casi, Stefano. 'Il teatro di *Salò*' per una tragedia personale.' In *Le giovani generazioni e il cinema di Pier Paolo Pasolini*. Rome: Associazione 'Fondo Pier Paolo Pasolini,' 1989.

– (ed.). *Desiderio di Pasolini*. Turin: La Sonda, 1990.

– *Pasolini: Un'idea di teatro*. Udine: Campanotto Editore, 1990.

Chaucer, Geoffrey. *The Canterbury Tales*. London: J.M. Dent and Sons, 1939.

Chiarini, Luigi. *Cinema e film*. Rome: Bulzoni, 1972.

Chiesa, A. 'Come Pasolini concilia cinema e letteratura.' *Paese Sera*, 20–21 September 1961.

Ciavolella, Massimo. *La 'malattia d'amore' dall'antichità al medioevo*. Rome: Bulzoni, 1975.

Cicchitti, Alejandro. 'Del pensiero selvaggio.' In *Le giovani generazioni e il cinema di Pier Paolo Pasolini*, 7–14. Rome: Fondo Pier Paolo Pasolini, 1989.

Coghill, Nevill. *The Poet Chaucer*. London: Oxford University Press, 1968 [1949].

Cohen, Keith. *Film and Fiction*. New Haven: Yale University Press, 1979.

Comolli, Jean Louis. 'Technique and Ideology: Camera, Perspective, Depth of Field.' *Film Reader* 2 (1977), 128–40.

Contini, Gianfranco. 'Testimonianze per Pier Paolo Pasolini.' *Il Ponte*, 30 April 1980.

Corrain, Lucia. 'La grammatica della duplicazione.' *Carte semiotiche* 1 (September 1985), 97–119.

Corti, Maria. 'Pasolini aveva ragione.' In Alfredo Todisco, ed., *Ma che lingua parliamo?* Milan: Longanesi, 1984.

Costa, Antonio. 'Pasolini's Semiological Heresy.' In Paul Willemen, ed., *Pier Paolo Pasolini*, 32–42. London: British Film Institute, 1977.

– 'Effetto dipinto.' *Cinema e cinema* 54–5 (January–August 1989), 37–48.

Costa-Lima, Luiz. *Control of the Imaginary: Reason and Imagination in Modern Times*. Minneapolis: University of Minnesota Press, 1988.

Cottino-Jones, M. *Order from Chaos: Social and Aesthetic Harmonies in Boccaccio's 'Decameron.'* Washington: University Press of America, 1982.

Coward, Rosalind. 'Lacan and Signification.' *Edinburgh Magazine*, no. 1 (1984), 6–21.

Crary, Jonathan. 'Spectacle, Attention, Counter-Memory.' *October* 50 (Fall 1989), 97–106.

– *Techniques of the Observer*. Boston: MIT Press, 1992.

Da Accattone a Salò. Bologna: Tip. Compositori, 1982.

De Facendes, D., and J. Mascotto. 'Entre le mythe et pragma: Place et fonction du mythe dans l'oeuvre de Pier Paolo Pasolini.' *Études Littéraires* 17, no. 1 (April 1984), 95–116.

De Giusti, Luciano (ed.). *Pier Paolo Pasolini. Il cinema in forma di poesia.* Pordenone, 1979.

– *I film di Pier Paolo Pasolini.* Rome: Gremese, 1983.

De Lauretis, Teresa. 'Language, Representation, Practice: Re-reading Pasolini's Essays on Cinema.' *Italian Quarterly* 82–3 (Fall/Winter 1981), 159–66.

– *Alice Doesn't: Feminism, Semiotics, Cinema.* Bloomington: Indiana University Press, 1984.

– *Technologies of Gender: Essays on Theory, Film, and Fiction.* Bloomington: Indiana University Press, 1987.

Deleuze, Gilles. *Cinema 1: The Movement Image.* Translated by Hugh Tomlinson and Barbara Habberjam. Minneapolis: University of Minnesota Press, 1986.

– *Cinema 2: The Time Image.* Translated by Hugh Tomlinson and Barbara Habberjam. Minneapolis: University of Minnesota Press, 1989.

D'Elia, Gianni. 'Senza Pasolini.' *Nuovi argomenti*, no. 27 (July–September 1988), 123–6.

Della Volpe, Galvano. 'Il verosimile filmico' [1952]. In G.P. Brunetta, ed., *Cinema e letteratura.* Bologna: Zanichelli, 1976.

De Mauro, Tullio. *Storia linguistica dell'Italia unita.* Bari: Laterza, 1976.

Derrida, Jacques. *Of Grammotology.* Translated by Gayatri C. Spivak. Baltimore and London: Johns Hopkins University Press, 1976.

De Santis, Gualtiero, et al. (eds). *Perché Pasolini?* Florence: Guaraldi Editore, 1978.

Di Giammatteo, Fernaldo. *Lo scandolo Pasolini.* Rome: Biblioteca del Centro Sperimentale Cinematografico, 1976.

Di Stefano, John. 'My Affair with Pasolini,' In M. Gever, J. Greyson, and P. Parmer, eds, *Queer Looks: Perspectives on Lesbian and Gay Film and Video*, 292–300. New York and London: Routledge, 1993.

Doane, Mary Anne, Patricia Mellencamp, and Linda Williams (eds). *Revision: Essays in Feminist Film Criticism.* Frederick, MD: University Publications of America and the American Film Institute, 1984.

Dondis, Donis A. *A Primer of Visual Literacy.* Cambridge, MA: MIT Press, 1973.

Duflot, Jean. *Il sogno del centauro.* Roma: Editori Riuniti, 1983.

Dyer, Richard. *Now You See It: Studies on Lesbian and Gay Film.* New York and London: Routledge, 1990.

– *The Matter of Images: Essays on Representations.* New York and London: Routledge, 1993.

Eco, Umberto. *L'opera aperta.* Milan: Bompiani, 1962.

– *Lector in fabula.* Milan: Bompiani, 1979.

– 'The Return of the Middle Ages.' *Faith in Fakes*, 56–85. Translated by W. Weaver. London: Secker and Warburg, 1986.

- 'The Comic and the Rule.' In *Faith in Fakes*. London: Secker and Warburg, 1986.
- 'Alcune verifiche: Il cinema e il problema della pittura contemporanea.' In *La struttura assente*, 149–63. Milan: Bompiani, 1989 [1968].

Eidsvik, C. 'Towards a "Politique des adaptations."' *Literature/Film Quarterly* 3 (1975), 255–63.

Eimerl, Sarel. *The World of Giotto*. New York: Time Inc., 1967.

Eisenstein, Sergei. 'Dickins, Griffith, and the Film Today.' In *Film Form*. Translated by Jay Leyda. New York: Harcourt, Brace, and Jovanovich, 1949.

Elbow, Peter. *Oppositions in Chaucer*. Middletown, CT: Wesleyan University Press, 1975.

Elias, Norbert. *The Civilizing Process*. 3 vols. Translated by Edmund Jephcott. New York: Pantheon, 1982.

'Énonciation et cinéma.' Special issue of *Communications*: 38 (1983).

Faldini, F., and G. Fofi (eds). *Il cinema italiano d'oggi: 1970–84. Raccontati dai suoi protagonisti*. Milan: Mondadori, 1984.

Ferrero, Adelio. *Il cinema di Pier Paolo Pasolini*. Venice: Marsilio, 1977.

Ferretti, Gian Carlo. 'Mio padre, quando sono nato ...' *Nuovi argomenti*, no. 8 (October–December 1983), 123–34.

Firpo, Luigi. 'Verso il tramonto della sessualità.' *La Stampa*, 8 October 1972.

Fortini, Franco. 'Carteggio inedito Pasolini–Fortini.' *Nuova Generazione*, October 1976: 15–31.
- 'Pasolini o il rifiuto della maturità.' In *Nuovi saggi italiani*, vol. 2: 208–16. Milan: Garzanti, 1987.
- *Attraverso Pasolini*. Turin: Einaudi, 1993.

Foster, Hal (ed.). *Vision and Visuality*. Seattle: Bay Press, 1988.

Foster, Harold M. *The New Literacy: The Language of Film and Television*. Urbana, IL: National Council of Teachers of English, 1979.

Foucault, Michel. *The Order of Things*. New York: Vintage, 1970.
- 'Les matins gris de la tolérance.' *Le Monde*, 23 March 1977.
- 'A Preface to Transgression.' In *Language, Counter-Memory, Practice*. Translated by Donald F. Bouchard and Sherry Simon. Ithaca: Cornell University Press, 1977.
- *Discipline and Punish: The Birth of the Prison*. Translated by Alan Sheridan. New York: Vintage, 1979.
- *History of Sexuality*, vol. 1. Translated by Robert Hurley. New York: Vintage, 1980.

Friedrich, Pia. *Pier Paolo Pasolini*. Boston: Twayne, 1982.

Gambetti, Giacomo. 'Pasolini da Boccaccio a Chaucer: Per una "Trilogia popolare, libera, erotica."' *Cineforum*, March 1974: 221–9.

Gardner, John. *The Poetry of Chaucer.* Carbondale: Southern Illinois University Press, 1977.

Gérard, Fabien S. *Pasolini ou le mythe de la barbarie.* Bruxelles: Éditions de l'Université de Bruxelles, 1981.

Gervais, Marc. *Pier Paolo Pasolini.* Paris: Seghers, 1973.

Gibson, Michael. *Bruegel.* Seacaucus, NJ: Wellfleet Press, 1989.

Giddings, R., K. Selby, and C. Wensley. *Screening the Novel: The Theory and Practice of Literary Dramatization.* London: MacMillan, 1990.

Gingras, Nicole. 'Peter Greenaway: The Photographic Effect and the Disquieting Stability.' *Parachute* 52 (1988), 23–8.

Le giovani generazioni e il cinema di Pier Paolo Pasolini. Rome: Associazione 'Fondo Pier Paolo Pasolini,' 1989.

Girard, René. *Violence and the Sacred.* Translated by Patrick Gregory. Baltimore: Johns Hopkins University Press, 1977.

Gittes, Katherine Slater. 'The *Canterbury Tales* and the Arabic Frame Tradition.' *PMLA* 98, no. 2 (March 1983).

Givens, Azzura B. *La dottrina d'amore nel Boccaccio.* Messina and Florence: G. D'Anna, 1968.

Godzich, Wlad. 'Afterword: Religion, the State, and Post(al) Modernism.' In S. Weber, *Institution and Interpretation,* 153–64. Minneapolis: University of Minnesota Press, 1987.

Goldmann, Lucien. *Per una sociologia del romanzo.* Milan: Bompiani, 1964.

Golino, Enzo. *Pier Paolo Pasolini: Il sogno di una cosa. Pedagogia, eros, letteratura dal mito del popolo alla società di massa.* Bologna: Il Mulino, 1985.

Gombrich, E.H. *Art and Illusion: A Study in the Psychology of Pictorial Representation.* Princeton: Princeton University Press, 1961.

Gondoni, Paola. 'Pier Paolo Pasolini tra cinema e realtà.' In *Le giovani generazioni e il cinema di Pier Paolo Pasolini,* 147–50. Rome: Fondo Pier Paolo Pasolini, 1989.

Gramsci, Antonio. *Quaderni del carcere.* Turin: Einaudi, 1975.

– *Selections from Cultural Writings.* Edited by David Forgacs and Geoffrey Nowell-Smith. Translated by William Boelhower. Cambridge, MA: Harvard University Press, 1985.

Grassi, Giovanna. 'Il *Decamerone* dei guaglioni.' *La Domenica del Corriere* 122 (24 November 1970).

Grazzini, Giovanni. 'Boccaccio sullo schermo.' *Studi sul Boccaccio* 7 (1973): 369–73.

– 'Al cinema col Boccaccio.' In *Boccaccio e d'intorni,* 323–6. Florence: Olschki, 1983.

Green, Martin. 'The Dialectic of Adaptation: The *Canterbury Tales* of Pier Paolo Pasolini.' *Literature/Film Quarterly* 4 (1976), 46–53.

Greene, Naomi. 'Art and Ideology in Pasolini's Films.' *Yale Italian Studies* 1, no. 3 (1977), 311–76.

- *Pier Paolo Pasolini: Cinema as Heresy*. Princeton: Princeton University Press, 1990.

Gregory, R.L. *The Intelligent Eye*. New York: McGraw-Hill, 1970.

Grignaffini, G. 'Rosso sangue.' *Cinema e cinema* 54–5 (January–August 1989).

Grossini, Giancarlo. *I 120 film di Sodoma: Analisi del cinema pornografico*. Bari: Edizioni Dedalo, 1982.

Harrington, John. *Film and/as Literature*. Englewood Cliffs, NJ: Prentice Hall, 1977.

Hastings, R. 'To Teach or Not to Teach: The Moral Dimension of the *Decameron* Reconsidered.' *Italian Studies* 44 (1989), 19–40.

Hauser, Arnold. *Mannerism: The Crisis of the Renaissance and the Origin of Modern Art*. 2 vols. Translated by Eric Mosbacher. London: Routledge and Kegan Paul, 1965.

Heath, Stephen. *Questions of Cinema*. Bloomington: Indiana University Press, 1981.

Heidegger, Martin. 'The Age of the World Picture.' In *The Question Concerning Technology and Other Essays*, 115–54. Translated by William Lovitt. New York: Harper, 1977.

Henderson, Brian. 'Towards a Non-Bourgeois Camera Style.' In G. Mast and E. Cohen, eds, *Film Theory and Criticism*. New York: Oxford University Press, 1979.

Hollander, Ann. *Moving Pictures*. New York: Knopf, 1989.

Horton, Andrew, and Joan Magretta (eds). *Modern European Filmmakers and the Art of Adaptation*. New York: Frederick Ungar, 1981.

Hutcheon, Linda. *A Theory of Parody*. London and New York: Methuen, 1985.

- *A Poetics of Postmodernism*. London: Routledge and Kegan Paul, 1988.

Iannucci, Amilcare. 'Dante, Television, and Education.' *Quaderni d'italianistica* 10, nos. 1–2 (Spring/Fall 1989), 1–34.

Jameson, Fredric. *The Political Unconscious: Narrative as a Socially Symbolic Act*. Ithaca: Cornell University Press, 1981.

- 'Postmodernism or the Cultural Logic of Late Capital.' *New Left Review* 146 (1984), 53–92.

- *Postmodernism or the Cultural Logic of Late Capital*. Durham: Duke University Press, 1990.

- *The Geopolitical Aesthetic: Cinema and Space in the World System*. Bloomington: Indiana University Press, 1992.

- *Signatures of the Visible*. New York and London: Routledge, 1992.

Jattarelli, Emidio. 'Pornografia a dispense con il Decamerone.' *Il Tempo*, 30 June 1971.

Jauss, Hans Robert. *Toward an Aesthetic of Reception.* Translated by Timothy Bahti. Minneapolis: University of Minnesota Press, 1982.

Jay, Martin. 'Scopic Regimes of Modernity.' In Hal Foster, ed., *Vision and Visuality*, 3–8. Seattle: Bay Press, 1988.

Jevolella, Massimo (ed.). *Le mille e una notte.* Translated by Armando Domenicis. Milan: Mondadori, 1984.

Jungmann, J.A. *Missarum Sollemnia.* Translated by Francis A. Brunner. Westminster, MD: Christian Classics, 1986.

Kendrick, Laura. *Chaucerian Play: Comedy and Control in the 'Canterbury Tales.'* Berkeley: University of California Press, 1988.

Koch, Gertrud. 'The Body's Shadow Realm.' *October* 50 (Fall 1989), 3–30.

Koch, Ludovica. 'Sul pastiche.' In *Le lettere rubate*, 7–26. Naples: Istituto Universitario Orientale, 1983.

Kracauer, Siegfried. 'Interlude: Film and Novel.' In *Theory of Film.* London: Oxford University Press, 1960.

Kuhn, Annette. *Women's Pictures: Feminism and Cinema.* London: Routledge and Kegan Paul, 1982.

Lacan, Jacques. *Écrits.* Translated by Alan Sheridan. New York: Norton, 1977.

Laclau, Ernesto. 'The Impossibility of Society.' *Canadian Journal of Political and Social Theory* 7, nos. 1–2 (Winter/Spring 1983).

Laclau, Ernesto, and Chantal Mouffe. *Hegemony and Socialist Strategy: Towards a Radical Democratic Politics.* London: Verso, 1985.

Landy, Marcia. 'Neorealism, Politics, and Language in the Films of the Tavianis.' *Annali d'Italianistica* 6 (1988), 236–51.

Lawrence, William W. *Chaucer and the 'Canterbury Tales.'* New York: Columbia University Press, 1950.

Lawton, Ben. 'Theory and Practice in Pasolini's Trilogy of Life: *Decameron.'* *Quarterly Review of Film Studies* 2, no. 4 (November 1977), 406–7.

– 'The Evolving Rejection of Homosexuality, the Sub-Proletariat and the Third World in the Films of Pier Paolo Pasolini.' *Italian Quarterly* 21 (1980), 167–73.

– 'The Storyteller's Art: Pasolini's *Decameron.'* In A. Horton and J. Magretta, eds, *Modern European Filmmakers and the Art of Adaptation.* New York: Frederick Ungar, 1981.

Lazagna, P. *Pasolini di fronte al problema religioso.* Bologna: Edizioni Dehoniane, 1970.

Le Goff, Jacques. *Your Money or Your Life: Economy and Religion in the Middle Ages.* Translated by Patricia Ranum. New York: Zone Books, 1988.

Longhi, Roberto. 'Giotto spazioso.' In *Da Cimabue a Morandi.* Milan: Mondadori, 1973.

– *Cinquecento classico e cinquecento manieristico.* Florence: Sansoni, 1976.

Lovell, Terry. *Pictures of Reality: Aesthetics, Politics and Pleasure*. London: British Film Institute, 1980.

Lukács, Gyorgy. 'Il romanzo come epopea borghese.' In *Problemi di teoria del romanzo*, 133–78. Turin: Einaudi, 1976.

Luperini, Romano. 'Semantica e interpretazione.' *Allegoria* 9 (1986), 11–66.

– *L'Allegoria del Moderno*. Rome: Editori Riuniti, 1990.

Luzi, Alfredo, and Luigi Martellini (eds). *Pier Paolo Pasolini*. Urbino: Argalia, 1973.

Lyotard, Jean-François. 'Interview.' *Diacritics*, Fall 1984.

– 'Acinema.' *Wide Angle* 2, no. 3 (1978), 52–9.

– *The Inhuman*. Translated by Geoffrey Bennington and Rachel Bowlby. Stanford: Stanford University Press, 1991.

– *Heidegger and 'the jews.'* Minneapolis: University of Minnesota Press, 1990.

MacCabe, Colin. 'Realism and the Cinema: Notes on Some Brechtian Theses.' *Screen* 15, no. 2 (Summer 1974), 7–27.

– 'Theory and Film: Principles of Realism and Pleasure.' *Screen* 17, no. 3 (Autumn 1976), 7–29.

– *Godard: Images, Sounds, Politics*. Bloomington: Indiana University Press, 1980.

Macciocchi, Maria-Antonietta. 'Pasolini: Assassinat d'un dissident.' *Tel Quel* 76 (Summer 1978).

– *Duemila anni di felicità*. Milan, 1983.

McLuhan, Marshall, and Hawley Parker. *Through the Vanishing Point: Space in Poetry and Painting*. New York: Harper and Row, 1968.

McNeil, John T., and Helena M. Gamer (eds). *Medieval Handbooks of Penance: A Translation of the Principal 'libri poenitentiales.'* New York: Columbia University Press, 1990 [1938].

Madeo, Liliana. 'Per il *Decamerone*, 80 denunce.' *La Stampa*, 11 February 1972.

Magrelli, Enrico. *Con Pier Paolo Pasolini*. Rome: Bulzoni, 1977.

Malone, Kemp. *Chapters on Chaucer*. Baltimore: Johns Hopkins University Press, 1951.

Mancini, Michele, and Giuseppe Perrella (eds). *Pier Paolo Pasolini: Corpi e luoghi*. Rome: Theorema Edizioni, 1981.

Mannino, V. *Il 'discorso' di Pasolini*. Rome: Argileto, 1973.

Maraini, Dacia. 'Il momento della negazione.' *Sipario*, August–September 1968.

Marcus, Millicent. *An Allegory of Form: Literary Self-Consciousness in the 'Decameron.'* Saratoga, CA: Anma Libri, 1979.

– 'The *Decameron*: Pasolini as a Reader of Boccaccio.' *Italian Quarterly* 82–3 (Fall/Winter 1980–1), 175–80.

– *Filmmaking by the Book: Italian Cinema and Literary Adaptation.* Baltimore: Johns Hopkins University Press, 1993.

Marcuse, Herbert. *The Aesthetic Dimension: Toward a Critique of Marxist Aesthetics.* Boston: Beacon Press, 1978.

Marino, Lucia. *The Decameron's 'Cornice': Allusion, Allegory, and Iconology.* Ravenna: Longo, 1979.

Martellini, Luigi (ed.). *Il dialogo, il potere, la morte.* Bologna: Cappelli, 1979.

Martini, S. 'La Mangano mi ricorda mia madre.' *Tempo Illustrato,* 16 April 1968.

Marx, Karl. *Capital,* vol. 1. New York: Vintage, 1977.

Massari, G. 'L'idea delle mille e una notte.' *Il Mondo,* 31 May 1973.

Mayne, Judith. *Private Novels Public Films.* Athens, GA, and London: University of Georgia Press, 1988.

Mazzotta, G. *The World at Play in Boccaccio's 'Decameron.'* Princeton: Princeton University Press, 1986.

Meccoli, Domenico. 'Nel nostro cinema il filone sociale non è ancora esaurito.' *Epoca* 22 (3 October 1971), 1097.

Melchiorre, Virgilio, and Anna Maria Cascetta (eds). *Il corpo in scena. La rappresentazione del corpo nella filosofia e nelle arti.* Milan: Vita e Pensiero, 1983.

Metz, Christian. *Film Language.* Translated by Michael Taylor. London: Oxford University Press, 1974.

– *The Imaginary Signifier.* Translated by Celia Britton. Bloomington: Indiana University Press, 1982.

Miccichè, Lino. 'Pasolini: La morte e la storia.' *Cinema sessanta* 121, May–June 1978.

– 'Contestazione e controcontestazione.' In *Per conoscere Pasolini,* 48–57. Rome: Bulzoni and Teatro Tenda, 1978.

– 'Cinema e letteratura.' In *La ragione e lo sguardo: saggi e note sul cinema,* 147–77. Cosenza: Lerici, 1979.

Michalczyk, John J. *The Italian Political Filmmakers.* London and Toronto: Associated University Presses, 1986.

Micheli, Sergio. 'Perpetuazione e sublimazione del "nudo" nei film di P.P. Pasolini.' *Salvo imprevisto* 3, no. 1 (January/April 1976).

Mieli, Mario. *Elementi di critica omosessuale.* Turin: Einaudi, 1977.

Moneti, Guglielmo. 'Per una lettura della *Trilogia della vita* di Pier Paolo Pasolini.' *Le giovani generazioni e il cinema di Pier Paolo Pasolini,* 37–50. Rome: Fondo Pier Paolo Pasolini, 1989.

Moravia, Alberto. 'La palisse fa il censore.' *L'Espresso,* 7 November 1973.

– *Al cinema.* Milan: Bompiani, 1975.

– 'Sade per Pasolini un sasso contro la società.' *Corriere della Sera,* 6 December 1975.

Morisette, Bruce. *Novels and Film: Essays in Two Genres.* Chicago and London: University of Chicago Press, 1985.

Mukarovsky, Jan. *Il significato dell'estetica.* Turin: Einaudi, 1973.

Mulvey, Laura. 'Visual Pleasure and Narrative Cinema.' *Screen* 16, no. 3 (1975), 6–18.

Mumford, Lewis. *The City in History.* New York: Harcourt, Brace and World, 1961.

Muzzioli, Francesco. 'Elementi sperimentali e conservazione delle strutture in Pasolini.' *Rapporti* 24–5 (January–June 1982), 29–42.

Naldini, Nico. *Nei campi del Friuli: La giovinezza di Pier Paolo Pasolini.* Milan: 1984.

– 'Pier Paolo, mio cugino.' *Nuovi argomenti,* no. 14 (April–June 1985), 127–31.

– *Pasolini: Una vita.* Turin: Einaudi, 1989.

Olson, Glending. *Literature as Recreation in the Later Middle Ages.* Ithaca: Cornell University Press, 1982.

Ong, Walter J. *Orality and Literacy.* London and New York: Methuen, 1982.

Orr, C. 'The Discourse on Adaptation.' *Wide Angle* 2 (1984), 72–6.

Oudart, Jean Pierre. 'Cinema and Suture.' *Screen* 18, no. 4 (Winter 1977–8), 35–47.

Ovid (P. Ovidius Naso). *The Art of Love.* Translated by Rolfe Humphries. Bloomington: Indiana University Press, 1957.

Padoan, Giorgio. 'Mondo aristocratico e mondo comunale nell'ideologia e nell'arte del Boccaccio.' *Studi sul Boccaccio* 2 (1964), 81–216.

Palumbo, Cesare. *Assassiniamo il poeta: Pier Paolo Pasolini.* Cosenza: Edizioni Pellegrini, 1978.

Panofsky, Erwin. *Renaissance and Renascences in Western Art.* Stockholm: Almquist and Wiksell, 1960.

Paolozzi, Letizia. 'Adesso ci parlo di Pasolini.' *Vie nuove* 25 (23 December 1970).

Pasolini, Pier Paolo. *Ragazzi di vita.* Milan: Garzanti, 1955.

– *Le ceneri di Gramsci.* Milan: Garzanti, 1957.

– 'Pasolini risponde a *Il Punto*: Letteratura e cinema non sono due componenti diverse di un'unica fenomenologia culturale.' *Il Punto,* 18 January 1958.

– *Una vita violenta.* Milan: Garzanti, 1959.

– 'Strumenti di governo (questionario del "libro e televisione").' *Leggere* 6 (October 1960).

– *La religione del mio tempo.* Milan: Garzanti, 1961.

– 'Confessioni tecniche.' *Paese Sera,* 27 September 1964.

– 'Cinema di prosa e cinema di poesia.' *Rinascita,* 2 April 1966.

– 'Dialogo 1.' *Cinema e film* 1, no. 1 (1966).

– 'Incontro con Pasolini.' *Inquadrature* 15–16 (Fall 1968), 33–7.

– 'Il sentimento della storia.' *Cinema nuovo* 205 (May/June 1970).

– 'Pasolini come Giotto.' *Epoca,* 18 October 1970.

- 'Al lettore nuovo.' In *Poesie*. Milan: Garzanti, 1970.
- *Le poesie*. Milan: Garzanti, 1971.
- 'La tentazione di parlare.' *Rivista del cinematografo* 5 (May 1971).
- 'Decameron.' *Avanti*, 19 September 1971.
- 'C'est le *Decameron* qui m'a choisi.' *La Galerie*, December 1971: 88–9.
- *Trasumanar e organizzar*. Milan: Garzanti, 1971.
- *Empirismo eretico*. Milan: Garzanti, 1972. [*Heretical Empiricism*. Translated by L. Barnett and B. Lawton. Bloomington and Indianapolis: Indiana University Press, 1988.]
- 'L'idea delle mille e una notte.' *Il Mondo*, 31 May 1973.
- 'Tetis.' In V. Boarini, ed., *Erotismo, eversione, merce*, 97–102. Bologna: Cappelli Editore, 1974.
- 'Il sesso come metafora del potere.' *Corriere della Sera*, 25 March 1975.
- 'Salò: L'intolleranza dello spettatore per cogliere l'anarchia del fascismo e del potere.' *Roma giovani* 2 (November 1975).
- *Scritti corsari*. Milan: Garzanti, 1975.
- *La divina mimesis*. Turin: Einaudi, 1975.
- 'Cinema and Literature.' Translated by Eugenia Wolfowicz. *Antaeus* (Winter 1976), 130–7.
- *Lettere luterane*. Turin: Einaudi, 1976.
- *Passione e ideologia*. Milan: Garzanti, 1977.
- *San Paolo*. Turin: Einaudi, 1977.
- *Le belle bandiere*. Rome: Editori Riuniti, 1977.
- *Cinema in forma di poesia*. Pordenone: Cinemazero, 1979.
- 'Poeta delle ceneri.' *Nuovi argomenti* 67–8 (July–December 1980), 3–26.
- *Trilogia della vita*. Milan: Mondadori, 1987.
- *Il portico della morte*. Edited by Cesare Segre. Rome: Associazione 'Fondo Pier Paolo Pasolini,' 1988.
- *Lettere 1955–1975*. Edited by Nico Naldini. Turin: Einaudi, 1988.
- *Alì dagli occhi azzurri*. Milan: Garzanti, 1989 [1965].
- *A Future Life*. Edited by Laura Betti and Lodovico G. Thorazzi. Rome: Associazione 'Fondo Pier Paolo Pasolini,' 1989.
- *Petrolio*. Turin: Einaudi, 1992 [1975].
- *Un paese di temporali e di primule*. Edited by Nico Naldini. Parma: Guanda, 1993.
Pasolini: Seminaire. Paris: Grasset, 1980.
Per Pasolini. Milan: Gammalibri, 1981.
Pedullà, Walter. 'L'italiano non è la lingua dei poveri.' *Mondo nuovo*, 22 November 1959.
Perelman, C., and L. Olbrechts-Tyteca. *Trattato dell'argomentazione: La nuova retorica*, vol. 2. Turin: Einaudi, 1982 [1966].

Peroni, L. 'Incontri con Pasolini.' *Inquadratura*, Autumn 1968.

Pestelli, Leo. 'Boccaccio a Napoli nel film di Pasolini.' *La Stampa*, 17 September 1971.

Petraglia, Sandro. *Pier Paolo Pasolini*. Florence: La Nuova Italia, 1974.

Petronio, Giuseppe. 'La posizione del *Decameron*.' In *L'Autore e il pubblico*, 19–47. Padova: Studio Tesi, 1981.

Pinsent, Pat. 'Chaucer's Critique of the Church in the General Prologue.' In L. Cookson and B. Loughrey, eds, *Critical Essays on the General Prologue to the 'Canterbury Tales,'* 39–49. Essex, England: Longman House, 1989.

Piromalli, A., and D. Scarfaglio (eds). *Volgar'eloquio di Pier Paolo Pasolini*. Naples, 1976.

Polese, Ranieri. 'Mille e un racconto per ricordare l'eros perduto.' *La Nazione*, 8 October 1982.

Porro, Maurizio. 'Pasolini e Delli Colli ancora insieme per il *Decamerone*.' *Photo 13 italiana* 2 (January 1971).

Potter, J. *Five Frames for the 'Decameron': Communication and Social Systems in the 'Cornice.'* Princeton: Princeton University Press, 1982.

Pucci, Piero. 'Lingua e dialetto in Pasolini e in Gadda.' In Giampaolo Borghello, ed., *Interpretazioni di Pasolini*, 50–7. Rome: Savelli, 1977.

Pudovkin, V. *Film Technique*. New York: Grove, 1970.

Purdon, Noel. 'Pasolini: The Film of Alienation.' In Paul Willemen, ed., *Pier Paolo Pasolini*, 43–55. London: British Film Institute, 1977.

Quintavalle, Arturo Carlo. *Prospettiva e ideologia: Alberti e la cultura del secolo XV*. Parma: Editrice Studium Parmense, 1967.

Ragland-Sullivan, Ellie. *Jacques Lacan and the Philosophy of Psychoanalysis*. Urbana: Illinois University Press, 1986.

Reed, Stanley. 'The Filmmaker and the Audience.' In Jean Creedy, ed., *The Social Context of Art*. London: Tavistock, 1970.

Richardson, R. *Literature and Film*. Bloomington: Indiana University Press, 1969.

Rinaldi, Rinaldo. *Pier Paolo Pasolini*. Milan: Mursia, 1982.

– *L'irriconoscibile Pasolini*. Rovito: Marra Editore, 1990.

Ropars-Wuilleumier, M.C. *De la littérature au cinéma: Genèse d'une écriture*. Paris: Colin, 1970.

Rose, Jaqueline. 'Sexuality and Vision: Some Questions.' In Hal Foster, ed., *Vision and Visuality*, 115–27. Seattle: Bay Press, 1988.

Rosen, Philip (ed.). *Narrative, Apparatus, Ideology: A Film Theory Reader*. New York: Columbia University Press, 1986.

Ross, Harris. *Film as Literature*. New York: Greenwood Press, 1987.

Rossi-Landi, Ferruccio. *Il linguaggio come lavoro e come mercato*. Milan: Bompiani, 1968.

– *Semiotica e ideologia*. Milan: Bompiani, 1972.

Roud, Richard. 'Roman Summer.' *Sight and Sound*, Autumn 1971.

Rumble, Patrick, and Bart Testa (eds). *Pasolini: Contemporary Perspectives*. Toronto: University of Toronto Press, 1994.

Russo, Vito. *The Celluloid Closet*. New York: Harper, 1981.

Salinari, C. 'L'empirismo ideologico del Boccaccio.' In *La critica della letteratura italiana*. Naples: Liguori, 1973.

Sanguinetti-White, Laura. *La scena conviviale e la sua funzione nel mondo di Boccaccio*. Florence: Olschki, 1983.

Santato, Guido. *Pier Paolo Pasolini: L'opera*. Vicenza: Neri Pozza Editore, 1980.

Sayce, Olive. 'Chaucer's "Retractions": The Conclusion of the *Canterbury Tales* and Its Place in Literary Tradition.' *Medium Aevum* 40 (1971), 230–48.

Scaglione, Aldo. *Nature and Love in the Late Middle Ages*. Berkeley: University of California Press, 1963.

Scalia, Gianni. 'Pasolini Corsaro.' In *Per conoscere Pasolini*. Rome: Bulzoni and Teatro Tenda, 1978.

Segre, Cesare. *Avviamento all'analisi del testo letterario*. Turin: Einaudi, 1968.

Shell, Marc. *Money, Language, and Thought: Literary and Philosophic Economies from the Medieval to the Modern Era*. Berkeley: University of California Press, 1982.

Shklovsky, Victor. 'Art as Technique.' In *Russian Formalist Criticism: Four Essays*. Lincoln: University of Nebraska Press, 1965.

– *Lettura del Decameron*. Bologna: Il Mulino, 1969.

– 'Poesia e prosa nel film.' In Edoardo Bruno, ed., *Film segno*, 23–6. Rome: Bulzoni, 1983.

Siciliano, Enzo. 'L'odiato Pasolini.' *Il mondo*, 14 July 1972.

– *Vita di Pasolini*. [*Pasolini*. Translated by John Shepley. New York: Random House, 1982.]

Silverman, Kaja. *The Subject of Semiotics*. New York: Oxford University Press, 1983.

Snyder, Joel. 'Benjamin on Reproducibility and Aura: A Reading of "The Work of Art in the Age of Its Technical Reproducibility."' In *Walter Benjamin: Philosophy, Aesthetics, History*, 158–74. Edited by Gary Smith. Chicago and London: University of Chicago Press, 1989.

Snyder, Stephen. *Pier Paolo Pasolini*. Boston: Twayne, 1980.

Sober, Elliot. 'Mental Representations.' *Synthese* 33, no. 1 (June 1976).

Sontag, Susan. 'Notes on Camp.' In *Against Interpretation*. New York: Delta, 1967.

Stack, Oswald. *Pasolini on Pasolini*. Bloomington: Indiana University Press, 1970.

Stam, Robert. *Subversive Pleasures: Bakhtin, Cultural Criticism and Film*. Baltimore and London: Johns Hopkins University Press, 1989.

Stone, Jennifer A. 'Cineastes' Texts.' *Yearbook of the British Pirandello Society* 3 (1983), 45–66.

Terracciano, Cenzo. 'La folgorazione figurativa nell'opera cinematografica di Pier Paolo Pasolini.' In *Le giovani generazioni e il cinema di Pier Paolo Pasolini*, 15–20. Rome: Fondo Pier Paolo Pasolini, 1989.

Thompson, Kristin. 'The Concept of Cinematic Excess.' In Philip Rosen, ed., *Narrative, Apparatus, Ideology: A Film Theory Reader*, 130–42. New York: Columbia University Press, 1986.

– *Breaking the Glass Armor: Neoformalist Film Analysis*. Princeton: Princeton University Press, 1988.

Tommasi, Wanda. 'La tentazione del neutro.' In *Diotima: Il pensiero della differenza sessuale*, 81–104. Milan: La Tartaruga, 1990.

Tyler, Parker. *Screening the Sexes: Homosexuality in the Movies*. New York: Da Capo, 1993 [1972].

Ulmer, Gregory. *Applied Grammatology*. Baltimore and London: Johns Hopkins University Press, 1985.

Vallora, Marco. 'Alì dagli occhi impuri: Come nasce il manierismo della narratività di Pasolini.' *Bianco e nero*, January–April 1976: 156–204.

– 'Pier Paolo Pasolini tra manierismo e metaletteratura.' In *Per conoscere Pasolini*, 117–33. Rome: Bulzoni and Teatro Tenda Editori, 1978.

Van Watson, William. *Pier Paolo Pasolini and the Theatre of the Word*. Ann Arbor and London: UMI Research Press, 1989.

Verdone, Mario. *Cinema e letteratura futurista*. Rome: Bianco e nero, 1967.

– 'Futurismo: Film e letteratura.' *Annali d'Italianistica* 6 (1988), 69–79.

Viano, Maurizio. *A Certain Realism: Making Use of Pasolini's Film Theory and Practice*. Berkeley: University of California Press, 1993.

Vitale, Maurizio. *La Questione della lingua*. Palermo: Palumbo, 1984.

Wagner, Geoffrey. *The Novel and the Cinema*. Rutherford, NJ: Farleigh Dickenson University Press, 1975.

Wagstaff, Christopher. 'Reality into Poetry: Pasolini's Film Theory.' *The Italianist* 5 (1985), 107–32.

Weber, Sam. *Institution and Interpretation*. Minneapolis: University of Minnesota Press, 1987.

White, John. *The Birth and Rebirth of Pictorial Space*. Cambridge, MA: Harvard University Press, 1987 [1957].

Willemen, Paul (ed.). *Pier Paolo Pasolini*. London: British Film Institute, 1977.

Zigaina, Giuseppe. 'Total Contamination in Pasolini.' *Stanford Italian Review* 4, no. 2 (Fall 1984), 267–85.

– *Pasolini e la morte*. Venice: Marsilio Editore, 1987.

Zumthor, Paul. *Speaking of the Middle Ages*. Lincoln, NB, and London: University of Nebraska Press, 1986.

Index

So, was it good?

Would you like to see a
Pasolini film together sometime soon?

Call me, because I would!

0032.2.734.06.89 or

my new phone number in Dublin,
......?